FIXED INCOME SECURITIES

Wiley Frontiers in Finance
Edited by Edward I. Altman

Damodaran on Valuation: Security Analysis for Investment and Corporate Finance
Aswath Damodaran (Book/Disk set also available)

Study Guide for Damodaran on Valuation: Security Analysis for Investment and Corporate Finance
Aswath Damodaran

Valuation: Measuring and Managing the Value of Companies, Second Edition
Tom Copeland, Tim Koller, and Jack Murrin (Book/Disk set also available)

Financial Statement Analysis, Second Edition
Martin S. Fridson

Style Investing: Unique Insight Into Asset Allocation
Richard Bernstein

The Stock Market, 6th Edition
Richard J. Teweles, Edward S. Bradley, and Ted M. Teweles

Fixed Income Securities: Tools for Today's Markets
Bruce Tuckman

FIXED INCOME SECURITIES
Tools for Today's Markets

Bruce Tuckman

John Wiley & Sons, Inc.
New York • Chichester • Brisbane • Toronto • Singapore

Copyright © 1995 by Bruce Tuckman

Published by John Wiley & Sons, Inc.

Library of Congress Cataloging-in-Publication Data:

Tuckman, Bruce.
    Fixed income securities: tools for today's markets / Bruce Tuckman.
       p.   cm.—(Wiley frontiers in finance)
    Includes index.
    ISBN 0-471-11214-3 (cloth : alk. paper)
    1. Fixed-income securities. I. Title. II. Series.
  HG4650.T83   1995
  332.63'2044—dc20   94-40576

Acknowledgments and Disclaimers

I would like to thank Pierluigi Balduzzi, Helen Edersheim, Raymond Hawkins, and Narasimhan Jegadeesh for reviewing the manuscript. I would also like to thank my wife, Katherine, for her help and support in preparing the manuscript.

This book was written before I left academics to work for Salomon Brothers Inc. Salomon is not responsible for any statements or conclusions herein, and no opinions, theories, or techniques presented herein in any way represent the position of Salomon Brothers Inc.

Preface

No book can describe all fixed income securities past, present, and yet to come. But this book is designed to make modern approaches to fixed income analysis accessible to practitioners. It will provide a set of concepts and tools with which they can meet the unknowns that they will inevitably face.

New breeds of fixed income securities are being created at a phenomenal pace. Moreover, the prices of these new instruments respond to interest rates quite differently from, and often more violently than, the prices of traditional fixed income securities. In this rapidly changing and increasingly risky environment, practitioners need to know how to think about pricing in these markets. Rules of thumb that have worked satisfactorily in the past may be quite misleading when applied to the new generation of securities. Imprecise analysis with respect to traditional instruments may not have dire consequences, but similar imprecision with respect to recent creations may be swiftly and severely punished.

The fast-paced evolution of these markets has been accompanied by great research achievements. Unfortunately, however, many of these achievements have not reached the general practitioner audience. Fixed income professionals often do not have the leisure, nor, in some cases, the mathematical background, to follow advances as they occur. Worse yet, many business schools have only recently begun to offer sophisticated and up-to-date courses on modern fixed income markets and analysis. This state of affairs is particularly regrettable because the ideas developed by the research community can be conveyed simply, intuitively, with a minimum of mathematics, and with an emphasis on useful applications.

WHO SHOULD BUY THIS BOOK

This book is based on an advanced MBA class at a top business school. As such, it is a challenging but rewarding read. The level of mathematics required to read the book has been kept to a minimum, but quantitative sophistication will be helpful. The intended audience for this book includes:

1. Practitioners who would like to solidify their understanding of the modern approach to fixed income analytics.
2. Practitioners who want to catch up on recent advances in fixed income pricing techniques, in particular, with arbitrage-free pricing of fixed income derivatives.
3. MBA students and Executive MBA students taking a course in fixed income securities.
4. Training program participants at banks and investment banks.
5. Mathematics and engineering professionals who have switched or who would like to switch into finance and fixed income.
6. Financial reporters who have never formally studied fixed income markets.

OVERVIEW OF CONTENTS

The term "fixed income" has become a terribly inaccurate misnomer. Bonds were originally called fixed income securities because they promised fixed cash flows over their lives. While such securities are still quite important in fixed income markets, newly created securities do not fit their "fixed income" classification: Their promised cash flows depend on the level of interest rates.

Part One of this book provides the basic ideas and tools for thinking about traditional fixed income securities, namely those with fixed cash flows. Many practitioners do not have a deep understanding of this material, despite its fundamental nature. Part Two introduces modern arbitrage-free techniques for pricing fixed income securities and derivatives whose cash flows depend on the level of interest rates. Part Three examines measures of price sensitivity essential for assessing portfolio risks, for asset-liability management, and for hedging. Part Four studies several fixed income securities and derivatives for their inherent importance and as illustrations of the concepts covered in the first three parts.

Contents

Part One
The Relative Pricing of Traditional Fixed Income Securities

Chapter 1
Bond Prices and Discount Factors

THE TIME VALUE OF MONEY

Any investor would prefer to receive $100 today than to receive $100 one year from today. Why? A sum of $100 received today can be deposited in a bank, earn interest, and provide more than $100 in a year's time. This is the principle of the *time value of money*: Anyone receiving a fixed sum of money wants it as soon as possible. Similarly, anyone paying a fixed sum wants to delay payment for as long as possible.

The principle of the time value of money is not particularly useful unless it can be quantified. How much would one pay today to receive $100 one year from now? How much would one pay to receive $5 a year for the next 30 years? More generally, how much would one pay to purchase a fixed income security that provides a particular set of cash flows?

By their nature, the answers to these questions are subjective. One investor may be willing to give up $95 today for a payment of $100 next year while, for whatever reason, another may be willing to give up only $94 for that same payment. Nevertheless, at any given time there will be only one market price for $100 to be received next year. If that price turns out to be $94.50, the first investor will purchase the security in question while the second will not. In fact, it is the collection of these individual decisions that determines the market price in the first place.

The rest of this chapter will demonstrate how to extract measures of the time value of money from U.S. Treasury bond prices. These measures will, by construction, reflect market prices rather than any particular individual's preferences. While an individual investor may ultimately choose to disagree with these market prices—viewing some securities as undervalued and some as overvalued— he must first process and understand all of the information contained in market prices.

Before proceeding, it should be noted that the discussion to follow assumes that securities are *default-free*, which means that any and all promised payments will be made. While this is quite a good assumption with respect to bonds sold by the U.S. Treasury, it is far less reasonable when applied to financially weak corporations that may default on their obligations to pay. But investors interested in pricing corporate debt must first understand how to value certain or default-free payments. The value of $50 promised by a corporation can be thought of as the value of $50 promised by the U.S. Treasury minus a default penalty. In this sense, the time value of money implied by prices of U.S. Treasury obligations is the foundation for pricing securities with *credit risk*, that is, with a reasonable likelihood of default.

TREASURY BOND QUOTATIONS

The cash flows from most Treasury bonds are completely defined by *face value* or *par value*, *coupon rate*, and *maturity date*. For example, buying a Treasury bond with a $10,000 face value, a coupon rate of 4 3/8 percent, and a maturity date of August 15, 1996, entitles the owner to an interest rate of 4.375 percent on $10,000, or $437.50 every year until August 15, 1996, and $10,000 on that date. By convention, however, the $437.50 due each year is paid in two installments, that is, $218.75 every six months. Noting that the Treasury did sell such a bond in the middle of August 1993, Figure 1.1 illustrates the cash flows from the bond.

Table 1.1 reports prices as of February 15, 1994, for several Treasury bonds paying coupons in February and August, or "on the February–August cycle."[1] The columns give a bond's coupon rate, maturity date, and price, respectively. Prices are expressed per $100 face value and the number after the ":" indicates 32nds. For example, the 4 3/8s due August 15, 1996, have a price of 99:15 or 99 + 15/32 = 99.46875 per $100 face value. So, selling $10,000 face of this bond will produce $10,000 x .9946875 or $9,946.88.

---

[1]Bid-ask spreads will be discussed in a later section.

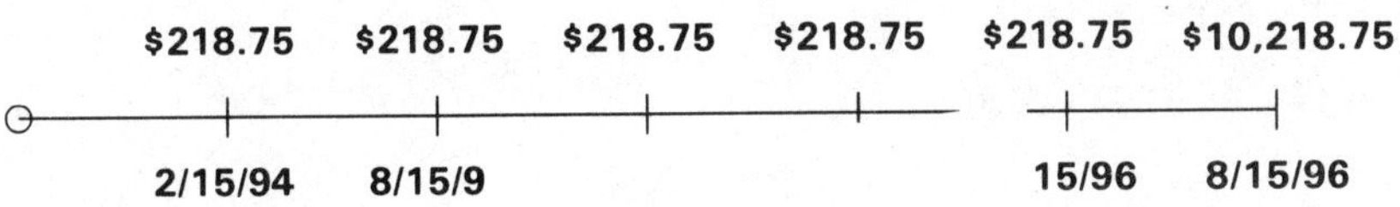

$218.75 $218.75 $218.75 $218.75 $218.75 $10,218.75

```
○───────┼────────────┼─────────────┼──────────┼───── ──┼────────┤
    2/15/94      8/15/9                                  15/96     8/15/96
```

FIGURE 1.1   Cash flows of the 4 3/8s due 8/15/96.

DISCOUNT FACTORS

The *discount factor* for a particular time period gives the value today, or the present value of $1 to be received at the end of that time. The discount factor for t years is written d(t). So, for example, if d(.5) = .9825, the present value of $1 to be received in six months is .9825. Discount factors provide answers to important questions about security prices. How much would one pay for a security that paid $105 six months from now? Well, since $1 to be received in six months is worth d(.5) = .9825 today, $105 to be received in six months is worth .9825 x $105 = $103.16.[2]

Discount factors can be used to compute *future values* as well as present values. Since $.9825 invested today grows to $1 in six months, $1 invested today grows to $1/d(.5) = $1/.9825 = $1.02 in six months. Therefore, $1/d(.5) is the future value of $1 invested for six months.

Discount factors can be extracted from Treasury bond prices. According to the first row of Table 1.1, the value of $100 principal amount of the 6 7/8s due August 15, 1994, is $101 20/32. Furthermore, since the bond matures in six months, on August 15, 1994, it will make the last interest payment of (1/2) x $6 7/8 plus the principal of $100 for a total of $103.44 on that date. Therefore, the present value of this $103.44 is $101 20/32. In terms of computing the discount factor d(.5), this means that

---

[2]For easy reading, prices throughout this book will often be rounded to the nearest cent. All calculations, however, have been done to greater precision. This means that readers may have to work a bit harder at reproducing some of the calculations presented.

Table 1.1   Selected U.S. Treasury Bond Prices on 2/15/94

Rate	Maturity	Price
6 7/8	8/15/94	101:20
5 1/2	2/15/95	101:18
4 5/8	8/15/95	100:21
4 5/8	2/15/96	100:12
4 3/8	8/15/96	99:15

$$101\frac{20}{32} = 103.44 \times d(.5)$$

Solving reveals that d(.5) is approximately equal to .9825.

The discount factor for cash flows to be received in one year can be found from the next bond in Table 1.1, the 5 1/2s due February 15, 1995. Payments from $100 face value of this bond are:

In six months: interest of 1/2 of $5.50, or $2.75
In one year: interest and principal of $102.75

The present values of these payments are $2.75 x d(.5) and $102.75 x d(1), respectively. So, in total, $100 face value of the bond is worth $2.75 x d(.5) + $102.75 x d(1). Since the present value of the bond equals its price of 101 18/32, it must be that

$$\$101\frac{18}{32} = \$2.75 \times d(.5) + \$102.75 \times d(1)$$

Knowing d(.5) = .9825 from the above calculations, this equation can be solved for d(1) to reveal that d(1) = .9621.

Continuing in this fashion, the prices in Table 1.1 can be used to solve for discount factors, in six-month intervals, up to two and one-half years. The resulting values are given in Table 1.2. Because of the time value of money, discount factors fall with maturity. The longer until the payment will be received, the less it is worth today.

Applying the techniques of Chapter 4, Figure 1.2 graphs the entire *discount function*, values of d(t) for all values of t, as of February 15, 1994. It is clear from this figure as well that discount factors fall with maturity. Note also that

Table 1.2   Discount Factors Derived from the Bond Prices Given in Table 1.1

t	d(t)
.5	.9824773
1	.9621478
1.5	.9398588
2.0	.9158669
2.5	.8920414

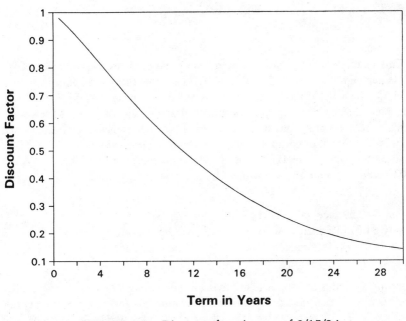

FIGURE 1.2   Discount function as of 2/15/94.

discounting substantially lowers the value of $1 to be received in the distant future. According to the graph, $1 to be received in 30 years is worth only about $.14 today.

ARBITRAGE AND THE LAW OF ONE PRICE

In the previous section the value of d(.5) derived from the 6 7/8s due August 1994 was used to discount the first coupon payment of the 5 1/2s due February 1995. This procedure implicitly assumes that d(.5) is the same for these two securities or, in other words, that the value of $1 to be received in six months does not depend on where that dollar comes from. This assumption is a special example of *the law of one price,* which, in general, states that two securities with exactly the same cash flows must sell for the same price.

To further illustrate the law of one price, consider a different one-year bond (not listed in Table 1.1), the 7 3/4s due February 15, 1994, with a price of 103:24 or $103.75. According to the law of one price the discount factors d(.5) and d(1), previously derived, can be used to discount the cash flows of the 7 3/4s. In that case, the value of $100 face value of the 7 3/4s is given by

$$3.875 \times d(.5) + 103.875 \times d(1) = 103.75$$

which matches the given market price.

This example shows that the law of one price predicts that the price of the 7 3/4s due February 15, 1995, will be $103.75 and that the market price is, in fact, $103.75. But what if the market price were $103.80 instead of $103.75? What guarantees that the law of one price accurately describes security prices? The answer is that a violation of the law of one price implies the existence of a profitable and riskless investment opportunity, called an *arbitrage opportunity*.[3]

Assuming that the market price of the 7 3/4s due February 15, 1995, is not $103.75 but $103.80, the following arbitrage opportunity arises:

Buy $10.59 face value of the 6 7/8s due August 15, 1994
Buy $1,010.95 face value of the 5 1/2s due February 15, 1995
Short $1,000 face value of the 7 3/4s due February 15, 1995

(Shorting a bond is the opposite of buying or being long a bond: The short seller receives money today and owes money in the future. So, for example, the investor shorting the 7 3/4s receives the price of the bond today of $1,038, but must pay $38.75 on August 15, 1994, and $1,038.75 on February 15, 1995.[4])

The following discussion proves that this arbitrage opportunity generates a positive cash flow today without generating any negative cash flows in the future. When the position is established, on February 15, 1994, the resulting cash flows in Table 1.3 total $.50.

On August 15, 1994, the cash flows from the arbitrage, shown in Table 1.4, total zero. Finally, on February 15, 1995, the cash flows from the closing of the arbitrage position also total zero, as seen in Table 1.5.

These last two sets of calculations reveal that the chosen portfolio of the 6 7/8s and the 5 1/2s has exactly the same future cash flows as $1,000 face value of the 7 3/4s. In such cases it is said that the chosen portfolio *replicates* the 7 3/4s. And it is because of this replication that buying the portfolio and shorting the 7 3/4s results in zero net cash flows.

It has now been shown that if the price of the 7 3/4s were $103.80, instead of $103.75, one could establish a position that generated $.50 today without

---

[3]Financial economists use the word "arbitrage" to mean a profitable and riskless opportunity. Market participants, perhaps because arbitrages in this sense are so rare, use the term more broadly to encompass investments that are highly likely to be profitable.

[4]This discussion ignores the costs of establishing and maintaining short positions. For a description of these costs and their effects on arbitrage activity, see, for example, Tuckman and Vila (1992).

Table 1.3   Arbitrage Cash Flows—Date One

Position	Calculation	Cash Flow
Buy the 6 7/8s	−$10.5850 × 101.6250%	−$10.757
Buy the 5 1/2s	−$1,010.9489 × 101.5625%	−$1,026.745
Short the 7 3/4s	$1,000 × 103.8000%	$1,038.000
Total		$0.50

Table 1.4   Arbitrage Cash Flows—Date Two

Position	Calculation	Cash Flow
Long the 6 7/8s	$10.5850 × 103.4375%	$10.9489
Long the 5 1/2s	$1,010.9489 × 2.7500%	$27.8011
Short the 7 3/4s	−$1,000 × 3.8750%	−$38.7500
Total		$0.00

Table 1.5   Arbitrage Cash Flows—Closing Date

Position	Calculation	Cash Flow
Long the 5 1/2s	$1,010.9489 × 102.750%	$1,038.75
Short the 7 3/4s	−$1,000.0000 × 103.875%	−$1,038.75
Total		$0.00

generating any liabilities in the future. It is, of course, no accident that the arbitrage profit is $.50 on a $1,000 face value transaction of the 7 3/4s. The price of the 7 3/4s was assumed to be $103.80 instead of the $103.75 predicted by the law of one price. This $.05 per $100 mispricing becomes a $.50 per $1,000 arbitrage profit.

Arbitrageurs would do the trade described "all day." In fact, since so many arbitrageurs will wish to sell the 7 3/4s and buy its replicating portfolio, the price of the 7 3/4s will be driven down and the prices of the 6 7/8s and 5 1/2s will be driven up. This process will continue until arbitrage profits are no longer available. The law of one price is ultimately obeyed.

A description of how one calculates the composition of the replicating portfolio, that is, $10.59 of the 6 7/8s and $1,010.95 of the 5 1/5s, can be found in the Appendix to this chapter.

BID-ASK SPREADS AND THE LAW OF ONE PRICE

The bid-ask spread is the difference between the price received when selling a bond and the price paid when buying a bond. This section considers the effects of bid-ask spreads on arbitrage and on the law of one price. Table 1.6 gives bond quotations as they appear in a newspaper or on a trading screen. The third column of the table gives the *bid price* of the bond, which is the price received when selling the bond. This price is typically below the *ask price*, the price paid when buying the bond. In exchange for his services, a broker or dealer keeps the difference between these two prices.

So far, this section has taken the average of the bid and the ask prices as the market price. While perhaps appropriate for quantifying the time value of money, trades take place at the bid or the ask price. As a result, the law of one price no longer gives an exact price for the 7 3/4s relative to the 6 7/8s and the 5 1/2s: It gives a permissible range of prices. If the bid price of the 7 3/4s is too high relative to the ask price of the replicating portfolio, an arbitrageur can profit by selling the 7 3/4s and buying the replicating portfolio. On the other hand, if the ask price of the 7 3/4s is too low relative to the bid price of the replicating portfolio, an arbitrageur can profit by buying the 7 3/4s and selling the replicating portfolio. As it turns out, if the bid and ask prices of the 6 7/8s and the 5 1/2s are as given in Table 1.6, the bid price of the 7 3/4s must be at most $103.78 and the ask price must be at least $103.72. For interested readers, the calculations behind these price bounds are also included in the Appendix at the end of this chapter.

TREASURY STRIPS

So far, the discussion of bond prices has considered securities that make regular coupon payments. Now consider *zero coupon* bonds, which are bonds that make no payments until they mature. Treasury STRIPS are zero coupon bonds issued by the U.S. Treasury. For example, $1,000 face value of a STRIP maturing on August 15, 1995, promises only one payment: $1,000 on August 15, 1995. STRIPS are created from "stripping" coupon and principal payments from a regular Treasury issue. Figure 1.3 illustrates this stripping process, as of February 15, 1994, for $1,000 face value of the Treasury's 10 1/2s due August 15, 1995. The three

Table 1.6 Selected U.S. Treasury Bond Price Quotations on 2/15/94

Rate	Maturity	Bid	Ask
6 7/8	8/15/94	101:19	101:21
5 1/2	2/15/95	101:17	101:19
7 3/4	2/15/95	103:23	103:25
4 5/8	8/15/95	100:20	100:22
4 5/8	2/15/96	100:11	100:13
4 3/8	8/15/96	99:14	99:16

Cash flows of the original bond:

$52.50 $52.50

2/15/94   8/15/94   2/15/95

Cash flows of the resulting zeros:

$52.50

$52.50

$52.50

$1,000.00

2/15/94   8/15/94   2/15/95   8/15/95

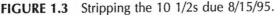

FIGURE 1.3   Stripping the 10 1/2s due 8/15/95.

remaining coupon payments and the one remaining principal payment are sold separately as four zero coupon bonds.

Table 1.7 lists the prices of selected Treasury STRIPS. The second column indicates whether the STRIPS come from a coupon payment or from a principal payment. The abbreviation "ci" stands for coupon income, "np" for note principal, and "bp" (not shown in the table) for bond principal.[5]

According to a strict interpretation of the law of one price, all STRIPS maturing on the same date should have the same price. Why should an investor care whether the $100 he receives was once interest or was once principal?[6] And yet, Table 1.7 shows that there are slight differences between interest and principal STRIPS prices. These differences are mostly due to *liquidity* differences across STRIPS. In other words, some STRIPS are easier to buy and to sell than others and, therefore, sell at a slightly higher price. Note, however, that no arbitrage opportunities are available from the prices listed in Table 1.7. For example, the principal STRIPS due

[5]Treasury notes have maturities from 1 to 10 years at issuance. Treasury bonds have maturities greater than 10 years at issuance. The distinction between notes and bonds makes little difference to investors in the Treasury market.
[6]Interest and principal STRIPS are taxed alike.

Table 1.7   Selected U.S. Treasury STRIPS Price Quotations on 2/15/94

Maturity	Type	Bid	Ask	Discount Factor
8/15/94	ci	98:09	98:09	.9828125
2/15/95	ci	96:06	96:07	.9620313
2/15/95	np	96:06	96:07	.9620313
8/15/95	ci	94:00	94:01	.9401563
8/15/95	np	93:31	94:00	.9398438
2/15/96	ci	91:18	91:20	.9159375
2/15/96	np	91:17	91:18	.9154688
8/15/96	ci	89:08	89:10	.8928125

February 15, 1996, with a bid of 91:18 and an ask of 91:20, seem cheaper than the interest STRIPS due on the same date, with a bid of 91:18 and an ask of 91:18. But, buying the principal STRIPS at the ask of 91:18 and selling the interest STRIPS at the bid of 91:18 clearly does not generate any arbitrage profit.

Since the price of STRIPS gives the value of $100 to be received on a particular date, the discount factor for that date is simply the STRIP price divided by 100. The fifth column of Table 1.7 gives discount factors of the various maturities based on the average of bid and ask STRIPS prices. Comparing these discount factors with those derived from bond prices (Table 1.2) generally confirms the validity of the law of one price. Despite small differences, the value of $1 to be received on a particular date is the same whether that $1 comes from bonds or from STRIPS.

Do the small differences between discount factors derived from Treasury bond prices and those derived from STRIPS give rise to arbitrage opportunities? Given the efficiency of these markets, the answer is usually no. Nevertheless, it is useful and instructive to check that relative prices are set correctly. As an example, consider buying a portfolio of STRIPS that replicates $100 face value of the 4 5/8s due August 15, 1995, and simultaneously selling $100 face value of the 4 5/8s. Since, by definition, these two portfolios have exactly the same cash flows, this transaction constitutes an arbitrage opportunity if the cost of buying the replicating portfolio is less than the proceeds from selling the 4 5/8s.

Table 1.8 provides the equivalent or replicating portfolio for the cash flows of $100 face value of the 4 5/8s.

Table 1.8   Replicating Portfolio

Cash flow of 4 5/8s	Replicating Portfolio
$2.3125 on 8/15/94	$2.3125 face value STRIPS due 8/15/94
$2.3125 on 2/15/95	$2.3125 face value STRIPS due 2/15/95
$102.3125 on 8/15/95	$102.3125 face value STRIPS due 8/15/95

According to the ask prices given in Table 1.7, the least costly way to buy this portfolio is to purchase the interest STRIPS due August 15, 1994, for 98:09 (the only ones available), the interest or principal STRIPS due February 15, 1995, for 96:07 (both can be bought for the same price), and the principal STRIPS due August 15, 1995, for 94:00 (since they cost less than the interest STRIPS due on that date). The cost of the replicating portfolio, therefore, is

$$.9828125 \times \$2.3125 + .9621875 \times \$2.3125 + .94 \times \$102.3125 = 100.67$$

According to Table 1.6, the 4 5/8s due August 15, 1995, can be sold for 100:20 = 100.625. Since this is less than the cost of purchasing the replicating portfolio, $100.67, one cannot earn an arbitrage profit from this set of transactions. More generally, small differences in the discount factors derived from Treasury bond prices and those derived from STRIPS do not usually indicate the existence of arbitrage opportunities.

APPENDIX 1A

Calculating the Replicating Portfolio and Deriving Arbitrage-Free Price Bounds

The first goal of this appendix is to calculate the face value of the 6 7/8s due August 15, 1994, and the face value of the 5 1/2s due February 15, 1995, that together replicate the cash flows of $1,000 face value of the 7 3/4s due February 15, 1995.

Let Z be the required face amount of the 6 7/8s and let Y be the required face amount of the 7 3/4s. The equations that must be satisfied are:

$$103.4535\% \times Z + 2.75\% \times Y = 38.75$$
$$102.75\% \times Y = 1038.75$$

The first equation states that the cash flows from the replicating portfolio on August 15, 1994, must match the cash flow from $1,000 face amount of the 7 3/4s on August 15, 1994. The second equation states that the cash flow from the portfolio on February 15, 1995, must match the cash flow from $1,000 face amount of the 7 3/4s on February 15, 1995. Solving these two equations for Y and Z gives, approximately, Y = $1,010.9489 and Z = $10.5850.

The second goal of this appendix is to derive arbitrage-free pricing bounds. First consider the case in which there is no bid-ask spread. Since the replicating portfolio has the same cash flows as $1,000 face value of the 7 3/4s, then, by the law of one price, the price of the replicating portfolio must equal the price of $1,000 face value of the 7 3/4s. So, given Y, Z, and the prices in Table 1.1, the price of $1,000 face value of the 7 3/4s must be

$$\$1,010.9489 \times 101.5625\% + \$10.585 \times 101.625\% = \$1,037.502$$

Per $100 face value, the 7 3/4s must be worth $103.75.

When there is a bid-ask spread, arbitrage is prevented by two rules. First, the bid price of the replicating portfolio must be less than the ask price of the 7 3/4s. Otherwise, an arbitrageur could buy the 7 3/4s, sell the replicating portfolio, and make a riskless profit. Second, the ask price of the replicating portfolio must be greater than the bid price of the 7 3/4s. Otherwise, an arbitrageur could buy the replicating portfolio, sell the 7 3/4s, and make a riskless profit.

Given the prices in Table 1.6, the bid price of the replicating portfolio, per $100 face value, is

$$\$1.0585044 \times 101.59375\% + \$101.09489 \times 101.53125\% = \$103.71828$$

Similarly, the ask price of the replicating portfolio is

$$\$1.0585044 \times 101.65625\% + \$101.09489 \times 101.59375\% = \$103.78213$$

Therefore, as mentioned in the text, the ask price of the 7 3/4s must be greater than 103.71828 and the bid price must be less than 103.78213.

Chapter 2
Bond Prices and Interest
Rates: Spot and Forward

Discount factors can be used to price any Treasury bond. Nevertheless, investors focused on rates of return often quantify the time value of money in terms of interest rates instead. This chapter defines two kinds of interest rates, namely, spot and forward rates, shows how these rates can be derived from bond prices, and explains the usefulness of these rates. As with discount factors, spot and forward rates are simply derived from market prices. However, the end of this section will discuss how fixed income investors can compare market rates with their own views on future interest rates and position themselves accordingly.

SEMIANNUAL COMPOUNDING

Telling an investor that he will earn an annual rate of 8 percent on his investment does not provide enough information with which to calculate his true rate of return. An investment of $100, for example, will earn $8 over the year, but when will that $8 be paid? The investment is worth less if the $8 is paid at the end of the year than if $4 is paid after six months and another $4 is paid at the end of the year. In the latter case, the $4 paid after six months can be reinvested for six months so that the investor accumulates more than $108 by year's end.

A complete specification of return tells an investor the annual rate and how often that rate will be *compounded* during the year. An annual rate of 8 percent, compounded semiannually, means that the investor receives 4 percent every six months which he can reinvest in the same investment to compound his interest, that is, to receive interest on interest. An annual rate of 8 percent, compounded quarterly, means that the investor receives .08/4, or 2 percent, every quarter while the same 8 percent, compounded monthly, means that the investor receives .08/12 = .67 percent every month. Because most bonds pay one half of their annual coupons every six months, bond market investors are particularly interested in the case of semiannual compounding.

If one invests $100 at an annual rate of 8 percent, compounded semiannually, at the end of six months one would have

$$\$100 \times \left(1 + \frac{.08}{2}\right) = \$104$$

where the term $(1 + .08/2)$ represents the per dollar payment of principal and semi-annual interest. If one invests the $100 at the same rate for one year instead, at the end of the year one would have

$$\$100 \times \left(1 + \frac{.08}{2}\right)^2 = \$108.16$$

The squared term results from taking the per dollar principal amount available at the end of six months, namely $1 + .08/2$, and reinvesting it for another six months, that is, multiplying again by $1 + .08/2$. Note that total funds at the end of the year are $108.16, $.16 greater than the total resulting from 8 percent paid annually. In other words, the $.16 represents interest on interest.

In general, investing $X at an annual rate of r, compounded semiannually, for T years, generates

$$\$X\left(1 + \frac{r}{2}\right)^{2T}$$

at the end of those T years. Note that the power in this expression is 2T since an investment for T years compounded semiannually is really an investment for 2T six-month periods. For example, investing $100 for 10 years at an annual rate of 8 percent, compounded semiannually, will be worth $100 (1.04)^{20}$ or approximately $219.11 after 10 years.

The above expression can also be used to calculate a semiannually compounded *holding period* return. What is the semiannually compounded return from investing $X for T years and having $Y at the end? Letting r be the answer, one needs to solve the following equation for r:

$$\$Y = \$X\left(1 + \frac{r}{2}\right)^{2T}$$

Solving shows that

$$r = 2\left[\left(\frac{Y}{X}\right)^{\frac{1}{2T}} - 1\right]$$

So, for example, an initial investment of $100 that grew to $250 after 15 years earned $2[(250/100)^{1/30} - 1]$ or approximately 6.20 percent, compounded semiannually.

SPOT RATES

The *spot rate* is the rate on a *spot loan*, a loan agreement in which the lender gives money to the borrower at the time of the agreement. The t-year spot rate is written $\hat{r}(t)$. One way to think about $\hat{r}(t)$ is as the semiannually compounded return from investing in STRIPS that mature t years from now. Table 1.7 reported that the average of the bid and ask prices for $100 face value of the STRIPS due August 15, 1996, was $89 9/32. This implies a semiannually compounded rate of return of

$$2\left[\left(\frac{100}{89\frac{9}{32}}\right)^{\frac{1}{5}} - 1\right] = 4.59\%$$

Therefore, $\hat{r}(2.5) = 4.59\%$.

More generally, the price of $1 face value of STRIPS maturing in t years is just d(t). Therefore,

$$\hat{r}(t) = 2 \times \left\{ \left[\frac{1}{d(t)} \right]^{\frac{1}{2t}} - 1 \right\}$$

Or, rearranging terms,

$$d(t) = \left\{ \frac{1}{\left[1 + \frac{\hat{r}(t)}{2} \right]^{2t}} \right\}$$

This last equation has the following interpretation. The value of $1 to be received in t years, d(t), equals the value of $1 *discounted for t years at the semiannually compounded rate* $\hat{r}(t)$.

Table 2.1 calculates spot rates based on the discount factors reported in Table 1.2. The resulting spot rates increase with maturity, starting at an annual rate of about 3.57 percent for six-month investments and increasing to about 4.62 percent for 2.5-year investments. The relationship between spot rates and maturity, or term, is often called the *term structure* of spot rates. When spot rates increase with maturity, as in Table 2.1, the term structure is said to be *upward-sloping*.

Figure 2.1 graphs the *spot rate curve*, which is the spot rates of all available maturities as of February 15, 1994. (This graph applies the techniques described in Chapter 4.) The term structure of spot rates slopes upward until a maturity of about 23 years at which point it becomes *downward-sloping* or *inverted*. The shape of the spot rate curve in Figure 2.1 is quite typical of the Treasury bond market.

It is important to emphasize that spot rates of different maturities are indeed different. Alternatively, the market provides a different holding period return for

Table 2.1   Spot Rates Derived from Discount Factors Given in Table 1.2

t	d(t)	$\hat{r}(t)$
.5	.9824773	3.567044%
1	.9621478	3.896186%
1.5	.9398588	4.178084%
2	.9158669	4.442840%
2.5	.8920414	4.622314%

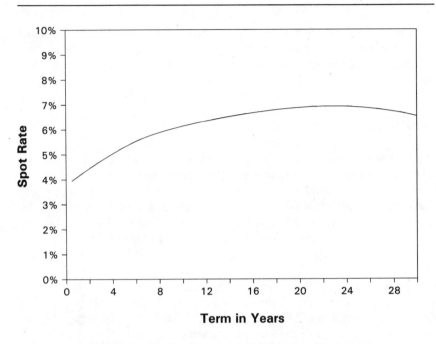

FIGURE 2.1   Spot rates as of February 15, 1994.

investments in two-year STRIPS than for investments in one-year STRIPS. Furthermore, since a coupon bond may be viewed as a particular portfolio of STRIPS, the existence of a term structure of spot rates indicates that each of a bond's payments must be discounted at a different rate.

To elaborate on this point, recall that the price of bonds can be written in terms of the discount factors. For example, as of February 15, 1994, the price of $100 face value of the Treasury's 4 5/8s of August 15, 1995, is given by the following expression:

$$2.3125 \times d(.5) + 2.3125 \times d(1) + 102.3125 \times d(1.5)$$

Or, using the relationship between discount factors and spot rates given above, the bond price can also be written as

$$\frac{2.3125}{1+\frac{r(.5)}{2}} + \frac{2.3125}{\left[1+\frac{\hat{r}(1)}{2}\right]^2} + \frac{102.3125}{\left[1+\frac{\hat{r}(1.5)}{2}\right]^3}$$

Writing bond prices in this way clearly shows that each cash flow is discounted at a rate appropriate for that cash flow's payment date. Said another way, an investor earns a different rate of return on bond cash flows received on different dates.

FORWARD RATES

Table 2.1 showed that, as of February 15, 1994, the six-month spot rate was about 3.567 percent and the one-year spot rate was about 3.896 percent. This means that an investor in a six-month STRIP would earn .5 of 3.567 percent over six months. Similarly, an investor in a one-year STRIP would earn .5 of 3.896 percent over the first six months and .5 of 3.896 percent over the following six months. But why do two investors, with equal market access, earn different rates of interest over the same six-month time period?

The answer, of course, is that the investor in the one-year STRIP earns the higher annual rate of 3.896 percent over the six months only because he has committed to roll over his balance at the end of six months for another six months. This type of commitment is an example of a *forward loan*. More generally, a forward loan is an agreement made to lend money at some future date. The rate of interest on a forward loan, specified at the time of the agreement (as opposed to the time of the loan), is called a *forward rate*. Therefore, an investor in a one-year STRIP has simultaneously made a spot loan for six months and a loan, six months forward, with a term of six months.

Let $r(t)$ be the semiannually compounded rate earned on a six-month loan t minus .5 years forward. So, for example, $r(4.5)$ is the semiannually compounded rate on a loan made four years forward, (that is, the loan is made four years from now and repaid 4.5 years from now). Figure 2.2 illustrates the difference between spot rates and forward rates: Spot rates are applicable from now to some future date while forward rates are applicable from some future date to six months beyond that future date.[7]

The discussion now turns to the computation of forward rates. A six-month loan zero years forward is simply a six-month spot loan. Therefore, $r(.5) = \hat{r}(.5) = 3.567$ percent, where the second equality simply reports a result from Table 2.1. The next forward rate, $r(1)$, is computed as follows. Since the one-year spot rate is $\hat{r}(1)$, a one-year investment of $1 grows to $(1 + \hat{r}(1)/2)^2$ at the end of the year. Alternatively, this investment can be viewed as a combination of a six-month loan zero years forward at an annual rate of $r(.5)$ and a six-month loan six months

---

[7]Here, all forward rates are taken to be six-month rates applicable some number of semiannual periods from now. However, one can define forward rates over any term applicable at any future time. Examples include a three-month rate two-years forward, a one-month rate 13 months forward, etc.

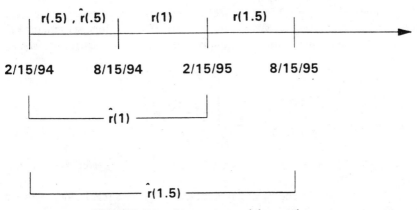

FIGURE 2.2   Spot rates and forward rates.

forward at an annual rate of r(1). Therefore, a one-year investment of $1 grows to $(1 + r(.5)/2) \times (1 + r(1)/2)$. Spot rates and forward rates will be consistent measures of return only if the $1 investment grows to the same amount regardless of which measure is used. Therefore, r(1) is determined by the following equation:

$$\left[1 + \frac{r(.5)}{2}\right] \times \left[1 + \frac{r(1)}{2}\right] = \left[1 + \frac{\hat{r}(1)}{2}\right]^2$$

Since r(.5) and r(1) are known, this equation can be solved to show that r(1) is about 4.226 percent.

Before proceeding with these calculations, the rates of return on six-month and one-year STRIPS can now be reinterpreted. The spot rate interpretation of the prior section was that six-month STRIPS earn an annual 3.567 percent over the next six months and that one-year STRIPS earn an annual 3.896 percent over the next year. The forward-rate interpretation is that both six-month and one-year STRIPS earn an annual 3.567 percent over the next six months. One year STRIPS, however, go on to earn an annual 4.226 percent over the following six months. The one-year spot rate of 3.896 percent, therefore, is a blend of its two forward-rate components.[8]

The same argument used to calculate r(1) can be invoked to calculate

---

[8]The exact statement is the following: The spot rate plus 1 is the geometric average of the relevant forward rates plus 1.

r(1.5). Investing \$1 for 1.5 years at the spot rate $\hat{r}(1.5)$ must result in the same final wealth as investing for six months at r(.5), for six months, six months forward at r(1), and, finally, for six months, one year forward at r(1.5). Mathematically,

$$\left[1+\frac{r(.5)}{2}\right] \times \left[1+\frac{r(1)}{2}\right] \times \left[1+\frac{r(1.5)}{2}\right] = \left[1+\frac{\hat{r}(1.5)}{2}\right]^3$$

Since r(.5), r(1), and $\hat{r}(1.5)$ are known, this equation can be solved to reveal that r(1.5) = 4.743%.

Generalizing this reasoning to any term t, the algebraic relationship between spot rates and forward rates is

$$\left[1+\frac{r(.5)}{2}\right] \times \ldots \times \left[1+\frac{r(t)}{2}\right] = \left[1+\frac{\hat{r}(t)}{2}\right]^{2t}$$

Table 2.2 reports the values of r(.5) through r(2.5) based on this equation and the spot rates reported in Table 2.1.

Figure 2.3, applying the techniques discussed later in Chapter 4, graphs the spot and forward rate curves as of February 15, 1994. Note the following behavior of these two curves. When the forward rate curve is above the spot rate curve, the spot rate curve is rising or sloping upward. On the other hand, when the forward rate curve is below the spot rate curve, the spot rate curve slopes downward or is falling. For the interested reader, an algebraic proof of these propositions can be found in Appendix 2A. The text, however, continues with a more intuitive explanation of this behavior.

The equation relating spot and forward rates can be rewritten in the following form:

Table 2.2 Forward Rates Derived from Spot Rates Given in Table 2.1

t	$\hat{r}(t)$	r(t)
.5	3.567044%	3.567044%
1	3.896186%	4.225860%
1.5	4.178084%	4.743053%
2	4.442840%	5.239167%
2.5	4.622314%	5.341787%

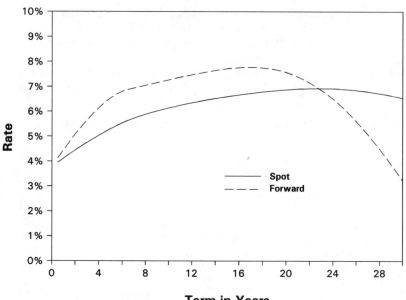

FIGURE 2.3   Spot and forward rates as of February 15, 1994.

$$\left[1+\frac{\hat{r}(t-.5)}{2}\right]^{2t-1}\times\left[1+\frac{r(t)}{2}\right]=\left[1+\frac{\hat{r}(t)}{2}\right]^{2t}$$

For concreteness, let t = 2.5 so that the equation becomes

$$\left[1+\frac{\hat{r}(2)}{2}\right]^{4}\times\left[1+\frac{r(2.5)}{2}\right]=\left[1+\frac{\hat{r}(2.5)}{2}\right]^{5}$$

The intuition behind this equation is that the proceeds from a $1 investment over the next 2.5 years (the right-hand side) must equal the proceeds from a spot loan over the next two years combined with a six-month loan two years forward (the left-hand side). Thus, the 2.5-year spot rate, $\hat{r}(2.5)$, is a blend of the two-year spot rate, $\hat{r}(2)$, and the six-month rate two-years forward, r(2.5).

If r(2.5) is above $\hat{r}(2)$, any blend of the two will be above $\hat{r}(2)$. Therefore, $\hat{r}(2.5) > \hat{r}(2)$. Hence, because the forward rate is above the spot rate, the spot rate curve is increasing. Similarly, if r(2.5) is below $\hat{r}(2)$, the blend $\hat{r}(2.5)$ will also be below $\hat{r}(2)$. Hence, because the forward rate is below the spot rate, the spot rate curve is decreasing. This completes the explanation of Figure 2.3.

Before concluding this section, the discussion returns to bond-pricing equations. Bond prices have previously been expressed as a function of discount factors and as a function of spot rates. But because forward rates are just another measure of the time value of money, bond prices can be expressed in terms of forward rates as well. Recall that, as of February 15, 1994, the price of $100 face value of the Treasury's 4 5/8s of August 15, 1995, is given by

$$2.3125 \times d(.5) + 2.3125 \times d(1) + 102.3125 \times d(1.5)$$

when using discount factors and by

$$\frac{2.3125}{1 + \dfrac{r(.5)}{2}} + \frac{2.3125}{\left[1 + \dfrac{\hat{r}(1)}{2}\right]^2} + \frac{102.3125}{\left[1 + \dfrac{\hat{r}(1.5)}{2}\right]^3}$$

when using spot rates. The corresponding expression using forward rates is

$$\frac{2.3125}{1 + \dfrac{r(.5)}{2}} + \frac{2.3125}{\left[1 + \dfrac{r(.5)}{2}\right]\left[1 + \dfrac{r(1)}{2}\right]} + \frac{102.3125}{\left[1 + \dfrac{r(.5)}{2}\right]\left[1 + \dfrac{r(1)}{2}\right]\left[1 + \dfrac{r(1.5)}{2}\right]}$$

These three bond-pricing expressions have slightly different interpretations, but they all perform the same task: that of transforming future cash flows into a price to be paid or received today. And, of course, all three expressions produce the same market price.

APPLICATION: SHORT-TERM VS. LONG-TERM BOND PRICES

Are bonds of longer maturity worth more or less than bonds of shorter maturity? As it turns out, the answer depends on the bonds' coupon rates relative to the forward rates.

For discussion purposes, focus on the following more structured question. Consider five 4 3/4 percent coupon bonds with maturities of six months, one year, one and one-half years, two years, and two and one-half years. As of February 15, 1994, which bond had the greatest price?

One could, of course, simply calculate the price of each of the five bonds. Doing these calculations produces Table 2.3 and reveals that the one and one-half-year bond has the greatest price. But why is that so?

Think about extending maturity from six months to one year. The coupon rate earned over that additional six-month period is 4.75 percent, but the forward rate for loans over that extension period, $r(1)$, is only 4.226 percent. So, by extending maturity from one-half year to one year, investors can earn an above-market rate on a six-month loan six months forward. This opportunity makes the one-year bond more desirable than the six-month bond and, equivalently, makes the one-year bond price of $100.83 greater than the six-month bond price of $100.58.

The same argument holds for the maturity extension from one year to one and one-half years, although the advantage is not as great. The coupon rate is, of course, still 4.75 percent, and the rate on a six-month loan one year forward is 4.743 percent. So extending maturity does allow for investment at above-market rates, but the advantage is small. As a result, the 1.5-year bond price of $100.84 is greater than the one-year bond price of $100.83, but not by much.

The same argument, however, does not hold for extending maturity out another six months. The rate on six-month loans one and one-half years forward is 5.239 percent, which is greater than the coupon rate of 4.75 percent. Therefore, extending maturity from one and one-half to two years makes a forward loan at below market rates. Therefore, the two-year bond price of $100.61 is less than the one and one-half-year bond price of $100.84.

More generally, price increases as maturity increases whenever the coupon rate exceeds the forward rate over the period of maturity extension. Price decreases as maturity increases whenever the coupon rate is less than the forward rate.

APPLICATION: SHORT-TERM VS. LONG-TERM BOND RETURNS

When will short-term bonds prove a better investment than long-term bonds and when will long-term bonds prove a better investment than short-term bonds? The

Table 2.3 Prices of 4 3/4 Percent Bonds of Various Maturities Using Discount Factors Given in Table 1.2

Years to Maturity	Price
.5	100.5811
1	100.8333
1.5	100.8365
2	100.6125
2.5	100.3486

answer, of course, depends on what happens to interest rates after the investment decision has been made. But, with the help of forward rates, much more can be said in response to this question.

Consider the following problem. Investor A chooses to invest $100 in six-month STRIPS, rolling over his investment every six months for the next two and one-half years. Investor B chooses to invest $100 in a 4 3/4 percent 2.5-year bond and to roll over his coupon receipts into six-month STRIPS. If both investors begin their strategy on February 15, 1994, under what conditions will investor A have more money 2.5 years later and under what conditions will investor B have more money?

The six-month rate on February 15, 1994, reported in Table 2.2, is about 3.567 percent. Assume for the moment that the six-month rate, over time, happens to match the forward rates as of February 15, 1994 (given in Table 2.2). In other words, assume that the six-month rates will be as shown in Table 2.4 on the given dates.

Given this very particular interest rate scenario, one can compute the wealth of investors A and B after 2.5 years.

Investor A, who begins with $100 and rolls over six-month STRIPS, will have

$$\$100 \times \left(1 + \frac{.03567}{2}\right) \times \left(1 + \frac{.04226}{2}\right) \times \left(1 + \frac{.04743}{2}\right) \times \left(1 + \frac{.05239}{2}\right)$$

$$\times \left(1 + \frac{.05342}{2}\right) = \$112.10$$

at the end of the 2.5 years.

Investor B begins with $100 as well, purchasing a 4 3/4 percent bond maturing in 2.5 years. As reported in Table 2.3, the price of this bond is 100.35 per $100 face value. So, with $100, investor B can buy $100/1.0035 = $99.65 face value of the bond.

Every six months investor B receives a coupon payment of $99.65 x 4.75%/2 = $2.37 which he reinvests at the six-month rate. So, for example, the first coupon,

Table 2.4   An Interest Rate Scenario

Date	6-month Rate
8/15/94	4.226%
2/15/95	4.743%
8/15/95	5.239%
2/15/96	5.342%

paid on August 15, 1994, is reinvested four times while the penultimate coupon, paid on February 15, 1996, is reinvested once. His total proceeds from coupons and their reinvestment over the two and one-half years are

$$\$2.37 \times \left(1 + \frac{04226}{2}\right) \times \left(1 + \frac{.04743}{2}\right) \times \left(1 + \frac{.05239}{2}\right) \times \left(1 + \frac{.05342}{2}\right)$$

$$+\$2.37 \times \left(1 + \frac{.04743}{2}\right) \times \left(1 + \frac{.05239}{2}\right) \times \left(1 + \frac{.05342}{2}\right)$$

$$+\$2.37 \times \left(1 + \frac{.05239}{2}\right) \times \left(1 + \frac{.05342}{2}\right)$$

$$+\$2.37 \times \left(1 + \frac{.05342}{2}\right)$$

$$+\$2.37 = \$12.45$$

Adding the principal return of $99.65 to this sum gives $112.10, which is exactly the same result as achieved by investor A.

It is no coincidence that, when the six-month rate evolves according to the initial forward rate curve, short-term and long-term investors perform equally well. Recall that an investment in a long-term bond is equivalent to a series of forward loans at rates given by the forward rate curve. In this example, the long-term bond locks in a six-month rate of 4.226 percent on August 15, 1994, a six-month rate of 4.743 percent on February 15, 1995, and so on. So, if the six-month rate does turn out to be 4.226 percent on 8/15/94, 4.743 percent on February 15, 1995, and so on, then the long-term bond locks in the actual succession of six-month rates. Equivalently, investors in long-term bonds do exactly as well as investors who roll over short-term bonds.

When does investor B, the long-term bond investor, do better than investor A? Say, for example, that the six-month rate, over the next 2.5 years, never moves from its initial value of 3.567 percent. Then investor B certainly does better than investor A. Investor B has locked in six-month rates of 4.226 percent, 4.743 percent, and so on, while investor A has to keep reinvesting at 3.567 percent. In general, investors in long-term bonds do better when the six-month rate, over time, remains below the initial forward rates.

When does investor A, the short-term bond investor, do better than investor B? Say, for example, that short-term rates rise as shown in Table 2.5. These rates are all above the initial forward rates. Therefore, investor B, by buying a long-term bond, has locked in what turned out to be relatively low six-month rates. Investor A, on the other hand, invests at the relatively high realized values of the six-month

Table 2.5   Another Interest Rate Scenario

Date	6-month Rate
8/15/94	4.5%
2/15/95	4.8%
8/15/95	5.4%
2/15/96	5.5%

rate. In general, investors in short-term bonds do better when the six-month rate, over time, rises above the initial forward rates.

These general results can be used by an investor with a view on rates, that is, one who is willing to invest based on his interest rate forecasts. A comparison of his view with the forward rate curve will reveal which bond maturities he ought to be buying. It should be cautioned, however, that the risks of investing in short-term and long-term bonds can be quite different. This issue will be studied extensively in Part Three.

APPENDIX 2A

On the Relations between Spot Rates, Forward Rates, and the Slope of the Term Structure

The first proposition states that if forward rates exceed spot rates then the term structure of spot rates is upward-sloping.

Proposition: If $r(t + .5) > \hat{r}(t)$ then $\hat{r}(t + .5) > \hat{r}(t)$
Proof: Since $r(t + .5) > \hat{r}(t)$,

$$1 + \frac{r(t + .5)}{2} > 1 + \frac{\hat{r}(t)}{2}$$

Multiplying both sides by $(1 + \hat{r}(t)/2)^{2t}$,

$$\left[1 + \frac{\hat{r}(t)}{2}\right]^{2t}\left[1 + \frac{r(t + .5)}{2}\right] > \left[1 + \frac{\hat{r}(t)}{2}\right]^{2t+1}$$

But, by the relation between spot and forward rates given in the text, the left-hand side can be written in terms of $\hat{r}(t + .5)$:

$$\left[1 + \frac{\hat{r}(t + .5)}{2}\right]^{2t+1} > \left[1 + \frac{\hat{r}(t)}{2}\right]^{2t+1}$$

Or equivalently,

$$\hat{r}(t + .5) > \hat{r}(t)$$

as was to be proved.

The second proposition states that if forward rates are less than spot rates, then the term structure of spot rates is downward-sloping.

Proposition: If $r(t + .5) < \hat{r}(t)$ then $\hat{r}(t + .5) < \hat{r}(t)$

Proof: As in the first proposition, with the inequalities reversed.

Chapter 3
Yield-to-Maturity

Unlike the term structure of interest rates, *yield-to-maturity* is one number used to describe the rate at which a bond's cash flows should be discounted. Some think of it as a measure of relative value. In other words, if one 10-year security has a higher yield than another, the former is a better buy. Others think of yield-to-maturity as a measure of a bond's realized, or *ex post,* return if held to maturity. A typical statement along these lines is that holding a coupon bond to maturity will earn a return equal to the bond's initial yield-to-maturity. This unit shows that yield-to-maturity is a good measure neither of relative value nor of realized return. As one number it simply cannot describe bond prices and returns as accurately as the entire term structure. In fact, in the opinion of many sophisticated practitioners, yield should be used only as another way to quote price.

DEFINITION AND COMMENTS

Yield-to-maturity is the one rate such that the discounted value of a security's cash flows at that rate equals the security's market price. For example, Table 1.1 reported that, as of February 15, 1994, the average of the bid and ask for the Treasury's 4 5/8s due August 15, 1996 was 100:12 or 100.375. Taking this value as the market price, the yield-to-maturity of the bond, y, is defined such that

$$\frac{2.3125}{1+\dfrac{y}{2}} + \frac{2.3125}{\left(1+\dfrac{y}{2}\right)^2} + \frac{2.3125}{\left(1+\dfrac{y}{2}\right)^3} + \frac{102.3125}{\left(1+\dfrac{y}{2}\right)^4} = 100.375$$

Solving for y by trial and error shows that the yield-to-maturity of this bond is about 4.427 percent.[9] Note, too, that given yield instead of price, one can easily solve for price. Because of the ability to move easily from price to yield and back, yield-to-maturity may be viewed as an alternate way to quote price.

While computers make price and yield calculations quite painless, there is a simple and useful formula with which to compute price given yield. The definition of yield-to-maturity implies that the price of a T-year bond with a coupon rate of c and a $1 face value is[10]

$$P = \frac{c}{2} \sum_{t=1}^{2T} \left(1 + \frac{y}{2}\right)^{-t} + \left(1 + \frac{y}{2}\right)^{-2T}$$

(The power in the last term is 2T because a T-year bond matures in 2T semiannual periods.) It can be shown that the above equation, in turn, implies that[11]

$$P = \frac{c}{y} \left[1 - \left(1 + \frac{y}{2}\right)^{-2T} \right] + \left(1 + \frac{y}{2}\right)^{-2T}$$

Several results follow immediately from writing the price-yield relationship in this form. First, when $c = y$, $P = 1$. In words, when the coupon rate equals the yield-to-maturity, the bond sells for its face value. Second, when $c > y$, $P > 1$ while when $c < y$, $P < 1$. This result says that if the coupon rate exceeds the yield, the bonds sells at a *premium* to par, that is at more than face value. Conversely, if the yield exceeds the coupon, the bond sells at a *discount* from par, that is at less than face value. Third, very long maturity bonds, those with large values of T, have prices that approach c/y. In fact, the price of a *perpetuity*, a bond that pays coupon payments forever, is exactly c/y.

Returning to the analysis of yield-to-maturity, previous sections showed that each of a bond's cash flows must be discounted at a rate corresponding to the

---

[9] If there are more than four payment dates, one cannot analytically solve the bond-pricing equation for yield-to-maturity. But numerical solutions are easily generated by calculators or computer programs.
[10] For a more general formula, valid for bonds with first coupons due in less than six months, see Chapter 4.
[11] To perform simplifications of this type, the following rule is invoked:

$$\sum_{t=a}^{b} z^t = [z^a - z^{b+1}]/[1 - z]$$

To apply this rule to the problem in the text, set $z = 1/(1 + y/2)$, $a = 1$, and $b = 2T$.

timing of that particular cash flow. Combining this fact with the sample yield-to-maturity equation given previously shows that

$$\frac{2.3125}{1+\dfrac{y}{2}} + \frac{2.3125}{\left(1+\dfrac{y}{2}\right)^2} + \frac{2.3125}{\left(1+\dfrac{y}{2}\right)^3} + \frac{102.3125}{\left(1+\dfrac{y}{2}\right)^4}$$

$$= \frac{2.3125}{1+\dfrac{\hat{r}(.5)}{2}} + \frac{2.3125}{\left[1+\dfrac{\hat{r}(1)}{2}\right]^2} + \frac{2.3125}{\left[1+\dfrac{\hat{r}(1.5)}{2}\right]^3} + \frac{102.3125}{\left[1+\dfrac{\hat{r}(2)}{2}\right]^4}$$

This equation clearly demonstrates that yield-to-maturity is a summary of all the spot rates that enter into the bond-pricing equation. Recall from Table 1.2 that these four spot rates have values of 3.567 percent, 3.896 percent, 4.178 percent, and 4.443 percent. Thus, this bond's yield-to-maturity of 4.427 percent is a blend of these four rates. Furthermore, this blend is closest to the two-year spot rate of 4.443 percent because most of this bond's value comes from its principal payment, that is, its cash flow to be received in two years' time.

To develop this last point further, consider three fictional, 2.5-year securities. The securities and their cash flows in six months, 1.5 years, and 2.5 years are given in the first four columns of Table 3.1. The prices of the three securities, as of February 15, 1994, can be computed using the discount factors in Table 1.2. Then, using these prices, yields can be calculated. For example, the price of security A is

$$.9825 \times \$100 + .9399 \times \$1 + .8920 \times \$1 = \$100.08$$

The yield-to-maturity of security A is 3.628 percent since

Table 3.1   Cash Flows, Price, and Yield for Three Fictional Securities

| Security | Cash Flows | | | Price | Yield |
	in 6 Months	in 1 1/2 Years	in 2 1/2 Years		
A	$100	$1	$1	100.08	3.628%
B	$1	$100	$1	95.86	4.183%
C	$1	$1	$100	91.13	4.617%

$$\frac{100}{1+\frac{.03628}{2}} + \frac{1}{\left[1+\frac{.03628}{2}\right]^3} + \frac{1}{\left[1+\frac{.03628}{2}\right]^5} = 100.08$$

Prices and yields of the three securities are recorded in the fifth and sixth columns of Table 3.1.

The important lessons from Table 3.1 are that the yields of the three 2.5-year securities are all different and that these differences can be explained by their cash flow patterns. Most of the value of security A comes from its six-month cash flow. Therefore, the blend of spot rates making up security A's yield will most heavily weight the six-month spot rate. Table 3.1 supports this reasoning: Security A's yield is 3.628 percent while the six-month spot rate is 3.567 percent. One can also explain why the yield on security A exceeds the six-month spot rate. Since the 1.5-year and 2.5-year spot rates are larger than the six-month spot rate, any blend of the three spot rates, such as the yield on security A, will also exceed the six-month spot rate.

Security B, which pays most of its value in 1.5 years, has a yield-to-maturity of 4.183 percent. This value is quite close to the 1.5-year spot rate of 4.178 percent. Finally, security C, which pays most of its value in 2.5 years, has a yield of 4.617 percent which is very close to the 2.5-year spot rate of 4.622 percent.

To summarize, securities with the same maturity will not generally have the same yield-to-maturity. Yields of individual securities depend on cash-flow patterns as well as the term structure of interest rates. Therefore, it is incorrect to say that, of securities with the same maturity, the one with the highest yield is "best." All three securities in the example are priced fairly, that is, according to prevailing discount factors or spot rates. Security C has the highest yield only because its main cash flow is discounted at the highest spot rate.[12]

THE COUPON EFFECT

This section discusses the relative value of certain types of bonds and a common situation in which yield-to-maturity can be mistaken for a measure of relative value. Using the discount function on February 15, 1994, Figure 3.1 graphs the yields on three different types of securities as a function of their maturities.

Before interpreting the graph, consider the three types of securities and how

---

[12]Readers already familiar with duration might think that security C has the highest yield because it has the longest duration. This is not correct. If the term structure of spot rates were downward-sloping, then security C would have the lowest yield even though it would still have the longest duration.

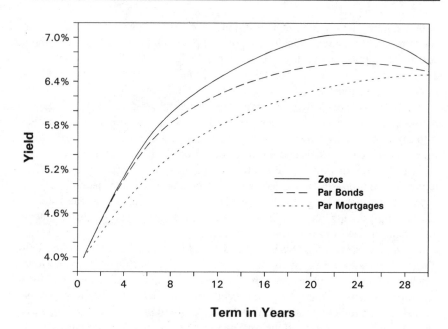

Term in Years

FIGURE 3.1   Yields on zeros, par bonds, and par mortgages.

each line is generated. The solid line represents the yield-to-maturity on zero-coupon bonds. The price of a zero-coupon bond is simply the present value of its single cash flow. Using the spot rate representation of present value, the price of a zero-coupon bond is given by

$$P = \frac{F}{\left(1 + \dfrac{\hat{r}(T)}{2}\right)^{2T}}$$

where P is the price, F is the face value, and T is the number of years to the zero's maturity. Recall that yield-to-maturity is the one rate that, when used to discount a security's cash flows, gives the security's price. It follows immediately from the above pricing equation that the yield-to-maturity of a zero-coupon bond is simply the appropriate spot rate. The top curve of Figure 3.1, therefore, is just the spot rate curve.

A par bond is a bond with a price equal to its face value, so the yield is equal to the coupon rate. Constructing the middle curve of Figure 3.1 requires the following steps. First, for each maturity find the coupon rate such that a coupon bond of that maturity will sell at par. This is done, of course, by finding the coupon rate such that the discounted value of coupon and principal payments, all discounted at their appropriate spot rates, equals the bond's face value. Second, given these are par bonds, their yields equal these coupon rates. Third, graph these yields as a function of maturity.

The bottom curve of Figure 3.1 graphs the yields on non-prepayable mortgages. A complete discussion of mortgage math will appear in Part Four. For now, suffice it to say that the cash flows of a traditional mortgage are level; that is, the cash flow on each date is the same. Furthermore, a newly issued mortgage is priced fairly if the present value of the mortgage payments equals the loan amount. The bottom curve is constructed as follows. For each maturity, calculate the mortgage payment that makes the present value of the mortgage equal to its face value or outstanding principal amount. Then, calculate each mortgage's yield-to-maturity and graph the result as a function of maturity.

All three securities depicted in Figure 3.1 are fairly priced. In other words, their present values are properly computed using the discount function or the term structure of spot or forward rates. Nevertheless, zeros, coupon bonds, and mortgages of the same maturity have different yields-to-maturity. Therefore, as discussed in the previous section, it is incorrect to say that zeros are the best buys because they have the highest yields. The impact of coupon level on the yield-to-maturity of coupon bonds with the same maturity has been called the *coupon effect*. The phenomenon that securities of the same maturity have different yields appears whenever securities have different cash-flow patterns.

The next lesson of the figure is that, for a given maturity, par bonds have lower yields than zeros. Why? The yield of a zero with T years to maturity is simply the T-year spot rate. On the other hand, since coupon bonds make payments before maturity, their yields will be a blend of spot rates, in six month intervals, up to and including the T-year spot rate. But, since the term-structure of spot rates is upward-sloping, this blend must be below the T-year spot rate. Therefore, the yield-to-maturity of coupon bonds will be below the yield on zero-coupon bonds.

Note from Figure 3.1 that, at long maturities, the relationship between zero yields and coupon yields narrows and may reverse. This happens because the spot rate curve eventually becomes downward-sloping. To understand fully why zero-coupon yields behave in this manner, consider the extreme case of a spot rate curve that is downward-sloping for all maturities. In that case, the blend of spot rates up to and including the T-year spot rate will be above the T-year spot rate and, therefore, the yield on the coupon bond will be above the yield on the zero. In Figure 3.1, the falling spot rate curve lowers the zero yields much faster than it lowers the coupon yields because coupon yields are blends of many shorter-term spot rates.

A final lesson from Figure 3.1 is that mortgages have the lowest yields of all three securities. Given their level payments, mortgages have more of their total value discounted at shorter-term spot rates than do coupon bonds. Therefore, the blend of spot rates that determines their yields is more heavily weighted toward the lower spot rates than the blend which determines coupon bond yields. As a result, non-prepayable mortgages have lower yields than coupon bonds. As before, this relationship can reverse itself as the spot rate curve slopes downward. In that case, the yield on mortgages falls more slowly than the yield on coupon bonds because mortgage yields are more heavily weighted toward the earlier spot rates.

YIELD-TO-MATURITY AND REALIZED RETURN

Yield-to-maturity is sometimes described as a measure of a bond's return if held to maturity. The argument is made as follows. As defined in the beginning of this chapter, the yield to maturity, y, of the Treasury's 4 5/8s due February 15, 1996 is given by

$$\frac{2.3125}{1+\frac{y}{2}} + \frac{2.3125}{\left(1+\frac{y}{2}\right)^2} + \frac{2.3125}{\left(1+\frac{y}{2}\right)^3} + \frac{102.3125}{\left(1+\frac{y}{2}\right)^4} = 100.375$$

Multiplying both sides of this equation by $(1 + y/2)^4$ gives

$$2.3125\left(1+\frac{y}{2}\right)^3 + 2.3125\left(1+\frac{y}{2}\right)^2 + 2.3125\left(1+\frac{y}{2}\right) + 102.3125 = 100.375\left(1+\frac{y}{2}\right)^4$$

The interpretation of the left-hand side of this equation is as follows. On August 15, 1994, the bond makes its first coupon payment of 2.3125. Reinvesting that payment at rate y through February 15, 1996, the bond's maturity date, will produce $2.3125(1 + y/2)^3$. Similarly, reinvesting the bond's second coupon payment, received on February 15, 1995, through the maturity date at rate y will produce $2.3125(1 + y/2)^2$. Continuing with this reasoning reveals that the left-hand side of the equation equals the sum of money one would have on February 15, 1996, assuming a coupon reinvestment rate y. The equation shows that this sum equals $100.375(1 + y/2)^4$, the purchase price of the bond invested at a semiannually compounded rate of y for two years. Hence it is claimed that yield-to-maturity is a measure of the bond's realized return.

Unfortunately, there is a terrible flaw in this argument. There is absolutely no reason to assume that coupons will be reinvested at the initial yield-to-maturity of the bond. The reinvestment rate of the first coupon will be the 1.5-year rate that prevails six months from now. The reinvestment rate of the second coupon will be the one-year rate that prevails one year from now, and so forth. The realized return from holding the bond and reinvesting coupons depends critically on these unknown future rates. If, for example, all of the reinvestment rates turn out to be higher than the original yield, then the realized yield-to-maturity will be higher than the original yield-to-maturity. If, at the other extreme, all of the reinvestment rates turn out to be lower than the original yield, then the realized yield will be lower than the original yield. In any case, it is extremely unlikely that the realized yield of a coupon bond held to maturity will equal its original yield-to-maturity. The uncertainty of the realized yield relative to the original yield because coupons are invested at uncertain, future rates is often called *reinvestment risk*.

Chapter 4
Real Data Issues

The concepts and calculations introduced in the previous chapter are extremely useful in thinking about fixed income markets. But, when applying them to real data, some complications arise. First, unlike the implicit assumption of the previous chapter, every bond does not make its next cash flow in exactly six months. The first section of this chapter discusses the adjustments that need to be made for first payments due in less than six months.

Second, the techniques presented so far allow for the calculation of discount factors corresponding to the payment dates of traded bonds. But investors may need to know other values of the discount function. If, for example, traded bonds make payments in six months, 1 year, 1.5 years, and so on, one cannot deduce the value of d(.75) or d(1.25) from bond prices. But these unobtainable values may be required for other pricing purposes such as the pricing of nontraded securities, a starting point for the pricing of securities with credit risk or, as will be seen in Part Two, the pricing of any derivative fixed income security. In short, there is a need to complete the discount function obtained from traded bonds.

The third real-data complication is that bond prices are subject to "error." The word "error" may mean that someone quoted or transcribed an inaccurate price by mistake, but it also refers to any effect that is not part of the model presented in previous sections. For example, since all bonds do not trade at every instant, some price quotations in a data set may be old or "stale" and, therefore, not directly comparable with other prices. Another example would be liquidity differences. Some bonds, because they are traded extremely frequently and at very high volumes, are particularly desirable and can command higher prices than would be indicated by the models of previous sections. A third example of left-out effects would be features of the tax code that treat one security differently from another.

The second and third sections of this chapter introduce smoothing techniques as a means to complete discount functions and to handle the problems of data subject to error.

COUPONS IN THE MIDST OF SEMIANNUAL INTERVALS

Say that on February 15, 1994, an investor purchases $10,000 face value of the Treasury's 8 7/8s due July 15, 1995. Since this bond matures in July, it pays coupons on the January–July cycle and the next coupon will be paid on July 15, 1994. It can be argued that the purchaser is not entitled to the entire July 15, 1994, semiannual coupon payment of $10,000 x 8 7/8%/2 = $443.75 because, at that time, he will have held the bond for only five of the six months in the coupon period. Taking this reasoning one step further, it can be said that the purchaser is entitled to 5/6 of the semiannual coupon, or 5/6 x $443.75 = $369.79. In the same vein, the seller is entitled to one month of interest or 1/6 x $443.75 = $73.96 since he held the bond for one month since the last coupon payment on January 15, 1994. This last amount, the amount of interest thought due to the seller, is called *accrued interest*. In light of this reasoning, market convention dictates that, at the time of purchase, the buyer pays the seller accrued interest. So, when the next coupon is paid, the buyer keeps it all. Figure 4.1 illustrates the working of this market convention.

The quoted ask price of the 8 7/8s due July 15, 1995, on February 15, 1994,

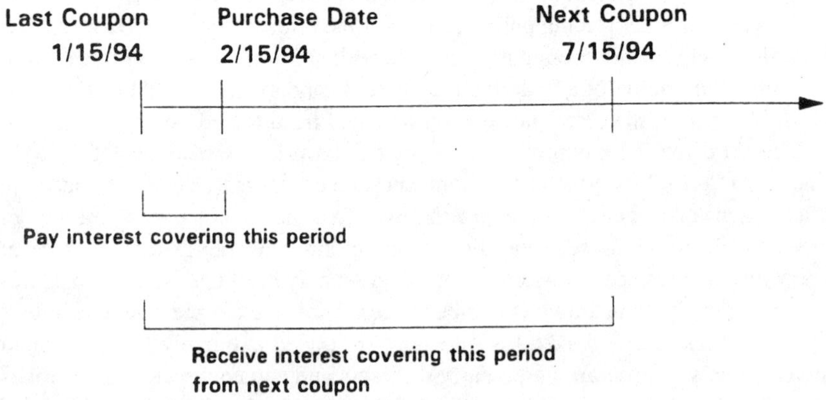

Last Coupon	Purchase Date	Next Coupon
1/15/94	2/15/94	7/15/94

Pay interest covering this period

Receive interest covering this period
from next coupon

FIGURE 4.1 Accrued interest.

was 106:15 or 106.46875. Adding the accrued interest to this price gives the total cost to the buyer of $10,000 x 1.0646875 + $73.96 = $10,720.84.[13]

How does the accrued interest convention affect the pricing equations of previous sections? It is still true that a bond's value equals the present value of its cash flows. Only now, the bond's true price includes accrued interest. Letting P be a bond's quoted price, AI a bond's accrued interest, and PV() the present value function, the following equation must hold:

$$P + AI = PV(\text{future cash flows})$$

This equation reveals an important principle about accrued interest. Tax effects aside, the particular market convention chosen for accrued interest calculations does not really matter. If accrued interest is too high, that is, if, in any sense, the seller receives "too much" of the anticipated coupon from the buyer, then the quoted price will fall to ensure that the above equation holds. Similarly, if accrued interest is in any sense too low, the quoted price will rise to restore equality. All that matters is that everyone know how accrued interest is calculated.

The accrued interest convention makes the quoted price process smooth over time. In other words, quoted price does not fall because of a coupon payment. To see this, let P^b be the price of a bond right before a coupon payment of $c/2$ on date t. Since the coupon is just about to be paid, accrued interest or $AI = c/2$. Also, the present value of the next coupon payment equals the next coupon payment. Therefore, the pricing equation is

$$P^b + \frac{c}{2} = \frac{c}{2} + PV(\text{all cash flows after the date-t coupon})$$

Or,

$$P^b = PV(\text{all cash flows after the date-t coupon})$$

[13]The calculation of accrued interest is actually more complicated than described in the text. In the Treasury market, for example, the exact number of days since the last coupon payment and the exact number of days between coupon payments are used to calculate accrued interest. Other markets have different conventions. For municipal and corporate bonds, accrued interest is accrued based on a 360-day year of 12 months with 30 days each. For a discussion of these rules the reader should consult Stigum (1981).

Now let P^a be the price of the bond right after the coupon payment. In this case, accrued interest equals 0 and the pricing equation is

$$P^a + 0 = PV(\text{all cash flows after the date-t coupon})$$

Clearly $P^b = P^a$ so that the quoted price does not fall as a result of the coupon payment. This behavior differs from that of stocks, which do not have an accrued dividend convention. As a result, stock prices fall by approximately the amount of the dividend on the day ownership of the dividend payment is established. The accrued interest convention developed in bond markets but not in stock markets probably because dividend payment amounts are generally much less certain than interest payment amounts.

The adjusted bond pricing equation presented here requires that one be able to discount cash flows payable after any time interval. Until now, however, it was assumed that all cash flows were paid in six month intervals. Consider, once again, the Treasury's 8 7/8s due July 15, 1995. As of February 15, 1994, its three cash flows are payable in 5 months, in 11 months, and in 17 months. Recalling that d(t) is the present value of $1 to be received in t years, the bond price is given by

$$4.4375 \times d\left(\frac{5}{12}\right) + 4.4375 \times d\left(\frac{11}{12}\right) + 104.4375 \times d\left(\frac{17}{12}\right)$$

The techniques of Chapter 1, used to extract discount factors for six month intervals, such as d(.5), d(1), d(1.5), can be easily applied to bonds that make payments on any chosen dates, such as d(5/12), d(11/12), and so on. The general rule is that a set of bonds making payments on N dates can be used to discover the discount factors on each of those N dates.

However, with cash flows paid in intervals of other than six months, writing bond-pricing equations in terms of semiannual rates is not a straightforward procedure. For interested readers, Appendix 4A develops this point and introduces continuous compounding as a solution. But, since bond prices can always be written in terms of discount factors, readers are encouraged to price bonds using their discount factor representations. If forward and spot rates are desired for purposes other than bond-pricing, like comparing one's own interest rate predictions with the forward rate curve, one can use the techniques of the next section to obtain the entire discount function and then compute semiannually compounded rates.

For the purposes of computing yield-to-maturity, there is a market convention to discount cash flows at intervals other than six months using semiannual rates. Consider the 8 1/2s due November 15, 1995, selling for about 107. The first coupon payment after February 15, 1994, is on May 15, 1994, three months hence. The market convention is to discount this coupon payment by dividing by

$$\left(1+\frac{y}{2}\right)^{\frac{1}{2}}$$

since the first coupon is one-half of a semiannual period away. Similarly, the coupon due in nine months is discounted by dividing by

$$\left(1+\frac{y}{2}\right)^{1+\frac{1}{2}}$$

since the second coupon is 1.5 semiannual periods away. Discounting coupons that are further away in a similar fashion gives the following equation for the yield of the 8 1/2s:

$$\frac{4.25}{\left(1+\frac{y}{2}\right)^{\frac{1}{2}}}+\frac{4.25}{\left(1+\frac{y}{2}\right)^{1\frac{1}{2}}}+\frac{4.25}{\left(1+\frac{y}{2}\right)^{2\frac{1}{2}}}+\frac{104.25}{\left(1+\frac{y}{2}\right)^{3\frac{1}{2}}}=107$$

More generally, if a bond's first coupon payment is paid in a fraction τ of a semi-annual period and the bond matures N semiannual periods after that payment, then yield-to-maturity is given by

$$P=\frac{c}{2}\sum_{t=0}^{n}\left(1+\frac{y}{2}\right)^{-t-\tau}+\left(1+\frac{y}{2}\right)^{-N-\tau}$$

Appendix 4A briefly comments on this market convention.

AN INTRODUCTION TO SMOOTHING TECHNIQUES

As mentioned at the beginning of this chapter, smoothing techniques are used to derive complete discount functions from a set of bond price quotations and to control the effects of imperfections in those quoted prices. Figures 4.2 and 4.3 illustrate the data error problem. Figure 4.2 is a plot of the discount function on February 15, 1994, obtained directly from prices of STRIPS maturing in six-month intervals. Figure 4.3 is a graph of the spot rates and forward rates on that date, obtained from these same prices and the techniques presented in Chapter 2.

Figure 4.2 makes it appear that the discount function is quite smooth and relatively well-behaved, despite the fact that it has been created from raw data. On the other hand, there is one glaring problem: At the longest maturities, the discount function seems to increase with maturity. In other words, the time value of money seems to become negative at long maturities! The graph has to be considered in relation to the data from which it is created. In this case, there is another, more believable explanation. The most recently issued coupon bonds, referred to as the *on-the-run* or *current* coupon bonds, sell for more than older, less-liquid bonds of similar maturities. The longest maturity zero-coupon bond stripped from the 30-year current coupon inherits the liquidity price premium. In summary, use of raw data without liquidity corrections may give misleading impressions about the discount function.

The spot rate curve in Figure 4.3 seems relatively smooth, though not as smooth as the discount function. Furthermore, there is a noticeable dip in the long end because of the premium that the long-term zero commands. The forward rates,

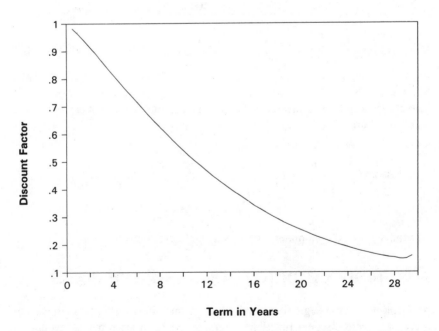

FIGURE 4.2   Discount factors from zero prices as of February 15, 1994.

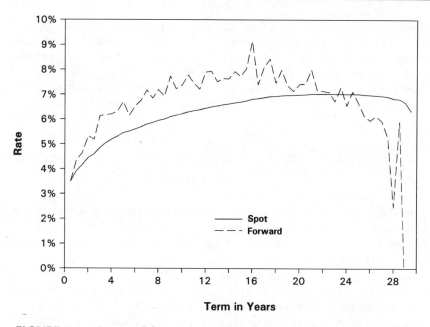

FIGURE 4.3   Spot and forward rates from zero prices as of February 15, 1994.

however, are very poorly behaved. Recalling from Chapter 2 that the forward rates are related to changes in the spot rates, the jaggedness of the forward rate curve indicates that the spot rate curve and, in turn, the discount function are not as smooth as they appear to be.

It is generally true that, when calculated from raw data, the discount function is the smoothest curve, followed by the spot rate curve and, as a distant third, the forward rate curve. To understand why this is true, consider the following example. The price of a 10-year STRIP, as of February 15, 1994, was quoted at 54.1875. If that quotation were in error by .1, so that the true price were 54.0875, then the true discount factor would be .540875 while it would be thought to be .541875. So, a percentage error in the STRIP price of .1/54.0875 = .1848 percent translates into the same percentage error in the discount factor of .001/.540875 = .1848 percent. That same pricing error, however, has a larger effect on the spot rate. Recalling from Chapter 2 that

$$\hat{r}(10) = 2\left\{\left[\frac{1}{d(10)}\right]^{\frac{1}{20}} - 1\right\}$$

the 10-year spot rate using the inaccurate discount factor is 6.222 percent while the true spot rate is 6.241 percent. The error in the spot rate, therefore, is $(.06241 - .06222)/.06241 = .304$ percent. Finally, it can be shown that the percentage error in the forward rate is much larger still. As it happens, the 9.5-year discount factor is .561875. Also, recall from Chapter 2 that the forward rate, $r(10)$, is given by

$$\left[1 + \frac{\hat{r}(9.5)}{2}\right]^{19}\left[1 + \frac{r(10)}{2}\right] = \left[1 + \frac{\hat{r}(10)}{2}\right]^{20}$$

These facts can be used to compute that the true forward rate is 7.7651 percent while the forward rate computed from the erroneous data is 7.3817 percent. The difference between these two numbers implies a percentage error of $(.077651 - 073817)/.077651 = 4.94$ percent.

To summarize, errors in discount factors are of the same magnitude as errors in prices. The computation of spot rates from discount factors compounds these errors and results in larger percentage errors. Finally, the computation of forward rates, which are related to changes in spot rates, leads to much larger percentage errors.

EXAMPLES OF SMOOTHING TECHNIQUES

One common but highly unsatisfactory technique of filling in missing discount factors is *linear yield interpolation*. This technique begins with a short list of bonds spanning the maturity range. For reasons to become apparent shortly, bonds best suited for this list are those that sell near par and those for which accurate prices are available. Since on-the-run issues usually satisfy both of these criteria, data points for this technique usually fall at the maturities of bonds sold by the Treasury. In any case, an example of such a list is given in Table 4.1.

The next step is to construct a yield curve by connecting the few data points with straight lines. This procedure is illustrated in Figure 4.4. Since, as shown in Chapter 3, yield depends on coupon level, this yield curve does not contain enough information from which to derive discount factors, spot rates, or forward rates. It is assumed, therefore, that this figure represents a *par yield curve*, that is, the yields on coupon bonds that sell for their face values. Since the yield of a par bond equals its coupon rate, being given a par yield curve is equivalent to being given a set of bonds and their prices. In that case, discount factors and rates can be extracted. By the way, the necessity of assuming that the yield curve has been constructed from par bonds is why it is best, in the first place, to select bonds that do, in fact, sell near par.

Table 4.1   List of Bonds Used in Linear Yield Interpolation

Coupon	Maturity	Yield
6 7/8	8/15/94	3.47
5 1/2	2/15/95	3.85
4 5/8	2/15/96	4.41
4 3/4	2/15/97	4.77
8 1/8	2/15/98	5.11
8 7/8	2/15/99	5.33
7 3/4	2/15/2001	5.64
5 7/8	2/15/2004	5.87
11 1/4	2/15/2015	6.54
7 1/8	2/15/2023	6.55

Figure 4.4 looks innocuous enough. But spot and forward rates implied by this yield curve usually behave quite badly. Figure 4.5 graphs the spot and forward rate curves implied by the par yields in Figure 4.4. Aside from being quite bumpy, the spot rate curve segments are convex, so that any line connecting two points on a segment is above the segment. In this particular graph, this effect is most notice-

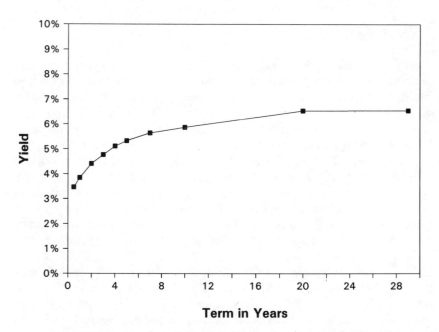

FIGURE 4.4   Linear yield interpolation on February 15, 1994.

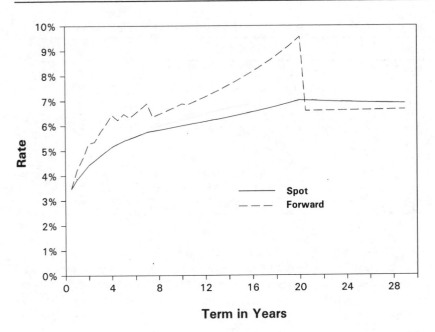

FIGURE 4.5   Spot and forward rates as of February 15, 1994: yield interpolation.

able for maturities between 7 and 20 years. The convexity of this constructed spot rate curve is a problem because the true spot rate curve is normally concave, so that any line connecting two points is below the curve. (See, for example, Figure 4.3 constructed from a set of STRIPS prices.) In fact, if one sees a spot rate curve with convex segments, there is a very good chance that it was constructed by linear yield interpolation.

The forward rate curve generated from the yield curve of Figure 4.4 is also quite unsatisfactory. It is extremely bumpy, where each bump corresponds to a particular bond in the data set. Because the slope of the estimated spot rate curve changes by so much at a maturity of 20 years, the forward rate curve takes a particularly large jump at that point. Furthermore, as in the case of the spot rate curve, the forward rate curve is convex where it should be concave. In short, neither of the two rate curves is believable.

A more satisfactory approach for estimating smooth rate curves and discount functions is to assume a *functional form* for the discount function and then estimate the *parameters* of that functional form from a set of bond prices. For example, an extremely simple functional form for the discount function would be a cubic polynomial:

$$d(t) = 1 + at + bt^2 + ct^3$$

where a, b, and c are parameters to be estimated. Note that this functional form imposes the condition that $d(0) = 1$; in other words, the value of \$1 to be received immediately is \$1 no matter what values of a, b, and c are ultimately chosen.

To estimate the parameters a, b, and c, one writes the bond prices in the data set as a function of the chosen functional form. Say, for example, that the price of the Treasury's 8 7/8s of July 15, 1995, was 106.40. Then, in terms of the discount function, its pricing equation is

$$4.4375 \times d\left(\frac{5}{12}\right) + 4.4375 \times d\left(\frac{11}{12}\right) + 104.4375 \times d\left(\frac{17}{12}\right) = 106.4$$

But, given the assumed functional form, each discount factor can be rewritten in terms of a, b, and c. For instance,

$$d\left(\frac{5}{12}\right) = 1 - a\left(\frac{5}{12}\right) - b\left(\frac{5}{12}\right)^2 - c\left(\frac{5}{12}\right)^3$$

Doing the same for $d(11/12)$ and $d(17/12)$, substituting the results into the pricing equation, and collecting terms gives the following version of the pricing equation:

$$153.87a + 214.10b + 300.67c = 6.91$$

In this way, the pricing equation for each bond in the data set can be written in terms of the unknown parameters.

At this point some statistical technique can be used to estimate the unknown parameters. A common choice is *least squares*. Another choice, which is less common but often useful, is *least absolute deviations*. A brief description of these two procedures can be found in Appendix 4B, but interested readers without any previous exposure to these tools are advised to consult an elementary statistical text.

The discussion here focuses first on the selection of a functional form for the discount function. On one hand, the more complex the functional form, and the greater the number of parameters, the better the discount function will be able to describe the data. On the other hand, the more complex the functional form, the more it is likely to *overfit* the data, which means capturing the errors in the data along with the indications of true prices. Figure 4.6 is an example of a spot and forward rate curve derived from an overfitted discount function.[14] While, as it turns out, they fit bond price data on February 15, 1994, quite well, the oscillations, sharp jumps, and negative values of the forward rate curve are far from satisfactory. Many practitioners, therefore, prefer an economically sensible discount function that fits the data relatively well to an economically unreasonable discount function that fits the data extremely well.

The cubic polynomial described above is too simple a functional form to be used in practice because it does not have sufficient flexibility to fit the data well enough. A common choice that works better is a *piecewise cubic polynomial*, which means that d(t) is assumed to be a different cubic polynomial over several maturity ranges. Put another way, the parameters a, b, and c change from one maturity region to another. Appendix 4C describes piecewise cubic polynomials in more detail.

Figure 4.7 graphs smoothed spot and forward rate curves using four joined

---

[14]The discount function in this case was computed using least squares to estimate a piecewise cubic polynomial with 10 segments.

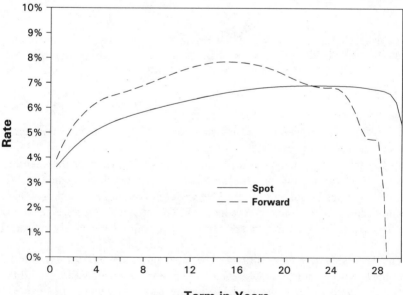

Term in Years

FIGURE 4.6   Spot and forward rates as of February 15, 1994: overfitting the data.

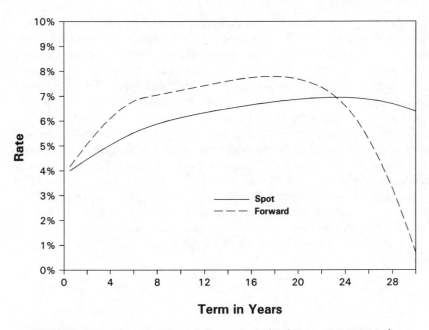

Term in Years

FIGURE 4.7   Spot and forward rates as of February 15, 1994: least squares.

cubic segments[15] estimated by least squares on a data set of zero and coupon bond prices prevailing on February 15, 1994. These curves fit the data very well, are quite smooth, and have relatively appealing shapes. The only drawback is that the forward rate curve seems to drop off too rapidly. In other words, the forward rates at the long-end of the maturity spectrum seem too low.

As it turns out, these low forward rates can be explained by liquidity considerations. The most recently issued long-term bonds command a substantial liquidity premium because of the ease with which one can establish and unwind large positions in those bonds. But since these bonds are not really comparable with those of adjacent maturities, their relatively high prices push spot and forward rates down below reasonable levels.

A difficult but potentially rewarding solution to this problem is to model the liquidity differences across bonds. A quicker solution is to use an estimation technique that is not as affected by a few special bonds as is least squares. Least absolute deviations is such a technique. Basically, least squares estimates are like taking an

[15]The functional form chosen is actually a cubic spline. See Appendix 4C for a description of this special case.

average. If, for example, one or two observations are much larger than the rest of the sample, the average will be too large to be representative of the sample. Least absolute deviations, however, is like taking a median. Several observations can be far away from the rest without affecting the median very much.

Applying least absolute deviations to the same data used to generate Figure 4.7 gives Figure 4.8. The curves are still smooth and shaped well, but the forward rate curve behaves much better at the longer maturities.

Before concluding this discussion, the reader should be cautioned that these smoothing techniques have to be monitored closely and frequently. The inexperienced and unwary can be easily caught. For example, using these techniques on coupon bond data alone often leads to unreliable forward rate curves. This effect is shown in Figure 4.9. The reason for this behavior is that there are no noncallable Treasury bonds maturing from February 2007 to November 2014. As a result, estimation techniques allow very oddly shaped rate curves in this region. Using zero-coupon data provides information on this maturity region and avoids the problem.

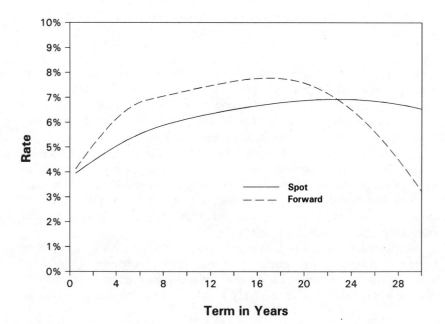

Term in Years

FIGURE 4.8   Spot and forward rates as of February 15, 1994: least absolute deviations.

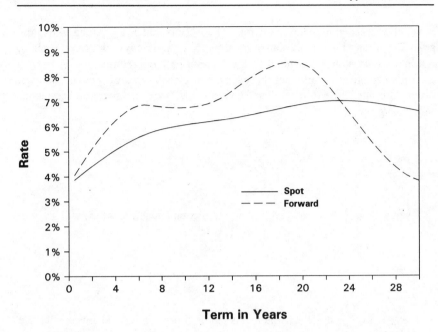

FIGURE 4.9   Spot and forward rates as of February 15, 1994: coupon bond data.

APPENDIX 4A

Rate Calculations When Cash Flows Occur in the Midst of Semiannual Intervals and Continuous Compounding

What is the present value of $1 to be received in five months when the five-month semiannually compounded spot rate is 4 percent? One might be tempted to answer the question with the following expression:

$$\frac{1}{\left(1+\dfrac{.04}{2}\right)^{\frac{5}{12}}}$$

But this is not very satisfactory. Raising $(1 + r/2)$ to the third power, for example, means that the semiannual interest payment is paid three times. A power of 5/12 has no such interpretation.

One approach to this difficulty might be to switch to monthly compounding, in which case a denominator of the form $(1 + r/2)^5$ would be a meaningful expression. But, if any bond makes a payment in 15 days, 45 days, and so on (that is, not in a whole number of months), the original problem returns.

A mathematically consistent approach is to use *continuously compounded* rates. To explain this concept, recall that \$1 invested at rate r, compounded semiannually, will grow to

$$\left(1+\frac{r}{2}\right)^{2T}$$

in T years. Analogously, \$1 invested at rate r, compounded monthly, will grow to

$$\left(1+\frac{r}{12}\right)^{12T}$$

in T years. More generally, if interest is paid n times per year, \$1 invested at rate r will grow to

$$\left(1+\frac{r}{n}\right)^{nT}$$

in T years.

It can be proven that if one lets n get very large, so that interest is paid every instant—that is, if r is continuously compounded—then the \$1 will grow to

$$e^{rT}$$

in T years, where $e = 2.71828\ldots$, the base of the natural logarithms. Equivalently, the present value of \$1 to be received in T years is e^{-rT}. Therefore, using continuous compounding, the spot rate, $\hat{r}(t)$, is defined such that

$$d(t) = e^{-\hat{r}(t)t}$$

Deriving the forward rate, $r(t)$, is harder. In the case of semiannual compounding,

$$\left[1 + \frac{\hat{r}(t)}{2}\right]^{2t} \left[1 + \frac{r(t + .5)}{2}\right] = \left[1 + \frac{\hat{r}(t + .5)}{2}\right]^{2t+1}$$

Using the relation between spot rates and discount factors, this equation can be rewritten as

$$d(t)\left[1 + \frac{r(t + .5)}{2}\right] = d(t + .5)$$

Analogously, in the case of compounding n times per year, this equation becomes

$$d(t)\left[1 + \frac{r\left(t + \frac{1}{n}\right)}{n}\right] = d\left(t + \frac{1}{n}\right)$$

Solving for the forward rate, r(t + 1/n), gives

$$r\left(t + \frac{1}{n}\right) = \frac{d\left(t + \frac{1}{n}\right) - d(t)}{\frac{1}{n}} \frac{1}{d(t)}$$

In the case of continuous compounding, n gets very large. Taking limits of both sides of the above equation as n goes to infinity shows that

$$r(t) = \frac{d'(t)}{d(t)}$$

where d'(t) is the derivative of the discount function with respect to its argument, t.

This appendix has shown that, given the discount function d(t), one can calculate spot rates and forward rates in a mathematically consistent way. And the smoothing techniques of this chapter can be used to estimate the function d(t) from bond data sets.

While continuous compounding allows for a mathematically consistent way of calculating rates of all terms, it sacrifices correspondence with the reality of semi-annual bond interest payments. Therefore, one may wish to calculate bond prices directly from the discount function obtained with the techniques of Section 2 of this chapter. If rates are required, whether semiannual rates at six-month intervals or monthly rates at one-month intervals, and so on, they can be computed from this discount function.

APPENDIX 4B

Least Squares and Least Absolute Deviations

A data set consists of observations on a *dependent variable* (that is, a variable to be explained by other variables), and on one or several *independent variables* (that is, variables used to explain the dependent variable). For example, one might like to explain daily changes in the price of a mortgage-backed security by changes in the price of a short-term Treasury bond and by changes in the price of a long-term Treasury bond. In this example, the dependent variable is the change in the price of the mortgage-backed security and there are two independent variables, namely changes in short-term and long-term Treasury bond prices, respectively. Therefore, each observation consists of three numbers: the change in the price of a mortgage-backed security on a particular day, the change in the price of a short-term Treasury on that day, and the change in the price of a long-term Treasury on that same day.

Say that there are N observations and k independent variables. Let y_n be the nth observation on the dependent variable and let x_{in} be the nth observation on the ith independent variable. The relationship between the dependent variable and the independent variables, for all observations, is assumed to be

$$y_n = \beta_1 x_{1n} + \beta_2 x_{2n} + \ldots + \beta_k x_{kn}$$

where $\beta_1, \beta_2, \ldots, \beta_k$ are coefficients to be estimated.

If the number of observations, N, were equal to the number of independent variables, k, there would be a particular choice of coefficients that would fit all the data exactly. Usually, however, N is much bigger than k so that there is no set of coefficients that fits the data exactly. The goal, therefore, is to select coefficients that, in some sense, best describe the data.

A particularly popular criterion for measuring how well a model describes the data is called *least squares*. To understand the least squares criterion, let e_n be the error of the model in predicting the nth observation of the dependent variable from the independent variables. Mathematically,

$$e_n = y_n - \beta_1 x_{1n} - \beta_2 x_{2n} - \ldots - \beta_k x_{kn}$$

Then, the *sum of squared errors* is given by

$$e_1^2 + e_2^2 + \ldots + e_n^2$$

The least squares criterion is to select the coefficients so as to minimize the sum of squared errors.

The text gives an example of a bond pricing equation

$$6.91 = 153.87a + 214.10b + 300.67c$$

For this particular observation, the value of the dependent variable is 6.91 and the values of the three independent variables are 153.87, 214.10, and 300.67. Given four or more such bond-pricing equations, a computer package can be used to calculate the values of a, b, and c that minimize the sum of squared errors of the model. Say that these values turn out to be $\hat{a}$, $\hat{b}$, and $\hat{c}$, respectively. Then, the least squares estimate of the discount function is given by

$$d(t) = 1 + \hat{a}t + \hat{b}t^2 + \hat{c}t^3$$

Least absolute deviations is another criterion by which to judge how well a model fits the data. In this case, the coefficients $\beta_1, \beta_2, \ldots, \beta_k$ are chosen so as to minimize the sum of the absolute values of the errors. Mathematically, least absolute deviations chooses coefficients to minimize

$$\mid e_1 \mid + \mid e_2 \mid + \ldots + \mid e_n \mid$$

As described in the text, least absolute deviations has the advantage that its estimates are not seriously affected by data points far away from the rest of the sample. On the other hand, least absolute deviation estimates are more difficult to compute. For a discussion of their computation, see Amemiya (1985): 77–78.

APPENDIX 4C

Piecewise Cubics

Say that it has been decided to represent the discount function from terms of 0 through 30 years by three cubic polynomials. The first cubic describes the discount function for maturities between 0 and 10, the second for maturities between 10 and 20, and the third for maturities between 20 and 30. Denote these cubics by $p_1(t)$, $p_2(t)$, and $p_3(t)$, respectively, such that

$$p_i(t) = a_{i0} + a_{i1}t + a_{i2}t^2 + a_{i3}t^3 \quad i = 1, 2, 3$$

where the $\{a_{ij}\}$, j=0, . . .,3, are parameters to be estimated.

It is customary to place some constraints on parameter values. For example, to avoid jumps in the discount function at terms of 10 and 20 years, it must be the case that

$$p_1(10) = p_2(10)$$

and

$$p_2(20) = p_3(20)$$

Or, in terms of the parameters,

$$a_{10} + 10a_{11} + 100a_{12} + 1000a_{13} = a_{20} + 10a_{21} + 100a_{22} + 1000a_{23}$$

and

$$a_{20} + 20a_{21} + 400a_{22} + 8000a_{23} = a_{30} + 20a_{31} + 400a_{32} + 8000a_{33}$$

A popular set of constraints leads to *piecewise cubic splines*. These constraints are that the piecewise cubic representation of the discount function is twice continuously differentiable. In other words, neither the discount function, nor its derivative, nor its second derivative, jumps at the points that join the cubic segments together.

For further discussions of piecewise cubics, see Conte and de Boor (1980). The reader planning to implement these techniques should be aware that one has to estimate the parameters in a numerically stable manner. For a discussion of this point, see de Boor (1978).

Part Two
The Relative Pricing of Interest Rate Contingent Claims

INTRODUCTION

Part One described how to price fixed income securities with fixed cash flows relative to other securities with fixed cash flows. While many such securities do trade in fixed income markets, there are very many fixed income securities whose cash flows are not fixed. Consider a European call option on $1,000 face value of a particular bond with a strike price of par. This security gives the holder the right, but not the obligation, to buy $1,000 face value of the bond for $1,000 on the maturity date of the option. If the price of the bond on that maturity date turns out to be $1,050, the holder will choose to exercise his call by paying $1,000 for a security worth $1,050. In that case, the cash flow from the option is $50. But, if the price of the bond on that maturity date turns out to be $950, the holder will choose not to exercise his call and the cash flow from the option is $0. Thus, the cash flow from an option depends on the value of an *underlying security* or, more generally, on the level of bond prices and, equivalently, on the level of interest rates.

Any security whose cash flows depend on the level of bond prices is called an *interest rate derivative* or an *interest rate contingent claim*. The purpose of this Part is to explain the pricing of interest rate contingent claims relative to the prices of securities with fixed cash flows. Chapter 5 introduces the arbitrage pricing of derivatives in a two-date setting, showing why such pricing is possible and pointing out that, unlike pricing securities with fixed cash flows, pricing derivatives requires strong assumptions about the future evolution of interest rates. Chapter 6 describes *risk-neutral* pricing, a commonly used but not so very well understood short-cut in the pricing of contingent claims. In fact, risk-neutral pricing is one of the most subtle ideas in modern finance theory. Chapter 7 extends the methodology of Chapters 5 and 6 beyond their simplified two-date setting.

Together, Chapters 5 through 7 explain the science of arbitrage pricing and term-structure modeling. While this science is essential for the development of a theoretically correct and internally consistent pricing model, it is far from sufficient for the development of a pricing model that accurately portrays market prices. Such models require a careful selection of assumptions regarding the future, random evolution of interest rates and are called *term-structure models*. Chapter 8 describes the art of term-structure modeling, that is, the principles that guide the choice of assumptions. The approach of Chapter 8 is to present such considerations in the context of several well-known term-structure models.

Chapters 5 through 8 focus on arbitrage-free models, which are most commonly used by practitioners. Chapter 9 introduces another class of models, called *equilibrium models*, and weighs the relative merits of the two classes.

Some readers may be familiar with the pricing of stock options and, more generally, of equity derivatives. While the material presented in this Part shares many ideas with that line of research, there are important differences. So, before turning to the main business of Part Two, it seems worthwhile to describe the special problems of fixed income contingent claims and, at the same time, explain why models used in the stock market cannot normally be used in fixed income markets. Readers not particularly interested in this perspective can skip to Chapter 5.

The famous Black-Scholes pricing analysis of stock options can be summarized as follows. Under the assumption that the stock price evolves according to a particular random process and that the short-term interest rate is constant, it is possible to form a portfolio of stocks and short-term bonds that replicates the payoffs of an option. Therefore, by arbitrage arguments like those of Part One, the price of the option must equal the (known) price of the replicating portfolio.

Say that an investor wants to price an option on a five-year bond by a direct application of the Black-Scholes logic. The investor would have to begin by making an assumption about how the price of the five-year bond evolves over time. But this is considerably more complicated than making assumptions about how the price of a stock evolves over time. First, the price of a bond must converge to its face value at maturity while the random process describing the stock price need not be constrained in that way. Second, because of the maturity constraint, the volatility of a bond's price must eventually get smaller as the bond approaches maturity. The Black-Scholes stock analysis, making the simpler assumption that the stock volatility is constant, will certainly not do in the fixed income context. Third, in the stock option context it may be relatively harmless to assume that the short-term interest rate is constant. However, simultaneously assuming that the bond price follows some random process and that the interest rate is constant makes little economic sense.[16]

These objections led researchers to make assumptions about the random evolution of the interest rate rather than of the bond price. In that way bond prices would naturally approach par, price volatilities would naturally approach zero, and the interest rate would no longer be assumed constant. But this approach raises another set of questions. Which interest rate is being assumed to evolve in a certain way? Making assumptions about the five-year rate's behavior over time is not particularly helpful for two reasons. First, five-year coupon bond prices depend on shorter rates as well. Second, pricing an option on a five-year bond requires assumptions about that bond's future possible prices. But, knowing how the five-year rate evolves over time does not meet this requirement because, in a very short time, the option's underlying security will no longer be a five-year bond! So it seems that one must make assumptions about the evolution of the entire term structure of interest rates to price bond options. But that entails making reasonable assumptions about how each rate moves relative to others. In short, despite the enormous importance of the Black-Scholes analysis, the fixed income context demands some special attention.

---

[16]These three objections are less important in the case of short-term options on long-term bonds. Since the underlying security is far from its maturity, the constraints that its price approach par and that its price volatility approach zero are not of great significance. Also, since the option expires shortly, the assumption of a constant short-term rate is as good or bad an approximation as in the case of stock options. In light of these considerations, some practitioners do apply the Black-Scholes analysis in this particular fixed income context.

Chapter 5
An Introduction to Arbitrage-Free Pricing of Derivatives

This chapter begins with a simple model to illustrate the technique of arbitrage-free pricing. Assume that the six-month and one-year spot rates are 3.99 percent and 4.16 percent, respectively. Also assume that, six months from now, the six-month rate will be either 4 percent or 4.5 percent with equal probabilities. This assumption can be represented by a *binomial interest rate tree* for the six-month rate, where "binomial" refers to the fact that only two future values are possible:

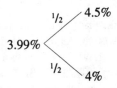

This tree represents an assumption about the evolution of the six-month rate over the next six months. Since this chapter and the next are concerned with pricing given a term-structure model, the reader should not concern himself at this point with the realism of this interest rate tree. Chapters 7 and 8 will take up that point.

Given the current term structure of spot rates (that is, the current six-month and one-year rates) and the six-month rate tree, one can compute trees for the prices of six-month and one-year zero-coupon bonds. The price tree for $1,000 face value of the six-month zero is

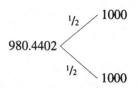

since $1000/(1 + .0399/2) = 980.4402$. Note that columns in the tree represent dates: The 980.4402 entry is a price as of February 15, 1994, which will be called date 0, while the two 1000 entries are prices as of the next date, date 1 or August 15, 1994. As of date 0 the security described by the tree is a six-month zero. As of August 15, 1994, however, six months have passed and the security described by the tree is a maturing zero. Rows in the tree represent different possible outcomes on a particular date. As of August 15, 1994, there are two possible outcomes or *states of the world*; namely, the six-month rate has risen to 4.5 percent, the "up-state," or to 4 percent, the "down-state." In both states, however, the price of a maturing zero is simply 1000.

The price tree for $1000 face value of the one-year zero is the following:

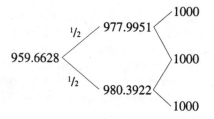

Since the one-year spot rate as of date 0 is 4.16 percent, the price of the one-year zero in the first tree column is $1000/(1 + .0416/2)^2 = 959.6628$. As of date 1 the one-year zero has become a six-month zero. If the six-month rate has risen to 4.5 percent, the now six-month zero is worth $1000/(1 + .045/2) = 977.9951$. If, however, the six-month rate is 4 percent on date 1, the now six-month zero is worth $1000/(1 + .04/2) = 980.3922$. At maturity, of course, the zero is worth 1000.

This model of interest rate movements captures one particularly important feature of bond markets. The average or *expected* value of the one-year zero's price on date 1 is

$$\frac{1}{2}\,977.9951 + \frac{1}{2}\,980.3922 = 979.1937$$

Discounting the resulting value to date 0 at the current six-month rate gives on *expected discounted value* of

$$\frac{979.1937}{1 + \dfrac{.0399}{2}} = 960.04$$

But the market price of the one-year zero is 959.6628. Why are these two numbers different?

The answer is that investors do not price securities by discounting expected values. Over the next six months, the one-year zero is a risky security; it will be worth 977.9951 half of the time and it will be worth 980.3922 the other half of the time, for an average or expected value of 979.1937. But, investors do not like this risk, or, put another way, they would prefer a security that was worth 979.1937 on date 1 with certainty. That security would sell for 979.1937/(1+.0399/2) = 960.04 as of date 0. But the one-year zero is penalized for its riskiness and valued at only 959.6628.

The discussion now turns to the pricing of an interest rate contingent claim. What is the price of a call option, maturing on August 15, 1994, to purchase $1,000 face value of a six-month zero for $978.50? Begin the analysis by drawing the price tree for this call option:

If, on date 1, the six-month rate is 4.5 percent and the price of a six-month zero is 977.9951, then the right to buy the zero for 978.50 is worth nothing. On the other hand, if the six-month rate turns out to be 4 percent and the price of a six-month zero is 980.3922, then the right to buy the zero is worth 980.3922 − 978.50 = 1.8922.

As discussed in Chapter 1, to value a security by arbitrage one must find and value its replicating portfolio. In the present case, the goal is to construct a portfolio of six-month and one-year zero-coupon bonds on date 0 that will be worth 0 on date 1 if the six-month rate rises to 4.5 percent but will be worth 1.8922 if the six-month rate rises to only 4 percent. Let F_5 and F_1 be the face value of six-month and one-year zeros in the replicating portfolio, respectively. Then, these values must satisfy the following two equations:

$$F_{.5} + .9779951F_1 = 0$$
$$F_{.5} + .9803922F_1 = 1.8922$$

These equations have the following interpretations. In the up-state (interest rate rises to 4.5 percent), the value of the replicating portfolio's now maturing six-month zeros is $1 per dollar face value. The value of the once one-year zeros, now six-month zeros, is $.9779951 per dollar face value. Since, by definition, the replicating portfolio contains $F_{.5}$ and F_1 face value of the once six-month and one-year zeros, the total value of the replicating portfolio in the up-state is $F_{.5}$ + .9779951F_1. Therefore, the first equation requires the value of the replicating portfolio in the up-state to equal 0, which is the value of the option in the up-state. By similar reasoning, the second equation requires the value of the replicating portfolio in the down-state to equal 1.8922, that is, the value of the option in the down-state.

Solving the previous two equations for $F_{.5}$ and F_1 reveals that $F_{.5} = -772.0005$ and $F_1 = 789.3705$. In words, the replicating portfolio is formed by buying about $789.37 face value of one-year zeros on February 15, 1994, and, at the same time, shorting about $772 face value of six-month zeros. But since the replicating portfolio is economically equivalent to the option itself, the law of one price requires that the price of the option must equal the price of the replicating portfolio. This portfolio's price is known and is equal to the current six-month zero price per dollar face value times $F_{.5}$ plus the current one-year zero price per dollar face value times F_1. Algebraically,

$$.9804402 \times -772.0005 + .9596628 \times 789.3705 = .63$$

Therefore, the price of the option must be $.63. Recall that this argument is based on arbitrage arguments. If the price of the option were less than $.63, arbitrageurs could buy the option, short the replicating portfolio, pocket the difference, and have no outstanding liabilities. Similarly, if the price of the option were greater than $.63, arbitrageurs could short the option, buy the replicating portfolio, pocket the difference, and have no outstanding liabilities. Thus, ruling out the potential for riskless arbitrage profits implies an option price of $.63.

It is important to emphasize that one could not have arrived at this option price by discounting the expected future value of the option. Since the option will be worth either 0 or 1.8922 on August 15, 1994, its expected future value is .5 x 0 + .5 x 1.8922 = .9461. Discounting this to February 15, 1994, gives a value of $.9461/(1 + .0399/2) = .9276$. The true option price is less than that value because investors dislike the risk of the call option and, as a result, will not pay as much as its discounted expected value.[17]

The careful reader will have noticed that the probabilities of up and down moves never entered into the calculation of the value of the option. The explanation for this somewhat surprising observation stems from the true meaning of arbitrage pricing. The arbitrage pricing argument requires that the value of the replicating portfolio match the value of the option in both the up-state and the down-state. So the composition of the replicating portfolio is the same whether the up-state occurs 20 percent of the time, 50 percent of the time, or 80 percent of the time. Furthermore, the price of each security in the replicating portfolio depends only on current prices. Therefore, calculating the price of the replicating portfolio or, equivalently, the price of the option, does not require knowledge of the probabilities of up and down states.

Having understood this last point, one must inquire as to how the probabilities do enter into the option price. After all, as it becomes more and more likely that rates increase to 4.5 percent and that future bond prices will be low, the value of options to purchase bonds should fall. The answer is that the probabilities are embedded into the current price of the one-year zero. Were the probability of an up-move to increase suddenly, the current value of a one-year zero would decrease. And since the replicating portfolio is long one-year zeros, the value of the option would decrease as well. In summary, an option depends on the probabilities of up and down moves only through current bond prices. Given bond prices, however, one need not know the probabilities to derive arbitrage-free option prices.

This Chapter illustrated arbitrage-pricing methodology through a call option. But it should be clear that this methodology can be used to price any security whose cash flows can be written as a function of the six-month rate. Say, for example, that one needed to price a security that, on August 15, 1994, was worth –$200 [18] in the up-state and $1,000 in the down-state. One would proceed as before. Construct the portfolio of six-month and one-year zeros that replicates these payoffs, price the replicating portfolio as of February 15, 1994, and conclude by arbitrage arguments that the price of the security equals the price of the replicating portfolio.

---

[17]It is not true that investors always value risky securities at less than their discounted expected values. Consider, for example, a put option struck at 979.89 so that the possible values of the option on August 15, 1994, are 1.89 in the up-state and 0 in the down-state. Similar arguments to those in the text show that the market price of this put option is about $1.23 whereas its discounted expected future value is only about $.92. In this case, therefore, investors will pay more than discounted expected future value for a risky security! The explanation for this is that put options are negatively correlated with bond prices, that is, they increase in value when bond prices fall. So, investors that penalize one-year zeros for their price fluctuations must reward put options for their fluctuations in the opposite direction. This phenomenon is analogous to the capital asset pricing model's result that assets with negative betas earn less than the risk-free rate.

[18]A negative number in this context means that the security generates a liability.

Chapter 6
Risk-Neutral Pricing

This chapter demonstrates a shortcut for the computation of arbitrage-free contingent claim prices. The setting of the discussion is the same as in Chapter 5. Assumptions have been made about the evolution of the six-month rate over the next six months and the goal is to price a six-month call option on $1,000 face value of a six-month zero-coupon bond struck at $978.50.

The tree for the price of a one-year zero over time, derived in the previous chapter, is reproduced here.

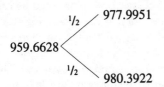

It has been noted that discounting the expected value of the zero's price on August 15, 1994, does not give the zero's price as of February 15, 1994. But, there are some "probabilities," called *pseudo-probabilities* or *risk-neutral probabilities* for which the discounted expected value does give the zero's current price. Let p be the pseudo-probability of an up-state and 1–p be the pseudo-probability of a down-state. Then, choose p such that

$$\frac{977.9951p + 980.3922(1-p)}{1+\dfrac{.0399}{2}} = 959.6628$$

In other words, find p such that the discounted expected value using the probability p instead of the real probability of .5 gives the current market price of 959.6628. Solving the above equation reveals that p = .661.

Now recall that the price tree of the option before solving for its current price is

Once again, one cannot price the option by discounting its expected value. But, what if one calculated an expected value using the pseudo-probability of p = .661? The resulting option price would be

$$\frac{.661 \times 0 + .339 \times 1.8922}{1 + \frac{.0399}{2}} = .63$$

But that is exactly the same option price computed in the previous chapter using the much more cumbersome replicating portfolio technology! And the fact that these two prices are the same is not a coincidence.

In general, *risk-neutral pricing* of contingent claims is accomplished as follows. Find the pseudo-probabilities that equate the price of the underlying securities to their discounted expected values. Then price the contingent claim by calculating its discounted expected value under these pseudo-probabilities.

The remainder of this chapter will explain why risk-neutral pricing works. The explanation is subtle and may require a number of readings before it is fully understood.

Step 1: Given trees for zero-coupon bond prices, the price of a security that is priced by arbitrage does not depend on investors' risk preferences. This assertion can be explained as follows.

A security is "priced by arbitrage" if one can construct a portfolio that replicates its cash flows. As demonstrated in Chapter 5, an option on a bond is clearly priced by arbitrage. On the other hand, a specific common stock, for example, is not priced by arbitrage because no portfolio of securities can mimic the idiosyncratic fluctuations in a common stock's market value.

If a security is priced by arbitrage and everyone agrees on the price evolution of the underlying securities, then everyone will agree on the replicating portfolio.

In the option example of Chapter 5, an extremely risk-averse retired investor and a free-wheeling bond trader would both agree that the option is replicated by buying $789.3705 face value of the one-year zeros and shorting $772.0005 of the six-month zeros. So, since they agree on the composition of the replicating portfolio and on the prices of the underlying securities, then they must also agree on the price of the contingent claim.

Step 2: Imagine an economy that is identical to our economy with respect to the current prices of bonds and the evolution of the six-month rate over time. But, everyone in that economy is risk-neutral—meaning that they do not penalize risk and, therefore, price securities by discounting expected cash flows.

The probability of an up-state in our economy has been given as .5. But what is the probability of an up-state in the imaginary economy? It is certainly not .5 because using that probability pricing is not risk-neutral. In other words, the discounted expected value of a one-year zero is not equal to the current market price. Mathematically,

$$\frac{.5 \times 977.9951 + .5 \times 980.3922}{1 + \dfrac{.0399}{2}} = 960.04 \neq 959.6628$$

What, then, is the probability of an up-state in the imaginary economy? It is the probability, p, that sets the discounted expectation of a one-year zero's value equal to its price. Mathematically, p satisfies the following equation:

$$\frac{977.9951p + 980.3922(1 - p)}{1 + \dfrac{.0399}{2}} = 959.6628$$

But this equation is the same as the one used earlier to compute the pseudo-probability of p = .661. It is now clear why p is also called a risk-neutral probability. It is the probability that prevails in a risk-neutral economy that has the same underlying security prices as our economy.

Step 3: The price of the option in the imaginary economy described in Step 2 is computed by discounting its expected cash flow. Since, as shown in Step 2, the probability of an up-state in the imaginary economy is .661, the price of the option in that economy is

$$\frac{.661 \times 0 + .339 \times 1.8922}{1 + \dfrac{.0399}{2}} = .63$$

Step 4: In the context of the option example, Step 1 says that, given the price of the six-month and one-year zeros, as well as the evolution of the six-month rate, the price of an option does not depend on the risk preferences of investors. Therefore, since the imaginary economy has the same bond prices and the same six-month rate evolution as our economy, option prices in the two economies must be the same. The fact that risk preferences in one economy are different from those of the other makes no difference with respect to the relative pricing arguments. Therefore, given the calculation in Step 3, the option price in our economy must be .63.

Chapter 7
Arbitrage-Free Pricing in a Realistic Setting

Chapters 5 and 6 introduced the arbitrage-free pricing framework in a two-date setting. This chapter shows how to place the framework in a realistic setting with respect to the number of dates and with respect to the time interval between dates.

The two-date setting required current values of the six-month and one-year spot rates and a tree describing the two possible values of the six-month rate in six months' time. To extend the model for another six months requires the current value of the 1.5-year spot rate and a tree describing the possible values of the six-month rate in one year's time. The current 1.5-year spot rate, available from the smoothed spot rate curve of Part One, Chapter 4, is about 4.33 percent.

Keeping with the assumption that the six-month rate can move either up or down, there are two possible shapes for the tree describing the evolution of the six-month rate over the next year. In the first, the "up-down" state is not forced to be the same as the "down-up" state; for example:

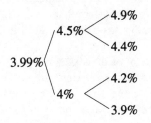

For obvious reasons, this type of tree is called a *non-recombining tree*. From an economic perspective, there is nothing wrong with assuming that the tree for the six-month rate takes this shape. But this assumption will be difficult or even impossible to implement. Note that after six months there are two possible interest rate values and that after one year there are four possible values. More generally, after N semiannual periods there will be 2^N possible values for the six-month rate. So, for example, a tree with semiannual steps capable of pricing 10-year securities will, in its rightmost column, have over 500,000 nodes. A semiannually spaced tree capable of pricing 20-year securities will, in its rightmost column, have over 500 billion nodes. Furthermore, as described later in this chapter, it is often desirable to reduce substantially the time interval between dates. In short, even with modern computers, trees that grow this quickly are computationally unwieldy.

The second type of tree is *a recombining tree*, meaning that the "up-down" and "down-up" states are forced to have the same rate value. An example of this type of tree is the following:

Note that the number of nodes after six months is two, after one year is three, and so on. A tree with weekly, rather than semiannual, steps capable of pricing a 30-year security would have only 52 x 30 + 1 = 1,561 nodes in its rightmost column. This number of nodes is much more manageable than the tree with nonrecombining nodes. As a result of this practical consideration, most practitioners restrict themselves to recombining trees.

As the trees grow, it becomes convenient to develop a notation with which to refer to particular nodes on a tree. A fairly common convention is as follows. The dates, representing columns of the tree, are numbered from left to right, starting from 0. The states, representing rows of the tree, are numbered from bottom to top, starting from 0 as well. For example, the six-month rate on date 2, state 0 in the above tree is 3.9 percent. The six-month rate on date 1, state 1 is 4.5 percent.

Having settled on the above tree for the evolution of the six-month rate, the trees for the price of six-month and one-year zeros over time are the same as shown in Chapter 5. The next step is to create the tree for the price of $1,000 face value of a 1.5-year zero. Several parts of the tree can be written down immediately:

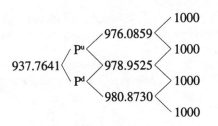

The value of the original 1.5-year zero after one and one-half years have elapsed is simply 1000. On date 2, when the original 1.5-year zero is a six-month zero, prices can be computed from the appropriate six-month rate. In state 2, the six-month rate is 4.9 percent and the value of the now six-month zero is $1,000/(1 + .049/2) = 976.0859$. In state 1, the six-month rate is 4.3 percent and the zero price is $1,000/(1 + .043/2) = 978.9525$. In state 0, the six-month rate is 3.9 percent and the zero price is 980.8730. Finally, the current or date 0 value of the 1.5-year zero is derived from the 1.5-year spot rate of 4.33 percent: $1000/(1 + .0433/2)^3 = 937.7641$.

P^u and P^d represent the possible prices of the 1.5-year zero after six months, when it has become a one-year zero. These values are not yet known because, as of this point in the discussion, possible values of the one-year spot rate in six months' time are not available.

The risk-neutral pricing technique requires the computation of probabilities that, when used to discount expected future values, generate market prices. From Chapters 5 and 6 it is already known that the risk-neutral probability of an initial up-move is .661. Letting q be the risk-neutral probability that the second move is up, the following tree can be drawn:

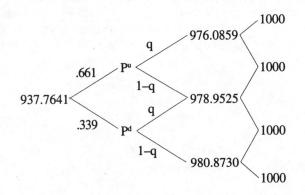

For ease of exposition, it has been assumed that the probability of an up-move from the up-state is the same as the probability of an up-move from the down-state. Since this chapter still focuses on the science of term-structure modeling, an extended discussion of this point is not appropriate. The following chapter will discuss the implications of choices of this sort.

By the definition of risk-neutral probabilities, discounted expected values, using the probability q, must reproduce market prices. With respect to the 1.5-year zero, this requires that

$$\frac{.661\,P^u + .339\,P^d}{1 + \dfrac{.0399}{2}} = 937.7641$$

where, by the same reasoning,

$$P^u = \frac{976.0859q + 978.9525(1 - q)}{1 + \dfrac{.045}{2}}$$

and

$$P^d = \frac{978.9525q + 980.8730(1 - q)}{1 + \dfrac{.04}{2}}$$

While these three equations may look complicated, substituting the definitions of P^u and P^d into the first equation gives a linear equation with only one unknown, namely q. Solving this equation reveals that q = .632. Substituting this value back into the definitions of P^u and P^d completes the specification of the 1.5-year zero price tree:

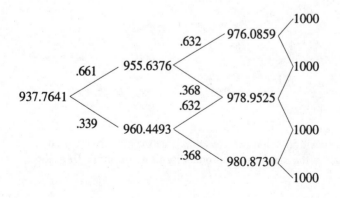

With the risk-neutral probabilities of .661 and .339 derived in Chapter 5, any security maturing in six months could be priced. Now, with the probabilities .632 and .368, any security maturing in one year can be priced. Consider, for example, an imaginary one-year security that is worth $500, $100, and –$10 on date 2, states 0, 1, and 2, respectively. Using the risk-neutral pricing technology, the price tree for this imaginary security over the coming year is the following:

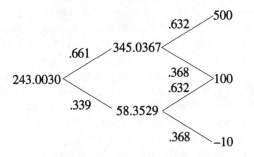

The valuation begins on date 2, when the prices are known to be 500, 100, and –10. Working backwards, prices are computed by discounting expected value under the risk-neutral probabilities. On date 1, state 1, the value is

$$\frac{.632 \times 500 + .368 \times 100}{1 + \dfrac{.045}{2}} = 345.0367$$

Similarly, on date 1, state 0, the value of the security is

$$\frac{.632 \times 100 + .368 \times -10}{1 + \dfrac{.04}{2}} = 58.3529$$

Finally, the value of the security today is

$$\frac{.661 \times 345.0367 + .339 \times 58.3529}{1 + \dfrac{.0399}{2}} = 243.003$$

Having extended the model from a two-date to a three-date setting, it should be clear how to extend the model to an arbitrary number of dates. Pricing securities that mature in n + 1 semiannual periods requires the following steps: (1) Obtain the current term structure, in six-month intervals; (2) Make assumptions about how the six-month rate evolves, in six-month intervals, over the next n semiannual periods; (3) Solve for the risk-neutral probabilities throughout the six-month rate tree. (When used in taking expectations, these probabilities force the discounted expected values of all zero-coupon bonds to match the initial term structure.); (4) Price the securities in question by starting with their maturity values and then pricing backwards by discounting expected values under the risk-neutral probabilities. Once again, guidance on selecting the assumptions of step 2 will be provided in Chapter 8. Applications of the pricing process itself, as in step 4, will be the subject of Part Four.

From the price tree of the 1.5-year zero, previously reported, one can extract the two possible values of the one-year spot rate six months from now. In six months, the now 1.5-year zero will be a one-year zero with the two possible prices, 955.6376 and 960.4493. But these prices imply one-year spot rates of about 4.59 percent and 4.08 percent, respectively. Since the current one-year spot rate is known to be 4.16 percent by assumption, the tree for the one-year spot rate is as follows:

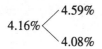

The fact that the one-year spot can be extracted in this manner is, at first, surprising. The starting point of this exercise was the initial six-month, one-year, and 1.5-year rates along with an assumption of how the six-month rate evolves over the coming year. So, the one-year spot rate is completely determined by the current term structure and the six-month rate process. In fact, since the one-year spot rate process was derived by arbitrage arguments, any specification of the one-year spot rate process that differs from the above tree will be inconsistent with the other assumptions in the sense of creating arbitrage opportunities within the model.

The fact that the one-year spot rate process follows from assumptions about the term structure and the six-month rate process follows from the *one-factor* nature of the model. By writing down a tree for the evolution of the six-month rate, it was implicitly assumed that prices of all fixed income securities could be determined by the evolution of the six-month rate. More precisely, the arbitrage arguments of Chapter 5 assumed that each state of the world is completely determined by the value of the six-month rate at that state. In an alternative, *multi-factor* approach, it would be assumed that the prices of all securities were determined not by the evolution of one random variable, but of several. Equivalently, it would be assumed that each state of the world is described by the value not of one random variable, but of several. For example, one well-known model assumes that states of the world are defined by the value of the short-term rate and of the short-term rate's volatility.[19]

One-factor models are quite popular because, relative to multi-factor models, they are relatively simple to implement. But, one-factor models do suffer from an important weakness. Because the random evolution of one factor governs all security prices, the returns on all security prices in the model are perfectly correlated. In the context of this chapter, returns on bonds of all maturities are perfectly correlated. For example, knowing the short-term return on a 5-year bond in a one-factor model is sufficient to determine the short-term return on a 10-year bond. This is not very realistic. While 5- and 10-year rates do tend to move up and down together, no rule completely describes their relationship. Technically, rates of different maturities are positively, but not perfectly correlated.

Multi-factor models break the perfect correlation between returns on bonds of different maturities. While in this way they are more realistic than one-factor models, they are also more complicated and difficult to implement. Since the goal of this book is to introduce the concepts of fixed income security pricing, the focus is almost exclusively on the simpler one-factor models.[20]

Trees with time steps of six months were chosen here for illustrative purposes only. In practice, there are two reasons to choose other, usually smaller, time steps. First, securities rarely make all of their payments in six-month intervals starting from today's date. But the pricing technology presented here can only value cash flows received at a particular set of nodes on the tree. Reducing the time step to a month, a week, or even a day can be used to ensure that all cash flows are sufficiently close to some node in the tree. Second, the assumption that the six-month rate can take on only two possible values in six months' time is too simplistic to give rise to accurate pricing models. Reducing the step size can make a model's assumption about possible future rates much more realistic.

Figures 7.1 through 7.4 illustrate the effect of step size on the assumed distribution of the six-month rate in six months' time. On the vertical axis is the probability of a particular rate's occurring. With quarterly steps (Figure 7.1), there are only three possible values for the six-month rate at the end of six months, so the probability distribution is still quite unrealistic. Decreasing the time step to one per month (Figure 7.2), one per week (Figure 7.3), and, finally, one per day (Figure 7.4) increases the number of possible values the six-month rate can take on in six months' time. The probability distributions arising from daily and weekly time steps are a giant leap in the direction of realism from the two-date model of Chapter 5.

Building an interest rate tree for time intervals shorter than six months entails technical rather than conceptual changes from the presentation thus far. First, term-

[19]See Longstaff and Schwartz (1992).
[20]See Boyle (1988) for a discussion of the construction of rate trees in two-factor models.

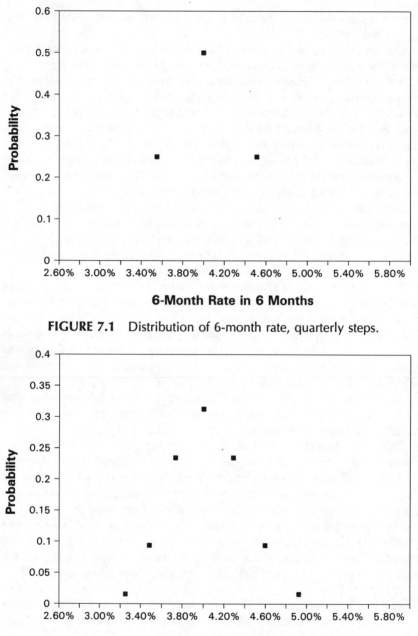

FIGURE 7.1   Distribution of 6-month rate, quarterly steps.

FIGURE 7.2   Distribution of 6-month rate, monthly steps.

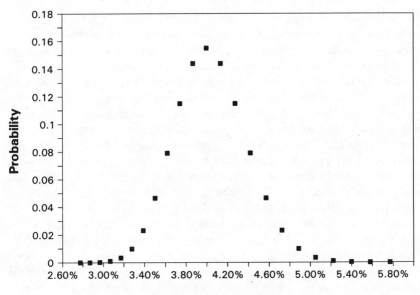

6-Month Rate in 6 Months

FIGURE 7.3 Distribution of 6-month rate, weekly steps.

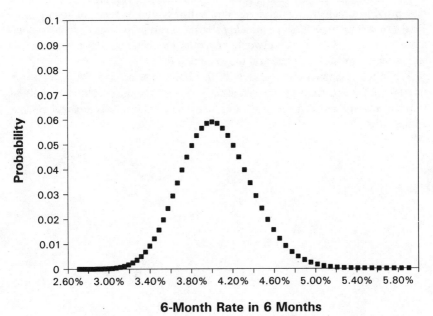

6-Month Rate in 6 Months

FIGURE 7.4 Distribution of 6-month rate, daily steps.

structure data must correspond to the time interval chosen for the model. So, for example, weekly time steps require the prices of zero-coupon bonds maturing every week. Such prices are typically not available and cannot even be inferred from traded bond prices, but the techniques of Chapter 4 can be used to fill in as many points of the discount function as are needed. Second, the interest rate tree must reflect the evolution of the rate corresponding to the time step. Said another way, the interest rate tree must always model the evolution of the short-term rate. In the presentation so far, the semiannual step size meant that the six-month rate was the short-term rate of the model. With weekly time steps, however, the short-term rate described by the interest rate tree must be the one-week rate. And, of course, discounting must be done to reflect the shorter time interval. Just as the semiannual rate was divided by two before being used for discounting, an annualized one-week rate, for example, needs to be divided by 52.

What determines the choice of a time step? It is not the case that smaller time steps are always better. First, as the time step decreases, computation time increases. Since many practitioners need models that provide answers in "real time," the time step cannot usually be made arbitrarily small. Second, the greater the number of computations required to price a security, the more attention one must pay to numerical issues like round-off error.

The best choice of step size really depends on the problem at hand. In trying to price a 30-year callable bond, for example, a model with monthly time steps may provide a realistic enough interest rate distribution to generate good prices. On the other extreme, the same monthly steps will certainly be inadequate to price a one-month bond option: That would be a return to the extremely unrealistic assumption of two possible rates on the valuation date.

While it is assumed through most of this book that the step size is the same throughout the tree, this need not be the case. The most sophisticated models allow step size to vary across dates to achieve an optimal balance between realism and computational concerns.

Chapter 8

The Art of Term-Structure Modeling

So far, the reader has been introduced to the science of term-structure modeling and arbitrage-free pricing. Given the current term structure and assumptions about the evolution of the short-term rate, there is a method to price contingent claims. The purpose of this Chapter is to describe how practitioners have gone about choosing assumptions in their quest to create reliable term-structure models. For readers not specifically interested in creating models, this chapter will provide a framework with which to evaluate competing models that might be in use.

This chapter will proceed by presenting some commonly used models. The first of the models is quite simple, since it was one of the earliest models developed. Each succeeding model introduces a new element that increases the realism and, hopefully, the accuracy of the model at a cost of increased complexity. As will become clear while reading the chapter, model users must decide on the level of complexity best suited to their respective purposes.

The description of each model is divided into two parts. The first describes the model's key features, strengths, and weaknesses. The second explains the details of the model's construction.

It is easiest to explain the arbitrage foundation of risk-neutral pricing by fixing the tree of short-term rates and adjusting the probabilities appropriately, as done in Chapters 6 and 7. But, when implementing these models, it is more convenient to take a slightly different approach. Namely, fix the probabilities at .5 throughout the tree but adjust the short-term rate tree so that the discounted expected values of zeros match their market prices. So long as the time step between dates is small enough, this approach is equivalent to the approach described in Chapters 5 through 7.

THE HO-LEE MODEL[21]

Description

The Ho-Lee model's strength is its simplicity. The interest rate at any time is determined by the previous interest rate plus or minus some random shock. An implication of this assumption is that the probability distribution of the short-term rate, at any time in the future, is approximately normally distributed. Put another way, the relative frequency of different short-term rates can be described by the well-known bell shape of the normal distribution.

One drawback of the Ho-Lee model and the normal distribution is that interest rates can become negative: When adding or subtracting random shocks to the interest rate, a large enough negative shock will drive the interest rate below zero. Some practitioners feel that this is a very serious drawback. Others feel that the purpose of these models is to provide good prices for contingent claims. If a model passes this test, then it does not matter much if some of its assumptions are unrealistic. Furthermore, this second group would say, good prices plus simplicity can compensate for the existence of negative interest rates in low-probability states of the model.

A second possible drawback of the Ho-Lee model, to be demonstrated below, is that the basis point volatility of the short-term rate does not depend on the level of the rate. More loosely put, the average random fluctuation in the interest rate is a constant number of basis points. Many practitioners believe, however, that the basis point volatility of a short-term rate when that rate is 10 percent is higher than when that rate is 4 percent. On the other hand, this is not a universally accepted empirical fact. In any case, other models assume that the basis point volatility of the short-term rate is positively related to the level of the short-term rate.

Model Construction

Let r be the current short-term rate and let τ be the time step in years. The binomial moves in the Ho-Lee model can be described by the following rate tree:

---

[21]This model appeared in Ho and Lee (1986). However, the presentation of the model here, written after a great deal of academic and industry research, bears little resemblance to the original presentation.

In words, the new short-term rate is found by adding a constant times the time step, $m\tau$, to the old short-term rate and by adding or subtracting another constant times the square root of the time step, $\sigma\sqrt{\tau}$. Since $m\tau$ is added to the rate in both the up- and down-states, it is called the *drift*, trend, or general tendency, of the short-term rate. Furthermore, since τ is measured in years, m itself is the annual drift. Since $\sigma\sqrt{\tau}$ is added in the up-state but subtracted in the down-state, it can be thought of as the random deviation of the short-term rate from its trend. In the up-state the short-term rate is above its trend by the amount $\sigma\sqrt{\tau}$ while, in the down-state, the short-term rate is below its trend by the amount $\sigma\sqrt{\tau}$. It will now be shown that $\sigma\sqrt{\tau}$ is the *volatility*, or standard deviation, of the short-term rate. Then, σ is the annual volatility of the short-term rate.[22]

Let r' be the random variable denoting the short-term rate after the move up or down; for example, r' = r + m + σ in the up-state and r' = r + m − σ in the down-state. Then, compute the expectation, or mean, of r', written E{r'}:

$$E(r') = \left(\frac{1}{2}\right)(r + m + \sigma) + \left(\frac{1}{2}\right)(r + m - \sigma) = r + m$$

Next compute the variance of r', written V{r'}:

$$V(r') = \left(\frac{1}{2}\right)[r + m + \sigma - E(r')]^2 + \left(\frac{1}{2}\right)[r + m - \sigma - E(r')]^2$$

Substituting r + m for E{r'} in the variance expression gives

$$V\{r'\} = \left(\frac{1}{2}\right)\{\sigma\}^2 + \left(\frac{1}{2}\right)\{-\sigma\}^2 = \sigma^2$$

[22]If there are N time steps each year, so that $\tau = 1/N$, then a single-step volatility of $\sigma\sqrt{\tau}$ is equivalent to an annual volatility of σ. The reasoning behind this is as follows. The change in an annual rate of r is made up of N single-step changes. If the variance of each of these changes is $\sigma^2\tau$, then, so long as the changes are independent, the variance of the annual change is $N\sigma^2\tau = \sigma^2$ and the volatility of the annual change is σ.

Since the standard deviation of r' is just the square root of the variance, the volatility of r' is just the constant σ, as was to be shown. Note that, in this model, volatility is measured in the same units as the interest rate, that is, basis points. This expression of volatility will be called *basis point volatility* to distinguish it from another expression of volatility presented later in the chapter.

The next step is to select the model's parameters m and σ. The objectives in parameter selection are to ensure that the model is arbitrage-free and to have the model accurately gauge contingent claims prices. Because the Ho-Lee model is particularly simple, it has only two parameters with which to achieve these goals. The volatility parameter σ is used to get "good" contingent claims prices. Its value can be chosen from a view on interest rate volatility, from historical data, or from some implied method.[23] Since contingent claim prices depend critically on volatility, it is hoped that a clever selection of σ will produce a useful model. For expositional purposes, set σ = .45 percent, that is, 45 basis points, and set a time step of six months so that τ = 1/2. Then, the single-step volatility σ√τ = .0045/√2 = .00318198.

To ensure that the interest rate model is arbitrage-free, the model's parameters must be chosen so that model prices for zeros match market prices. The six-month spot rate, used in Chapters 5 through 7, is 3.99 percent. Therefore, the current value of r is set to 3.99 percent. The one-year spot rate, also borrowed from previous sections, is 4.16 percent. This means that the model must price $1 face value of a one-year zero at $1/(1 + .0416/2)^2 = .959663$. The drift parameter, m, will be used to obey this constraint.

According to the model, the price-tree of a one-year zero is

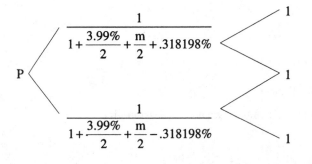

$$P \left\langle \begin{array}{c} \cfrac{1}{1 + \cfrac{3.99\%}{2} + \cfrac{m}{2} + .318198\%} \left\langle \begin{array}{c} 1 \\ 1 \end{array} \right. \\ \cfrac{1}{1 + \cfrac{3.99\%}{2} + \cfrac{m}{2} - .318198\%} \left\langle \begin{array}{c} 1 \\ 1 \end{array} \right. \end{array} \right.$$

---

[23]Selecting σ by an implied method means that σ is selected so that the model price for a particular contingent claim matches its market price. For example, one might select σ so that a particular callable bond's model price matches its market price. The hope here is that forcing the model to match a particular market price makes the model more realistic and, consequently, more capable of pricing other contingent claims. This hope is analogous to the practice of using implied volatility for pricing stock options.

where

$$P = \cfrac{.5 \cfrac{1}{1 + \cfrac{3.99\%}{2} + \cfrac{m}{2} + .318198\%} + .5 \cfrac{1}{1 + \cfrac{3.99\%}{2} + \cfrac{m}{2} - .318198\%}}{1 + \cfrac{.0399}{2}}$$

Note that P is the discounted "expected" value of the one-year zero in six months' time. The word "expected" is in quotation marks because the rates of the model are not the true possible values of the short-term rate. They are, like the pseudo-probabilities of the previous sections, artificial constructs used to make the model arbitrage-free and, consequently, usable for pricing contingent claims.

For the model to be arbitrage-free, P must equal the current price of the one-year zero, namely .959663. Hence,

$$.959663 = \cfrac{.5 \cfrac{1}{1 + \cfrac{3.99\%}{2} + \cfrac{m}{2} + .318198\%} + .5 \cfrac{1}{1 + \cfrac{3.99\%}{2} + \cfrac{m}{2} - .318198\%}}{1 + \cfrac{.0399}{2}}$$

Solving for the drift[24] reveals that m = .342089 percent or about 34 basis points. Substituting this value for m into the six-month rate tree, along with the chosen values for r and σ, gives the following tree,

which can be used for contingent claim valuation.

---

[24]While some of the equations in this section can be manipulated analytically to solve for parameter values, most have to be solved numerically, that is, by trial and error or some more sophisticated numerical analysis technique. Since applied models are almost always implemented on computers anyway, the necessity for numerical solutions should not trouble the reader very much.

To extend the tree another period, the Ho-Lee model assumes that the basis point volatility does not change over time or with the interest rate. The extended tree will, therefore, have the following form:

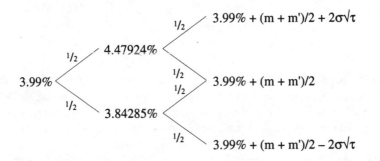

The total drift over the year is $(m + m')/2$, the drift over the first six months plus the drift over the second six months. To get the rate in the up-up state, one has to add two up-moves of $\sigma\sqrt{\tau}$ to the original rate plus the drift. The up-down state has perturbed the original rate up and down by $\sigma\sqrt{\tau}$, so the rate there is just the original rate plus the drift. Finally, the down-down state is the original rate plus the drift plus two moves of $-\sigma\sqrt{\tau}$.

Using the value for m obtained above, the tree becomes

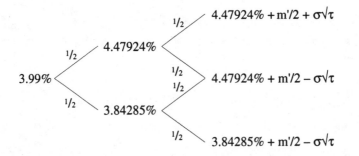

The up-down state has been written as a "down" perturbation from the up-state, but it could as easily have been written as an "up" perturbation from the down-state. In that case the rate at that node would be $3.84285\% + m'/2 + \sigma\sqrt{\tau}$. Note from the previous expression of this tree that the construction of the tree guarantees that an up-down sequence gives the same rate as a down-up sequence.

Substituting the value for σ into the rate tree above gives six-month rate values in one year of .0479744% + m'/2, .0416105% + m'/2, and 3.52465% + m'/2. To solve for m', find the value of m' that sets the price of a 1.5-year zero equal to its market price of $1/(1 + .0433/2)^3 = .937764$. Begin by writing the price-tree of 1.5-year zero as

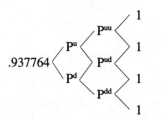

where $P^{uu} = 1/(1 + (.0479744 + m'/2)/2)$, $P^{ud} = 1/(1 + (.0416105 + m'/2)/2)$, $P^{dd} = 1/(1 + (.0352465 + m'/2)/2)$, $P^u = (.5 \times P^{uu} + .5 \times P^{ud})/(1 + .0447924/2)$, and $P^d = (.5 \times P^{ud} + .5 \times P^{dd})/(1 + .0384285/2)$. Then, for the model and market price of the 1.5-year zero to match, it must be that

$$.937764 = \frac{.5P^u + .5P^d}{1 + \frac{.0399}{2}}$$

While this equation is a bit messy to write down, there is only one unknown, namely m'. Solving, m' = 1.36176 percent. Substituting this value into the six-month rate tree produces the following tree:

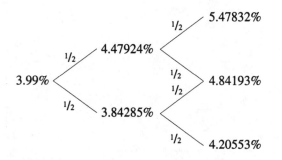

Continuing in this manner allows one to construct trees with any number of periods.

THE ORIGINAL SALOMON BROTHERS MODEL[25]

Description

The original Salomon Brothers model assumes that the new interest rate equals the old interest rate multiplied by a random shock. So, instead of an additive random shock, there is assumed to be a multiplicative random shock. This change replaces the normal distribution with the *lognormal distribution*. It also eliminates the possibility of negative interest rates and causes the basis point volatility of the short-term rate to be proportional to the level of that rate. Due to the latter change, the parameter σ in the Salomon model denotes the *proportional volatility*. The proportional volatility equals the basis point volatility divided by the interest rate. Alternatively, basis point volatility is found by multiplying the proportional volatility by the interest rate. So, for example, if $\sigma = .12$ and the current short-term rate is 4 percent, the basis point volatility equals $.12 \times .04 = 48$ basis points.

Figure 8.1 graphs the probability distribution of the six-month rate in 30 years'

[25]A description of this model appeared in Kopprasch *et al.* (1987). It is not to be inferred that Salomon Brothers uses this model presently.

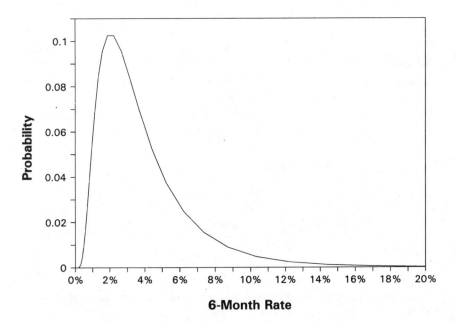

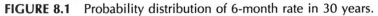

6-Month Rate

FIGURE 8.1   Probability distribution of 6-month rate in 30 years.

time using the Salomon Brothers model. Note that the lognormal distribution is not symmetric like the normal distribution; it is *skewed* to the left. More importantly for the present purpose, negative interest rates cannot occur.

The original Salomon model, like the Ho-Lee model, makes assumptions about the short-term rate volatility. The volatilities of all other rates, on the other hand, are set implicitly, rather than explicitly. Assuming that the proportional volatility of the six-month rate is 12 percent and using the smoother term structure of Chapter 4, Figure 8.2 graphs the *term structure of volatilities* implied by the Salomon model. Note that proportional volatility falls gradually from 12 percent for the six-month rate to 10.5 percent for the thirty-year rate.

Empirically, the term structure of volatilities does slope downward,[26] but at a faster rate than implied by the original Salomon model. Table 8.1, using data published by Ibbotson Associates, illustrates this point using data from 1950–1987 and terms of 1 month to 20 years. According to this table, the volatility of the twenty-year rate is 33 percent as large as the volatility of the one-year rate. According to the original Salomon model, however, the volatility of the twenty-year rate is about 93 percent as large as that of the one-year rate. While this is only a particular example of the Salomon model, it is generally true that the implied term structure of volatilities of the model is not sufficiently downward sloping. The next model improves on the original Salomon model by explicitly imposing a term structure of volatilities.

---

[26]One explanation for this phenomenon is as follows. Short-term rates are determined by current economic conditions while forward rates are determined by expectations of future short rates or, equivalently, future economic conditions. Furthermore, expectations or forward rates are much less volatile than current economic conditions or short-term rates: While current business conditions can change rapidly, one's expectation about the short-term rate in 20 years does not change much from day to day. Now, long-term rates, as discussed in Part One, are complex averages of short-term rates and forward rates. But since forward rates are less volatile than short-term rates, long-term rates will also be less volatile than short-term rates.

Table 8.1   The Term Structure of Volatilities: Historical Evidence, 1950–1987

Term	Proportional Volatility
1 month	15.1%
3 months	11.9%
1 year	10%
2 years	7.7%
5 years	5.2%
10 years	4.1%
20 years	3.3%

Source: Coleman, Fisher, and Ibbotson (1993).

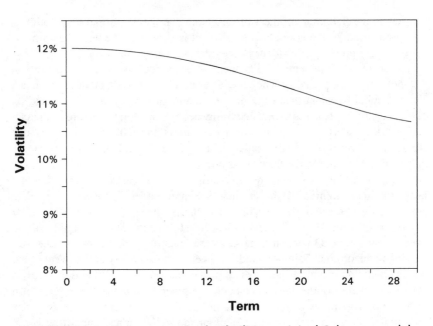

FIGURE 8.2   Term structure of volatilities: original Salomon model.

At this point it is worthwhile to state a general rule about model construction. Whatever is not imposed explicitly is imposed implicitly. Therefore, just because one does not have strong views about the term structure of volatilities does not mean that one can ignore the issue. Every term structure model, at least implicitly, imposes some term structure of volatilities.

Model Construction

The evolution of the short-term rate in this model takes the following form,

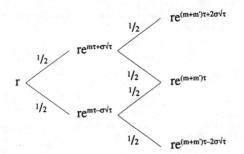

where e is the base of the natural logarithms.[27] If one took the natural logarithm of all rates in this tree, the following tree would emerge:

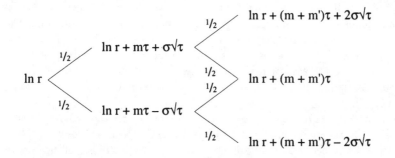

The exercise shows that this model applies the Ho-Lee structure of adding a drift and perturbing a volatility to the natural logarithm of the rates instead of to the rates themselves. Put another way, in this model the natural logarithm of the short-term rate will be approximately normally distributed. In statistics, a variable whose natural logarithm is normally distributed is said to have a *lognormal distribution*.

The short-term rate in this model always takes the form $re^{\mu\tau+i\sigma\sqrt{\tau}}$ for some drift μ and some integer i. So, if the original short-term rate, r, is positive, then all subsequent rates are also positive. It is in this manner that the lognormal distribution avoids negative interest rates.

Let r' be the random value of the short-term rate one period from now. The basis point volatility r' can be computed as described in the context of the Ho-Lee model. To show this,

$$E(r') = .5r\,[e^{m\tau+\sigma\sqrt{\tau}} + e^{m\tau-\sigma\sqrt{\tau}}]$$

$$V(r') = .25r^2\,[e^{m\tau+\sigma\sqrt{\tau}} + e^{m\tau-\sigma\sqrt{\tau}}]^2$$

So, the basis point volatility of the short-term rate is

$$.5r\,[e^{m\tau+\sigma\sqrt{\tau}} + e^{m\tau-\sigma\sqrt{\tau}}]$$

[27]The value of e is approximately 2.7182818. For the purposes of this discussion the reader should be aware of the mathematical rule that

$$\ln(re^x) = \ln(r) + x$$

for any values r > 0 and x.

Note that the basis point volatility depends on the level of the short-term rate. The higher the value of r, the higher the basis point volatility. In fact, as the time step decreases, it can be shown that the basis point volatility is approximately equal to $r\sigma\sqrt{\tau}$.[28] For small time steps, then, the basis point volatility of a lognormally distributed interest rate is approximately proportional to the level of the rate. The parameter σ in this model, therefore, is called the proportional volatility of the short-term rate.[29] While there is not a strong consensus on this point, many practitioners feel that the assumption of a constant proportional volatility is a more accurate description of reality than the Ho-Lee assumption of a constant basis point volatility.

As in the Ho-Lee model, the parameter σ is chosen in a way that will, hopefully, generate accurate contingent claim prices. For expositional purposes, σ is taken to be 12 percent and τ is again assumed to be .5. (Note that, at the current six-month rate of 3.99 percent, $\sigma = 12$ percent translates into an annual basis point volatility of .0399 x .12 = 47.88 basis points. At the initial level of rates, then, this volatility is similar to the 45-basis point assumption used in illustrating the Ho-Lee model.)

The initial value of r will be the six-month rate of 3.99 percent. The next step is to solve for m and m' so that the model matches the one-year and 1.5-year spot rates of 4.16 percent and 4.33 percent. Since the solution technique is very similar to that used to solve the unknown parameters of the Ho-Lee model, only the final tree will be produced here:

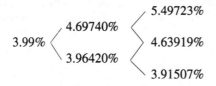

The proportional volatility of the six-month rate is set at 12 percent. In order to compute the term structure of volatilities, however, it is necessary to know how to calculate the volatility of rates of longer term. The discussion begins with the calculation of the volatility of the one-year rate.

The current one-year rate is given at 4.16 percent. What are the possible values

[28]If x is small, the e^x is approximately equal to $1 + x$. Using this approximation in the volatility expression gives the cited result.
[29]Readers who know the calculus can think of this result as follows. The differential of $\ln r$ equals dr/r. Therefore, the volatility of $\ln r$ equals the basis point volatility of r divided by r, that is, the proportional volatility.

for the one-year rate six months from now? Using the six-month rate tree given above, the price tree of a 1.5-year zero is as follows:

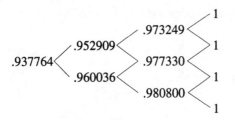

Since after six months a 1.5-year zero becomes a one-year zero, the one-year rate in six months can be extracted from the up-state and down-state prices of this tree. Let the one-year rate in the up-state and down-state be denoted by y^u and y^d, respectively. Then, by definition,

$$.952909 = \frac{1}{\left(1 + \dfrac{y^u}{2}\right)^2}$$

and

$$.960036 = \frac{1}{\left(1 + \dfrac{y^d}{2}\right)^2}$$

Solving, $y^u = 4.88222$ percent and $y^d = 4.12032$ percent. Therefore, the one-year rate tree is

4.16% $\Big\langle$
　4.88222%
　4.12032%

Using this tree, it can be computed that the proportional volatility of the one-year rate is $.5 \ln(y^u/y^d) = 8.48346\%$ semiannually,[30] or $8.48346\%/\sqrt{.5} = 11.99742\%$ annually.

Performing these computations to determine the rate trees for rates of longer term, one can calculate the volatility of any rate in this particular example of the original Salomon model.

THE BLACK-DERMAN-TOY MODEL[31]

Description

The chief advantage of the Black-Derman-Toy model over the original Salomon model is that it can capture a realistic term structure of volatilities. This is accomplished by allowing the short-term rate volatility to vary over time and by making the drift or trend in interest rate movements depend on the level of rates.

Many practitioners believe that interest rate drift is relatively low, or even negative, when rates are high but relatively high when rates are low. In other words, they believe that interest rates are characterized by *positive mean reversion* or just *mean reversion*. The name comes from the idea that the short-term rate is attracted to some central tendency. When the short rate is above this central tendency, the drift is negative; but, when the short rate is below this central tendency, the drift is positive. In addition, the further the short rate is from the central tendency, above or below, the faster the short rate tends to revert to its central tendency.

While the Black-Derman-Toy displays mean reversion, that property comes about through the term structure of volatilities. This means that the extent to which the drift depends on the level of rates depends completely on the short-term rate volatility process. The danger of this approach is that the model might have to portray both mean reversion and future short-rate volatilities *inaccurately* in order to replicate the desired term structure of volatilities. The fear, of course, is that

---

[30]Given a lognormal rate tree with up-state y^u and down-state y^d, let y' be the random rate at the next time step. As explained in the previous footnote, the proportional volatility of y' equals the standard deviation of ln r. The proof of the statement in the text now follows.

$E[\ln y'] = .5 \ln y^u + .5 \ln y^d$
$V[\ln y'] = .5 (\ln y^u - E[\ln y'])^2 + .5 (\ln y^d - E[\ln y'])^2$
$\qquad = .5 (.5 \ln y^u - .5 \ln y^d)^2 + .5 (-.5 \ln y^u + .5 \ln y^d)^2$
$\qquad = (.5 \ln y^u - .5 \ln y^d)^2$
$\qquad = .25 (\ln y^u - \ln y^d)^2$
$\qquad = .25 [\ln(y^u/y^d)]^2$

Taking the square root of this expression gives the volatility $.5\ln(y^u/y^d)$, as was to be shown.
[31]This model appears in Black, Derman, and Toy (1990).

these inaccuracies will adversely affect contingent claims pricing. Therefore, it might be more desirable to model mean reversion independently of the volatility process. The next model is one example of how this can be accomplished.

Model Construction

The Black-Derman-Toy model, like all other arbitrage-free models, must ensure that model prices for zero-coupon bonds match market prices. In addition, however, the Black-Derman-Toy model ensures that the model's term structure of volatilities matches an empirical or given term structure of volatilities. To accomplish this goal, the Black-Derman-Toy model allows the volatility of the short-term rate over the next time step, sometimes called the *local volatility*, to change over time.

Time-varying local volatilities create a bit of a problem, however, because they may lead to a non-recombining tree. For example, changing the original Salomon model to allow the volatility over the first six months, σ, to differ from the volatility over the second six months, σ', would lead to the following non-recombining tree:

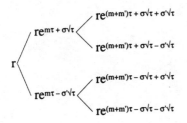

This tree does not recombine since the rates in the up-down and down-up states will be equal only if $\sigma = \sigma'$, which defeats the purpose of the exercise.

The way out of this problem is to allow the drift from the up-state to differ from the drift from the down-state. Letting m' be the drift from the up-state and m" the drift from the down-state, the short-term rate tree becomes the following:

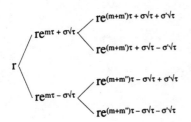

This tree will recombine if the up-down and down-up states are forced to generate the same rate. This condition requires that

$$re^{(m+m')\tau + \sigma\sqrt{\tau} - \sigma'\sqrt{\tau}} = re^{(m+m'')\tau - \sigma\sqrt{\tau} + \sigma'\sqrt{\tau}}$$

or,

$$(m'' - m')\sqrt{\tau} = 2(\sigma - \sigma')$$

To summarize, matching a term structure of volatilities in the Black-Derman-Toy model requires assumptions about future local volatilities and about how the drift responds to the level of interest rates.

While the above presentation of the Black-Derman-Toy model is useful for understanding its inherent interest rate dynamics, solving for the short-term rate tree is easiest from a slightly different perspective. For illustrative purposes, set the six-month, one-year, and 1.5-year rates to 3.99 percent, 4.16 percent, and 4.33 percent, as before. Keep the time step at $\tau = 1/2$ and the six-month rate volatility at 12 percent. But, unlike before, require the model to generate a one-year rate volatility of 11 percent.

Write the six-month rate tree as follows:

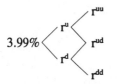

Solving for r^u and r^d is exactly as in the original Salomon model. In fact, since the term structure of interest rates and the six-month rate volatility are the same in this example as in the one used to illustrate the original Salomon model, the evolution of the six-month rate over the next six months is exactly as found before. So, the six-month rate tree is known to be as follows:

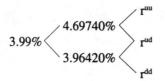

To solve for the remaining unknown rates, one must use three requirements of the model. First, the model value of a 1.5-year zero must equal its market price of $1/(1 + .0433/2)^3 = .937764$. Second, the annual volatility of the one-year rate must equal 11 percent. Third, the local volatility in the up-state equals the local volatility in the down-state, which is saying that σ' is the same both for moving from the up-state and for moving from the down-state. This condition is implicit in the structure of the Black-Derman-Toy model previously presented.

To write these three conditions mathematically, it is convenient to define the one-year rate tree as follows.

$$4.16\% \Big\langle \begin{array}{l} y^u \\[1em] y^d \end{array}$$

Then, using the six-month rate tree, y^u and y^d can be defined in terms of the six-month rates:

$$\frac{1}{\left(1+\dfrac{y^u}{2}\right)^2} = \frac{.5\left(\dfrac{1}{1+\dfrac{r^{uu}}{2}} + \dfrac{1}{1+\dfrac{r^{ud}}{2}}\right)}{1+\dfrac{.0469740}{2}}$$

$$\frac{1}{\left(1+\dfrac{y^d}{2}\right)^2} = \frac{.5\left(\dfrac{1}{1+\dfrac{r^{ud}}{2}} + \dfrac{1}{1+\dfrac{r^{dd}}{2}}\right)}{1+\dfrac{.0396420}{2}}$$

Having set up this notation, the three equations corresponding to the three required conditions are

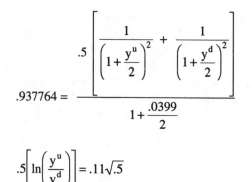

$$.937764 = \frac{.5\left[\dfrac{1}{\left(1+\dfrac{y^u}{2}\right)^2} + \dfrac{1}{\left(1+\dfrac{y^d}{2}\right)^2}\right]}{1+\dfrac{.0399}{2}}$$

$$.5\left[\ln\left(\frac{y^u}{y^d}\right)\right] = .11\sqrt{.5}$$

and

$$.5 \ \ln\left(\frac{r^{uu}}{r^{ud}}\right) = .5 \ \ln\left(\frac{r^{ud}}{r^{dd}}\right)$$

The first two equations can be solved to reveal that y^u = 4.85040 percent and y^d = 4.15161 percent. Then, substituting these values into the definitions of y^u and y^d, along with the third equation, gives a system of three equations and three unknowns. Solving this system shows that r^{uu} = 5.35998 percent, r^{ud} = 4.64827 percent, and r^{dd} = 4.03106 percent.

Although not necessary for contingent claims pricing, one can use the six-month rate values to solve for the underlying parameters of the interest rate process. Doing so gives m = 15.6730 percent, m' = 12.1437 percent, m" = 17.5917 percent, and σ' = 10.07381 percent.

THE BLACK-KARASINSKI MODEL[32]

Description

The Black-Karasinski approach explicitly models mean reversion by specifying a central tendency for the short-term rate and by specifying the speed at which the short-term rate reverts to that central tendency. The model can be used in a number of different ways. One can specify reasonable mean reversion parameters over time or, indeed, a single, constant speed of mean reversion, and then match the

[32]A description of this model appeared in Black and Karasinski (1991). Another model that breaks the Black-Derman-Toy link between mean reversion and the volatility process is Hull and White (1990).

term structure and term structure of volatilities using the model's other parameters. Alternatively, one could specify local volatility parameters and match the term structure and the term structure of volatilities with the remaining parameters.

A third alternative, suggested by the authors themselves, is to use the model's flexibility to match another set of market quantities, in particular, the *differential cap* curve.[33] The hope here is that matching the model's differential cap prices to the market's will endow the model with enough realism to price other contingent claims.

The Black-Karasinski model is a very flexible one-factor model, addressing many of the concerns practitioners have when creating models. Like all arbitrage-free term-structure models, it matches the current term structure of interest rates. As a lognormal model, rates are restricted to be positive and the volatility of rates is proportional to their level. Like the Black-Derman-Toy model it matches the current term structure of volatilities. In addition, the Black-Karasinski model allows for an independent specification of mean reversion behavior.

Model Construction

The goal of this model is to incorporate mean reversion independently of the volatility structure. Let μ be the central tendency of the short-term rate and let ϕ be the parameter of mean reversion. Then, the drift of the natural logarithm of the interest rate is taken to be

$$\phi \, (\ln \mu - \ln r) \, \tau$$

where, as before, r is the current level of the short-term rate and τ is the length of the time step. The parameter ϕ, which is almost always positive, gives the speed at which the short-term rate reverts back to its central tendency μ. This drift is the mathematical expression of mean reversion as described earlier: When $\mu > r$ the drift is positive while when $\mu < r$ the drift is negative. Furthermore, the magnitude of this corrective process depends on the size of the mean reversion parameter ϕ.

Adding a random shock with volatility σ gives rise to the following short-term rate process over the next time step:

$$r \Big\langle \begin{array}{l} re^{\phi(\ln \mu - \ln r)\tau + \sigma\sqrt{\tau}} \equiv r'e^{\sigma\sqrt{\tau}} \\[2mm] re^{\phi(\ln \mu - \ln r)\tau - \sigma\sqrt{\tau}} \equiv r'e^{-\sigma\sqrt{\tau}} \end{array}$$

[33]A differential cap pays the difference between the short rate and the strike, if positive, on some notional amount on a particular date. A cap is a collection of differential caps.

The definition $r' \equiv re^{\phi(\ln \mu - \ln r)\tau}$ is simply a notational convenience to be used presently.

In the Black-Derman-Toy model, the short-term rate tree recombines through the imposition of a specific relationship between drift and local volatility. Here, however, such a restriction is not possible because the modeling of mean reversion completely determines the drift. To illustrate this point, consider the following extension of the structure already described.

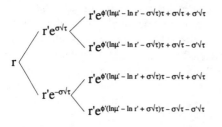

The parameters ϕ', μ', and σ' are the mean reversion, drift, and volatility parameters over the second time step. Note that the drift over the second time step is of the same form as the one over the first time step, that is, $\phi (\ln \mu - \ln r)\tau$. The differences are that ϕ' and μ' replace ϕ and μ, and that $r'e^{\sigma\sqrt{\tau}}$ or $r'e^{-\sigma\sqrt{\tau}}$ replace r. In any case, it can be shown that the tree does not recombine unless $\phi' = (\sigma - \sigma')/\sigma\tau$. But that restriction would put the model in the same class as Black-Derman-Toy: Mean reversion could not be specified independently of the volatility structure.

Specifying an independent mean reversion process clearly requires an extra degree of freedom, that is, another variable whose value can be freely set. For this purpose, Black-Karasinski allows the length of the time step to vary over time.[34] Letting τ' be the length of the time step over the second interval, the interest rate process previously discussed becomes the following:

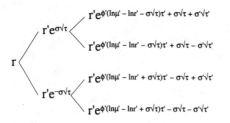

---

[34]Hull and White (1990) accomplish the same goal by using a trinomial instead of a binomial model. In other words, the additional degree of freedom is obtained by allowing the interest rate to take on three possible values on each subsequent date.

It can be shown that this tree will recombine so long as

$$\phi' = \frac{1 - \dfrac{\sigma'\sqrt{\tau'}}{\sigma\sqrt{\tau}}}{\tau'}$$

The length of the first time step, τ, can be selected arbitrarily, as in all previous models. By selecting τ' appropriately, however, the user of the Black-Karasinski model can recreate any desired ϕ', that is, any desired speed of mean reversion.

Chapter 9
Equilibrium vs. Arbitrage-Free Models

The models presented in Chapter 8 are all arbitrage-free models of the term structure and, as such, are set up so as to match the current term structure of interest rates. As discussed in Chapters 5 through 7, arbitrage-free models have the following property: If assumptions regarding the evolution of the short-term rate are correct, the model's contingent claim prices are supported by arbitrage arguments. Prices with such support are believable because there exist arbitrage strategies that allow one to profit from differences between market and model prices.

Another category of term structure models is *equilibrium models*. These models assume a process for the short-term rate, as do the arbitrage-free models, but do not constrain the model's zero-coupon prices to match the market's. One result of this difference is that all bond prices and contingent claim prices cannot be determined from the short-term rate process alone. Equilibrium models, therefore, make additional assumptions about how much extra expected return investors require to induce them to hold longer-term bonds that have more price risk. (Part Three discusses price risk in great detail.) The equilibrium approach thus differs from the arbitrage-free approach which, in essence, uses the current term structure to deduce this risk premium in expected returns.

Equilibrium models do not take bond prices as given whereas arbitrage-free models do. This fact leads some practitioners, for some purposes, to favor equilibrium models. The remainder of this chapter is devoted to a discussion of the relative merits of the arbitrage-free and equilibrium approaches.

Obtaining the inputs of the models.   With respect to the market price of interest rate risk, the arbitrage-free models require the term structure of spot rates as an input. These rates are very easy to obtain. On the other hand, equilibrium models require some measure of how much investors need to be compensated for bearing interest rate risk. This sort of information, which is much harder to obtain than spot rates, usually comes from a statistical examination of past price and rate movements. Therefore, regarding the ease with which inputs are obtained, arbitrage-free models have a great advantage.

Sensitivity to data or market imperfections.   The fact that arbitrage-free models take the term structure as given is also a weakness. As discussed in Chapter 4, quoted prices may differ from true values because of errors or special factors like liquidity. An arbitrage-free model would build any such discrepancies into the pricing model. An equilibrium model, however, would, in effect, shrug its shoulders at the odd price quotations, which is exactly the desired action.

This drawback of arbitrage-free models simply requires their users to be careful about imputed term structures. In fact, the techniques of Chapter 4 are exactly suited to this purpose, namely, to capture the truth contained in term structure data while ignoring, or at least deemphasizing, the noise.

Using the models for trading bonds with fixed cash flows.   Say that a trader wants to make money by purchasing one set of government bonds and selling another set. One example of this kind of trading is a yield curve bet in which a trader positions himself to profit from a steepening or flattening of the term structure. In any case, the trader needs some model to determine which bonds to buy and which to sell. While many traders carry such models in their heads, others might want to build a more formal model. For this purpose should they choose arbitrage-free or equilibrium models?

The answer is clearly equilibrium models. In fact, arbitrage-free models are completely useless for this purpose. Arbitrage-free models take the term structure as given. In other words, all bonds are assumed to be priced correctly. When asked about a strategy that buys one set and sells another set of bonds, an arbitrage-free model will always reply that there is no money to be made in such strategies.

Using the models for trading derivatives.   Trading derivatives means buying or selling derivatives while simultaneously hedging one's exposure using the underlying security or other derivative securities. The goal is to make money not on the level of interest rates nor on the level of one rate relative to another. The goal is to make money on relative mispricing, that is, on a divergence between a derivative's price and the price of its replicating portfolio. From this perspective, which class of models is more desirable?

Arbitrage-free models deliver exactly what a derivative trader wants. They indicate when derivatives prices are too high or too low relative to the market value of an underlying security or, in the case of multi-factor models, relative to the market values of an underlying set of securities. Equilibrium models, however, indicate when derivatives prices are too high or too low relative to model prices for the underlying securities. In other words, a derivatives trader using an equilibrium model would be making two bets. First, the model is right in assessing the value of the derivative relative to the value of the underlying securities. Second, the model is right in assessing the value of the underlying securities. While there is nothing wrong about making these two bets, most derivative traders are often interested in making only the first bet.

Using the models over time.   This point is about the internal consistency of models and, consequently, is a bit philosophical in nature. At every point of use, arbitrage-free models make assumptions about the drift, volatility, and mean reversion of the interest rate process. But there is no continuity between assumptions made one day and those made the next except for whatever continuity exists in the market quantities being matched. So, for example, drifts calculated on a particular day are assumed by the model to be relevant over the next 20 years while the user knows that a completely new drift process will be calculated the next day to fit that day's term structure of interest rates. In short, the use of arbitrage-free models is inconsistent over time.

A similar problem applies to the use of the Black-Scholes stock option pricing formula. The Black-Scholes model assumes that the stock volatility is constant over time. But users of the model often input the implied volatility of the previous day which, of course, changes every day. So, as with the arbitrage-free models of the term structure, the use of the Black-Scholes model contradicts its assumptions.

By contrast, equilibrium models, whose parameters are estimated from historical data or generated by strong beliefs, do not change from day to day. Their use over time, therefore, is internally consistent. On the other hand, many practitioners find that equilibrium models are not sufficiently accurate on a consistent basis. So, while the search continues for the "great model in the sky," arbitrage-free models are estimated anew over and over again in the pursuit of accurate contingent claim pricing.

For convenience, Table 9.1 summarizes the differences between the equilibrium and arbitrage-free approaches to term structure modeling.

Table 9.1   Equilibrium vs. Arbitrage-Free Models

Criterion	Equilibrium	Arbitrage-Free
Obtaining Inputs	Statistical Estimation	Market Prices
Sensitivity to Data	Deemphasizes Outliers	Accepts Outliers
Trading Bonds	Possible	Not Possible
Trading Derivatives	Two Bets	One Bet
Model Use Over Time	Stable Parameters	Inconsistent

Part Three
Measures of Price Sensitivity

INTRODUCTION

This Part describes how investors should think about the *price sensitivity* of fixed income securities; in other words, how they should think about price changes when interest rates change. In this discussion, as in the rest of the book, there is no analysis of whether rates will go up or down, or whether the term structure will unexpectedly flatten or steepen. The purpose of these measures is to calculate or estimate price changes for a given change in interest rates.

Measures of price sensitivity are used in many ways, three of which will be mentioned here. First, investors that have a view about future changes in interest rates need to calculate which securities will perform best if their view does, in fact, materialize. Consider, for example, an investor who expects all spot rates to fall over the next month. In order to choose between buying 30-year mortgage-backed securities and 10-year zeros, he needs to know how much the price of each of these securities will increase if rates do behave as he expects.

A second use of sensitivity measures is to determine price volatilities. Risk-averse investors often want to know how much a security's price can change for reasonable rate movements. Consider, for example, an investor who thinks that the chance of a 100 basis point increase in all rates over the next six months is remote but not out of the question. He might like to know how much he might lose by purchasing a particular security.

A third use of price sensitivity measures is in asset-liability management. An asset-liability manager usually raises money by incurring a set of liabilities and then investing that money at what is hoped will be a profit. Examples include banks that raise money through deposits and other short-term borrowings in order to lend to corporations, insurance companies that collect premiums and invest in a broad range of fixed income securities, and defined benefit pension plans that must pay money to retirees in the future but, in the interim, invest funds in financial markets. In any case, asset-liability managers need to know how the interest rate sensitivities of their assets and liabilities differ: Increases in the value of assets do no good if accompanied by more than offsetting losses due to increases in the value of liabilities.

The first, and by far best-known, measure of price sensitivity is *Macaulay duration*. While an important achievement that still has relevance today, this measure was developed under extremely restrictive assumptions and is applicable only to a very narrow class of fixed income securities. Put another way, the concept of measuring price sensitivity is far broader than indicated by Macaulay duration. Therefore, the chapters in this part will first discuss the broad concepts behind the measurement of price sensitivity and then analyze some special, well-known cases.

Chapter 10 introduces the price-rate function and its *derivative*. This derivative will turn out to be the basis for all measures of price sensitivity. Chapter 11 describes three of these measures, namely the price value of a basis point, duration, and convexity. In general, there does not exist a formula with which to calculate these measures. This chapter, therefore, shows how to calculate these measures numerically using term-structure models of the sort developed in Chapter 8. Chapter 12 presents a widely known and used simplified framework for analyzing price sensitivity that leads to *Macaulay duration* and *modified duration*. It is emphasized that this framework requires several restrictive assumptions and, more importantly, is only valid for analyzing securities with fixed cash flows. While many fixed income securities do not have fixed cash flows, it is worthwhile to spend some time on these sensitivity measures. First, the exercise develops one's intuition about price sensitivity in general. Second, the price sensitivity of simple securities is often a good benchmark with which to compare the sensitivities of more complicated securities. Chapter 13 introduces the need for multi-factor models of price sensitivity and presents one particular example of such a model, namely Ho's *key-rate durations*.

Chapter 10

The Price-Rate Function and its Derivative

Let the price of a fixed income security be P(y), where y is an interest rate factor that, together with a particular one-factor model, summarizes all of the information contained in the term structure of interest rates. For example, the curved, solid line in Figure 10.1 graphs the price of a 9 percent, 16-year bond that is callable at par any time after 3 years.[35] Prices are computed using the original Salomon Brothers model described in Chapter 8 but were graphed against the 10-year par yield, a common benchmark for intermediate-term securities, instead of the short-term rate.[36] When, for example, the 10-year par yield is 6.19 percent, the callable bond's price is 110.01 per $100 face value. However, when the 10-year par yield is much higher, at 13.38 percent, the price of the bond is only 68.52 per $100 face value. For ease of exposition, the following text will simply say "yield" instead of "10-year par yield."

Measures of price sensitivity, designed to describe how price changes when y changes, will be based on the derivative of P(y) with respect to y, written dP/dy. For those not familiar with the calculus, this expression can be read as the change in price divided by the change in y or, equivalently, the change in price per unit

---

[35]Part Four describes callable bonds and explains why their pricing functions have the shape shown in Figure 10.1. For now, however, the reader should simply take P(y) as given.

[36]One factor models assume that movements of the entire term structure can be summarized by movements in one particular interest rate factor, usually the short-term rate. But given the change in the short-term rate, the change in any other rate, like the 10-year par yield, can be easily determined from the model.

change in y. Graphically, the derivative of the pricing function at a particular rate level is the slope of the curve at that rate level, where the slope of the curve at a particular rate is defined as the slope of the line tangent to the curve at that rate.[37] Hence, since the line AA in Figure 10.1 is the line tangent to the curve at a yield of 6.19 percent, dP/dy at y = 6.19 percent equals the slope of AA. Similarly, the slope of BB equals dP/dy at a yield of 13.38 percent. Notice that the slope of the tangent line, and hence dP/dy, changes as yield changes. This is saying nothing more than that the price-yield curve is, in fact, a curve. The slope of a line is the same everywhere along the line, but the slope of a curve depends on location along the curve.

Because the derivative changes as yield changes, it is a *local* measure of price sensitivity. Figure 10.2 illustrates this point. Say that one knows the price of the callable bond at a yield of 6.19 percent and would like to estimate the price at a yield of 4 percent. Using the derivative at 6.19 percent as an estimate of the rate at which price changes, one would conclude that the price at a yield

[37]The slope of a line is the change in the vertical coordinate divided by the change in the horizontal coordinate. In the price-yield context, the slope of the line is the change in price divided by the change in yield.

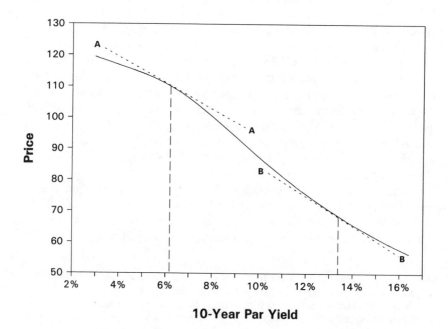

10-Year Par Yield

FIGURE 10.1 Price-yield curve of a callable bond.

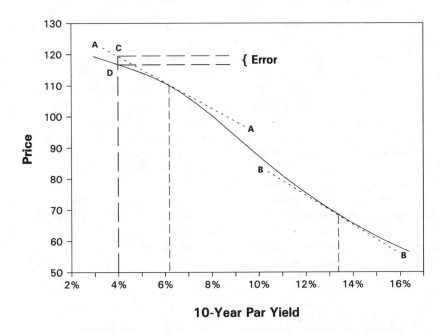

FIGURE 10.2   Price-yield curve of a callable bond.

of 4 percent was along the line AA at point C. The true price, however, is point D. The resulting estimation error is due to the fact that the derivative at 6.19 percent is not valid all the way from 6.19 percent to 4 percent. More specifically, the estimate of point C is above point D because the slope gradually flattens as yields fall from 6.19 percent to 4 percent. Consequently, the slope at 6.19 percent consistently overstates the increase in price as yield decreases. Note too that smaller rate changes would be more accurately estimated. At a yield of 5 percent the difference between the line AA and the price curve is less than it is at 4 percent.

The estimation of price changes using the slope can be expressed mathematically. The *first order Taylor approximation* to the price-yield curve is written as follows:

$$P(y') \approx P(y) + \left(\frac{dP}{dy}\right)(y' - y)$$

This equation states what was previously discussed. A new price can be estimated by starting at the old price and moving along the tangent line to the new yield. It is called a first order approximation, by the way, since the only derivative being used in the approximation is the first derivative.

If one has an explicit formula by which to compute price given y, then one can usually derive an explicit formula by which to compute price sensitivity, dP/dy, as well. An important example of this situation is the case of bonds with fixed cash flows, analyzed extensively in Chapter 12 of this Part. More generally, however, no such formulae exist. Practitioners price callable bonds and produce figures like Figure 10.1, for example, by models of the sort described in Part Two. The point is that for most fixed income securities, there does not exist an explicit formula by which to compute prices. And, in those cases, there also does not exist an explicit formula by which to compute price sensitivity, dP/dy.

It is generally possible, however, to estimate derivatives numerically from data about the price function. Recall that dP/dy represents the change in price divided by the change in y. Therefore, one can estimate dP/dy at a particular rate level, y, from prices at two rate levels near y. If y_0 and y_1 are two such rate levels and $P(y_0)$ and $P(y_1)$ are prices at those rate levels, respectively, then an estimate of dP/dy would be as follows:

$$\frac{dP}{dy} \approx \frac{P(y_1) - P(y_0)}{y_1 - y_0}$$

The data used to generate Figure 10.1 indicate that P(6.79%) = 107.27 and that P(6.65%) = 107.96. To estimate the derivative of the callable bond's pricing function for yields between 6.65 percent and 6.79 percent, one can apply the expression just given above:

$$\frac{dP}{dy} \approx \frac{107.96 - 107.27}{6.65\% - 6.79\%} = -492.86$$

The interpretation of the resulting value is that the price of $100 face value of this callable bond falls by 492.86 when the yield of 10-year par bonds increases by 1, which is 10,000 basis points. This is not a particularly useful way of expressing price sensitivity because 10,000 basis points is an impossibly large interest rate move. However, since dP/dy really expresses a rate of change, better interpretations are that price falls by about $0.49 for a 10 basis-point increase in yield and that price falls by about $0.049 for a 1 basis point-increase in yield.

Thinking of dP/dy in terms of price changes for relatively small interest rate changes is important for another reason. One can say with confidence that the slope of the curve between 6.65 percent and 6.79 percent is about –492.86. Recall, however, that the slope of a price curve changes as yield changes. Therefore, since the slope at 6 percent can be quite different from the slope at 8 percent, it is not very meaningful to estimate dP/dy between 6 percent and 8 percent. Mathematically, [P(8%) – P(6%)]/.02 does not measure slope at any particular point along the price curve.

Defining dP/dy in terms of "small" interest rate changes is intuitively correct. Nevertheless, its numerical calculation is not unique. Say that one is interested in dP/dy at a yield of 6.72 percent. One might choose yields of 6.65 percent and 6.79 percent, as above, to obtain a slope estimate of –492.86. On the other hand, one might just as easily have chosen yields of 6.69 percent and 6.75 percent to obtain a different slope estimate. There is not much that can be done about this ambiguity. But, so long as the two yields are not too far apart, the slope calculation should be sufficiently accurate and the particular choice of yields should not matter very much.[38]

---

[38]Were prices available without any error, it would be desirable to choose an infinitely small difference between the two yields and, in that way, estimate the derivative extremely accurately. But prices are usually not available without error. First, models of the sort developed in Part Two must perform many calculations and, therefore, are subject to some round-off error. Second, even if one has a formula for price, limits on calculation precision generate small errors. As a result, it is not a good idea to magnify these pricing errors by dividing by very small yield differences. In short, the yield difference selected should depend on the pricing accuracy, where more accurate pricing allows for smaller yield differences.

Chapter 11
Measures of Price Sensitivity

THE PRICE VALUE OF A BASIS POINT

The first measure of price sensitivity to be discussed here is called the *price value of a basis point* or PVBP.[39] As its name implies, it gives the dollar price change of a particular fixed income security for a one basis-point change in the interest rate.[40] Mathematically, the PVBP is defined as

$$\frac{-dP/dy}{10000}$$

Division by 10,000 simply transforms the derivative, which measures price change for a unit or a 10,000 basis-point change in y, to a measure for a one-basis-point change in y. The negative sign is a convention adopted because most, although not all, fixed income securities fall in price when rates increase. Mathematically, dP/dy is most often negative. To avoid having to quote negative measures most of the time, convention decrees that a positive value of sensitivity denotes the usual response of lower prices to higher rates. So the PVBP of the callable bond when yields are between 6.65 percent and 6.79 percent is about

---

[39]This measure is also known as the DV01, the dollar value of an 01.
[40]Industry convention defines changes in interest rates as changes in the yield-to-maturity of a security. But yield-to-maturity has no meaning for securities whose cash flows depend on the level of rates. Therefore, this book defines changes in interest rates as changes in the single factor used to summarize term-structure movements.

$$-\frac{-\$492.86}{10,000} = \$.049286$$

Alternatively, one could work directly with the price change data and divide by the change in basis points:

$$-\frac{\$107.96 - \$107.27}{665 - 679} = \$.049286$$

Table 11.1 lists this calculation as well as the calculation of the PVBP at two other yield levels. (The duration column will be discussed below.) When yields are between 10.85 percent and 10.99 percent, PVBP is $.0579, while when yields are between 14.20 percent and 14.33 percent, PVBP is $.0438. These different values illustrate the point made earlier: The interest rate sensitivity of fixed income securities depends on the level of rates. And, as will be seen in Part Four, callable bonds generally have the property exhibited in Table 11.1. Their PVBPs are relatively low when yields are high, are relatively high for intermediate yield levels, and are particularly low when yields are low.

Note that all of these calculations have assumed a position of $100 face value of the callable bonds. Were the position $1000 face value, then the price changes in Table 11.1 would be 10 times as large as would be the resulting PVBPs. So, for example, a callable bond with a $10,000 face value would, when yields are between 10.85 percent and 10.99 percent, have a PVBP of about $5.79.

PVBP is a particularly convenient measure of price sensitivity for hedging purposes. Say that a trader has just bought $10,000 face value of a callable bond that he thinks the market has undervalued. He calculates its current PVBP at $5.79.

Table 11.1 Measures of Price Change for the 9%, 16-Year Bonds Callable at Par in 3 Years

10-year Par Yield	Price	Price Change	Value of a Basis Point	Duration
6.65%	107.96			
6.79%	107.27	.69	.0493	4.57
10.85%	82.01			
10.99%	81.20	.81	.0579	7.05
14.20%	64.82			
14.33%	64.25	.57	.0438	6.76

Not wanting to speculate on the general level of interest rates, but only on the underpricing of the callable bond, he chooses to hedge his position by short selling some quantity of another bond issue with a PVBP of $2.895 per $10,000 face value. How many of these other bonds should he sell? The answer is $5.79/$2.895 = 2, or $20,000 face value. If, after shorting these bonds, interest rates rise by one basis point, he will lose $5.79 on his callable bond but win 2 x $2.895 = $5.79 on his short position. On the other hand, if rates fall by one basis point, he will gain $5.79 on his callable bond but lose 2 x $2.895 = $5.79 on his short position. So, the trader has immunized himself against interest rate changes. Regardless of how interest rates move in the near term, he will win if the callable bond's price rallies relative to the bond he shorted.

The caveat "in the near term," included in the previous sentence, is quite important. As has been shown, PVBPs change as the level of interest rates change. Therefore, after rates have moved, it is likely that the PVBP of the callable bond will no longer be twice the PVBP of the other bond issue. Put another way, the hedge ratio will change. To maintain a position that is neutral with respect to interest rate changes, the trader will have to adjust, or *rebalance*, his hedge position.

One result about the PVBP that can be useful in the hedging context is that the PVBP of a portfolio is simply the sum of the PVBPs of the individual securities in that portfolio.[41] This result is useful for the following reason. Say that a trader is considering purchasing various portfolios of fixed income securities for hedging purposes. Without the stated result, the trader would have to compute the PVBP for each proposed portfolio. If the portfolio contains many bonds, and if models of the type described in Part Two are needed for pricing, this can be an extremely time-consuming process. Armed with the stated result, however, the trader need compute the PVBP of each security only once. The PVBP of any portfolio is then obtained by simply adding the individual PVBPs.

The price value of a basis point measures the price response of a particular position size in a particular security. Assume that the PVBP of a position in callable bonds is $5.79 while the PVBP of a position in mortgage-backed securities is $4.00. One cannot tell whether the callable bonds are inherently more sensitive to interest rate change or whether the position in callable bonds happens to be larger than the position in mortgage-backed securities. It has been found useful, therefore, to develop a measure of price sensitivity that does not depend on position size and, consequently, can be used to compare the inherent riskiness of different fixed income securities.

---

[41]This result follows directly from the fact that the derivative of a sum equals the sum of the derivatives.

DURATION

Duration measures price changes per dollar of portfolio value or percentage price changes. Thus, unlike the PVBP, duration does not depend on position size. Therefore, duration can be used to compare the riskiness of different securities as opposed to the risk of different security positions.

The mathematical definition of duration is

$$-\frac{1}{P}\frac{dP}{dy}$$

or

$$-\frac{dP/P}{dy}$$

Since dP/P is the percentage change in price, duration may be interpreted as the percentage change for a unit change in y. As in the case of the PVBP, the negative sign is a convention to ensure that most fixed income securities, encompassing all those that increase in value when rates fall, have positive duration measures.

From Table 11.1, P(6.65%) = 107.96 and P(6.79%) = 107.27. Assuming that 6.65 percent is the starting yield, the percentage change in price is given by [P(6.79%) – P(6.65%)]/P(6.65%). Therefore, the duration of the bond at a yield of 6.65 percent is

$$-\frac{\dfrac{107.27-107.96}{107.96}}{6.79\%-6.65\%}=4.57$$

Of course, positions of $10,000 face value would have the same durations as these positions of $100 face value. In the former case duration equals –{[10,727 – 10,796]/ 10,796}/(6.79% – 6.65%) = 4.57, as just shown.

Just as dP/dy can be interpreted for rate changes of different magnitudes, so can duration. The most common interpretation of the value 4.57 is that the bond price falls by about 4.57 percent when the yield increases by 1 percent or 100 basis points. So, for example, a $5,000 position in the callable would lose about 4.57 percent x $5,000 = $228.50 if the yield rose by 100 basis points. But since, as discussed earlier, slope estimates can change significantly in a 100-basis-point range, it may be wiser to use duration for smaller rate changes. More generally then,

% change in price = $-D \times \Delta y$ [42]

If yield increases by .001, or 10 basis points, for example, then the same position would experience a percentage change in price of $-4.57 \times .001 = -.457$ percent or an absolute change of $-.457\% \times \$5,000 = -22.85$.

This expression for percentage price change indicates the sense in which acquiring duration is a bet on the direction of interest rates. If rates increase, so that Δy is positive, higher durations result in larger losses. On the other hand, should rates decrease, higher durations result in larger gains. The same argument, of course, applies to the PVBP.

Table 11.1 calculates duration at three different yield levels. As with the PVBP, duration depends on the level of interest rates, moving from 4.57 at yields of about 6 3/4 percent up to 7.05 at yields of about 10 7/8 percent and then down to 6.76 at yields of about 14 1/4 percent. Figure 11.1 fleshes out this story by graphing the callable bond's duration against the 10-year par yield. The pattern of interest rate sensitivity is quite complicated. When rates rise from about 3 percent to about 10 percent, the duration of the bond increases. If rates continue to increase, however, the duration of the bond falls off. Clearly, the price sensitivity of a fixed income security can depend, in a very complicated way, on the level of interest rates. Once again, Part Four will explain why the duration-yield curve of callable bonds has this particular shape.

Duration is often the preferred measure of interest rate sensitivity in the context of asset-liability management. Say that a life insurance company has taken in premiums of $1.05 million in exchange for assuming liabilities worth $1 million. The $.05 million profit can be paid out to shareholders or reinvested in the company's business. The other $1 million of premium revenue must be invested so that, when the liabilities come due, the insurance company will be able to meet its obligations.

Life insurance liabilities are, in aggregate, quite stable. Therefore, one can view life insurance liabilities as a fixed set of cash flows, like any traditional fixed income security. Assume that the duration of these liabilities is 5. How can the insurance company invest the $1 million so that, no matter what happens to interest rates, the net value of its position will not change from zero? This is the relevant question because, if it manages to keep the net value of its position equal to zero, it will be able to pay off its liabilities without requiring any additional cash inflows.

---

[42]This expression can be derived from the first order Taylor approximation. Subtracting P(y) from both sides and dividing by P(y) gives the following expression:

$$[P(y') - P(y)]/P(y) \approx \{dP/dy\}/P \times (y' - y)$$

Letting $\Delta y = y' - y$ and recalling the definition of duration, this can be rewritten as

% change in price = $-D\Delta y$

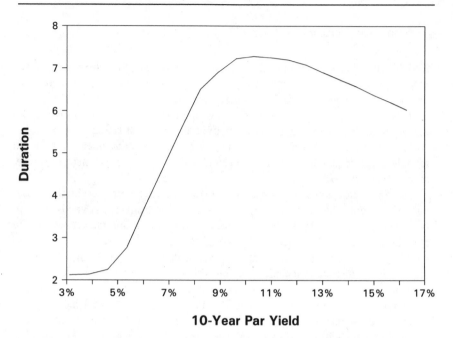

10-Year Par Yield

FIGURE 11.1   Duration-yield curve of a callable bond.

The answer is that the insurance company should buy assets with a duration of 5. If it does so, consider the consequences. If rates increase by 10 basis points, the value of both assets and liabilities will fall by 5 x .001 = .5 percent or $5,000. On the other hand, if rates decrease by 10 basis points, the value of assets and liabilities will both rise by $5,000. In either case, the net value of the insurer's position stays the same. Of course, as interest rates change, the duration of assets and the duration of liabilities will both change. Therefore, as when using the PVBP for hedging, the asset-liability manager must periodically rebalance assets so that they remain duration-matched with liabilities.

It should now be clear why duration is used so often in the asset-liability context. Because assets come from assuming liabilities, asset value often equals liability value. Therefore, matching the percentage price changes of assets and liabilities, that is, matching durations, immunizes an asset-liability manager against any dollar price changes due to interest rate moves. In the hedging context, however, the dollar value of the original position often differs from that of the hedging vehicle. As a result, matching percentage price changes does not guard against dollar losses; it is more convenient to use the PVBP than to use duration.

It should be emphasized that the choice between duration and the PVBP really is just a matter of convenience because both measures are based on dP/dy. One must simply exercise some care not to confuse percentage price changes with dollar price changes. So, for example, to use duration in a hedging context, or in any context where the dollar value of the two sides of a position differs, one needs to match duration times value, or D x P instead of duration itself. Since D x P = – dP/dy, matching that quantity is equivalent to matching the PVBP of the two sides.

Just as there is a relationship between the PVBP of a portfolio and the PVBPs of its constituent securities, there is an analogous relationship for duration. Let P and D be the price and duration of a portfolio while letting P_i and D_i be the price and duration of security i in that portfolio. Appendix 11A shows that the duration of a portfolio equals a weighted average of the individual security durations where the weights are the proportion of portfolio value contributed by each security:

$$D = \sum_i \frac{P_i}{P} D_i$$

Consider, for example, the portfolio described by Table 11.2. The prices of securities A, B, and C, are $25, $75, and $100, respectively, and their durations are 3, 5, and 10, respectively. The three securities are combined into a $200 portfolio. Therefore, the weights of the three securities in the portfolio are $25/$200 = 12.5%, $75/$200 = 37.5%, and $100/$200 = 50%. The duration of the portfolio is obtained by the following weighted average of the individual durations:

$$D = .125 \times 3 + .375 \times 5 + .5 \times 10 = 7.25$$

CONVEXITY

The PVBP and duration, based on the slope of the price-yield function, measure how price changes when interest rates change. Convexity is a measure of how the

Table 11.2   The Duration of a Portfolio

Security	Value	Fraction of Portfolio Value	Duration
A	$25	12.5%	3
B	$75	37.5%	5
C	$100	50%	10
Portfolio	$200	100%	7.25

slope itself changes as interest rates change. The change in slope, or convexity, measures the curvature of the price-yield graph.

The convexity measure is useful for two reasons. First, it can be used as a curvature correction to price sensitivity measures that are based on the derivative alone. Increasing the accuracy of these measures can improve performance in the hedging and asset-liability management contexts. Second, whereas increasing or decreasing the PVBP or duration of a portfolio can be viewed as betting on the direction of interest rates, changing the convexity of a portfolio can be viewed as a bet on the volatility of rates. Each of these uses is examined in turn.

Mathematically, convexity is defined as

$$\frac{1}{P} \frac{d^2P}{dy^2}$$

where d^2P/dy^2 is the *second derivative* of the price function. The second derivative, for those not familiar with the calculus, equals the change in the first derivative, or the slope, for a unit change in yield.

As in the case of duration and the PVBP, if there is an explicit formula for price given interest rates, there is usually an explicit formula for convexity. For most fixed income securities, however, such formulae do not exist and convexity must be calculated numerically. Table 11.3 shows how this is done.

Since the first derivative is the change in price for a change in yield, it is calculated by dividing price change by yield change. Similarly, since the second derivative is the change in the first derivative for a change in yield, it is calculated by dividing the change in the first derivative by the yield change.

Table 11.3   Convexity of the 9%, 16-Year Bonds Callable at Par in 3 Years

10-Year Par Yield	Price	First Derivative	Second Derivative	Convexity
6.65%	107.96			
6.79%	107.27	−492.86	−13,646.67	−127.22
6.94%	106.50	−513.33		
10.85%	82.01			
10.99%	81.20	−578.57	5100	62.81
11.13%	80.40	−571.43		
14.20%	64.82			
14.33%	64.25	−438.46	11,830.77	184.14
14.46%	63.70	−423.08		

Consider the convexity calculation in Table 11.3 for yields between 6.65 percent and 6.79 percent. The first derivative at y = 6.79 percent is estimated as

$$\frac{107.27 - 107.96}{.0679 - .0665} = -492.86$$

while the first derivative at y = 6.94 percent is estimated as

$$\frac{106.50 - 107.27}{.0694 - .0679} = -513.33$$

Then the second derivative at y = 6.79 percent, which is the rate of change in the first derivative, is estimated as follows:

$$\frac{-513.33 - (-492.86)}{.0694 - .0679} = -13,646.67$$

Finally, convexity at y = 6.79 percent is calculated by dividing the second derivative by the price at that point. The result is

$$\frac{-13,646.67}{107.27} = -127.22$$

Similar calculations reveal that convexity at y = 10.99 percent and at 14.33 percent is equal to 62.81 and 184.14, respectively.

The sign of the convexity measure can usually be seen from the price-yield curve. Consider the callable bond, whose price-yield curve is repeated, for convenience, in Figure 11.2. When rates are above about 10 percent, the price-yield curve is convex, which means it looks like a "smile." This shape is called *positive convexity*. On the other hand, when rates are below about 10 percent, the price-yield curve is concave and looks like a "frown." This latter shape is called *negative convexity*.

Recall from Chapter 10, Figure 10.2, that estimating price changes using the slope of the price-rate curve at a particular rate will not be very accurate because the slope changes along the curve. Therefore, one way to increase the accuracy of such estimates is to incorporate changes in the slope explicitly.

Figure 11.2 illustrates this enhanced approximation procedure. Recall that the

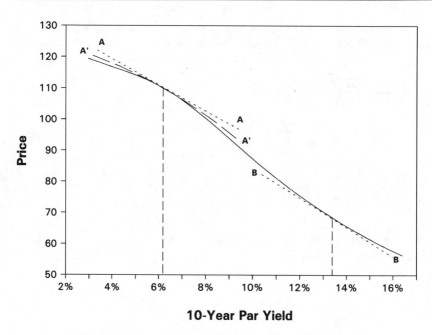

10-Year Par Yield

FIGURE 11.2   Price-yield curve of a callable bond.

line AA is the price estimate using the slope alone. It is a line because a first order approximation has a constant slope equal to the derivative of the price-yield function at 6.19 percent.

Furthermore, since the slope of the approximation is constant, its second derivative equals zero. By contrast, the approximating curve A'A' has a slope equal to the derivative of the price-yield function only at 6.19 percent. Elsewhere, the slope is governed by a rate of change equal to the second derivative of the price-yield curve at 6.19 percent. So, since the second derivative of A'A' is not zero, A'A' is, in fact, a curve. Mathematically, the curve A'A' is the *second order Taylor approximation*, written as follows:

$$P(y') \approx P(y) + \left(\frac{dP}{dy}\right)(y'-y) + .5\ \frac{d^2P}{dy^2}\ (y'-y)^2$$

It is called a second order approximation because it uses the first and second derivatives of the price function.

As evident from Figure 11.2, the curve A'A' is a much better approximation to the price-yield curve than is the line AA. In particular, A'A' is extremely close to the price-yield curve for a much larger range of yields. This suggests that hedgers and asset-liability managers can achieve greater protection against interest rate changes by basing their strategies on the first and second derivatives instead of the first alone. Consider an asset-liability manager who sets the duration and convexity of his assets equal to those of his liabilities. For any interest rate change, the change in the value of his assets will more closely resemble the change in the value of his liabilities than had he matched durations alone. Furthermore, since matching both durations and convexities will provide extremely similar price moves for a relatively large range of rate changes, he need not rebalance quite as often as in the case of matching only durations. The intuition behind this last point is that portfolios with the same durations and convexities will be alike not only in price response but in the response of slope as well. Therefore, the portfolios remain duration-matched over a relatively large yield range.

The second use of convexity is as a means to measure bets on the volatility of rates. Rewriting the equation for curve A'A' (the second order Taylor approximation) by subtracting and then dividing by P(y) gives the following expression:

$$\frac{P(y') - P(y)}{P(y)} \approx \frac{1}{P(y)} \frac{dP}{dy} (y' - y) + .5 \frac{1}{P(y)} \frac{d^2P}{dy^2} (y' - y)^2$$

Using the definitions of duration, D, and convexity, C, and letting $\Delta = (y' - y)$, this expression can be rewritten as follows:

$$\% \text{ change in price} \approx -D \, \Delta y + .5 \, C \, (\Delta y)^2$$

From the duration term it is clear that, as mentioned earlier, increasing the duration of a security or portfolio increases exposure to the direction of interest rates, for richer or for poorer. The convexity term, however, conveys a different message. Since $(\Delta y)^2$ is always positive, positive convexity contributes gains so long as interest rates move. The bigger the move, in either direction, the greater the gains from having positive convexity. Negative convexity works in the reverse. If C is negative, then rate moves, in either direction, contribute losses to a portfolio. In this sense, increasing convexity is a bet on volatility, that is, a bet that interest rates will be volatile. Decreasing convexity is a bet that interest rates will be stable.

To conclude this section, the convexity of a portfolio will be related to the convexity of its constituent securities. Not surprisingly, the relationship resembles that derived in the case of durations. If C is the convexity of a portfolio and C_i the convexity of individual security i, then

$$C = \sum_i \frac{P_i}{P} \, C_i$$

This result is proved in Appendix 11A.

THE COST OF CONVEXITY

The cost of increasing duration is clear: If rates rise, it will have been a bad idea to do so. Put succinctly, the higher the duration of a security or portfolio, the greater the short-term price risk.

The cost of convexity, however, is not as transparent. Given the discussion at the end of the last section, one might think that increasing convexity is always a good thing to do. After all, one gains from added convexity whether rates rise or fall.

This question will be strengthened before being answered. At a yield of about 7.51 percent, the callable bond graphed in Figure 10.1 has a price of 103.26 and a duration of 5.66. As it turns out, at this same yield, a 7.30 percent, 7.5-year noncallable bond has a price of 100.70 and a duration of 5.66. Note that, at a yield of 7.51 percent, these two bonds are duration-matched. Also note that 103.26/ 100.70 = 1.0254 of the noncallable bonds, or 102.54 face value, costs as much as 100 face value of the callable bonds. Figure 11.3 graphs the price of 100 face value of the callable bond, given by the solid line, and the price of 102.54 face value of the noncallable bond, given by the dashed line. As just pointed out, the price and the duration of the two bond positions match at a yield of 7.51 percent.[43]

From the figure it is evident that, at a yield of 7.51 percent, the convexity of the noncallable bond exceeds the convexity of the callable bond. In fact, the convexity of the callable bond at 7.51 percent is negative, so that its price sensitivity is increasing as yields increase, while the convexity of the callable bond is positive so that its price sensitivity is decreasing as yields increase. In any case, as a result of this convexity relationship, the noncallable bond has a higher price than the callable bond whether rates are higher or lower.

One might be tempted to conclude from Figure 11.3 that the noncallable bond is a better investment than the callable bond. After all, while both bonds have the same price today, at any future interest rate the callable bond's price exceeds that of the noncallable bond. But this analysis is faulty. Figure 11.3, along with duration and convexity measures, analyzes price moves assuming that the only vari-

---

[43]One can see from the graph that the duration matches. The slopes of the two curves look equal at a yield of 7.51%. And, since the prices of the two are equal at that yield level, an equal slope implies an equal duration as well.

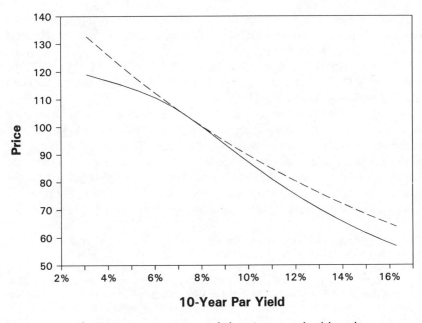

FIGURE 11.3   Price- and duration-matched bonds.

able that changes is the interest rate factor. The passage of time, however, is ignored by these measures.

The passage of time affects investment returns in two ways. First, even if rates do not change, the price of a bond changes as it matures. Second, as a coupon bond matures it makes coupon payments. A correct comparison of bond returns must be based on *total return*, which takes these effects into account in addition to the effect of changing interest rates. If P is the price of the bond at the beginning of the investment period, P' the price at the end of the investment period, and H the value of all intermediate cash flows at the end of the investment period,[44] then the equation for total return over that investment horizon is

$$\frac{H + P' - P}{P}$$

---

[44]If the investment horizon is six months and a coupon is paid at the end of those six months, then H is simply the coupon payment. If, however, the coupon is paid before the end of the investment horizon or if there are many intermediate coupon payments, then H is the accumulated value of all coupon payments reinvested, from the time of their respective receipts, until the end of the investment horizon. The selection of a particular reinvestment rate is ambiguous and is chosen in a manner most appropriate to the particular investment under consideration.

Figure 11.4 plots the total return of the callable and noncallable bonds over a six-month horizon as a function of the yield at the end of that horizon. The total return of the callable bond is above the total return of the noncallable bond when the yield does not move very much from its initial level of 7.51 percent. On the other hand, if the yield does move much, in either direction, the noncallable bond provides the higher total return.[45]

It is quite easy to explain why the noncallable bond does better when rates move up or down by a sufficient amount. The noncallable bond has higher convexity and, therefore, profits more from rate volatility. The reason that the callable bond fares better when rates do not move very much is more subtle. One could explain this fact by studying the particular term structure used in this example, the relative coupon rates of the two bonds, and so on. But the simpler and more accurate reason is that markets do not admit arbitrage opportunities.[46] If the noncallable

[45]Note that the domain (horizontal axis) of this graph has been limited to a more realistic range of possible interest rate values over a six-month horizon. The larger domain of Figure 11.3 was chosen to emphasize the convexity differences between the callable and noncallable bonds.
[46]This example, of course, does not use market prices. But the pricing model used to generate all of the numbers, as all those reviewed in Part Two, precludes arbitrage opportunities. For this reason the example inherits the property, characteristic of real markets, that securities do not dominate one another.

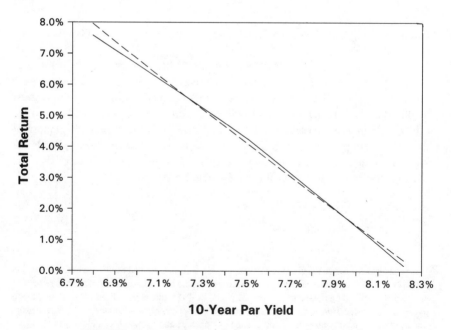

10-Year Par Yield

FIGURE 11.4   Price- and duration-matched bonds.

bond had a higher return than the callable bond in all scenarios, meaning if the noncallable bond *dominated* the callable bond, no one would buy the latter. Or, more dramatically, arbitrageurs would short the callable bond and buy the noncallable bond, earning riskless profits. In either case, the price of the callable bond would fall relative to the noncallable bond until its return was higher in at least some scenarios. At that point, presumably, some would find it a worthwhile purchase. In summary, since markets are generally characterized by the lack of riskless arbitrage opportunities, bond portfolios with relatively high convexities do better than duration-matched portfolios when yields change sufficiently, but worse when yields move little. This lower return in a stable yield environment may be called the *cost of convexity*.

APPENDIX 11A

The Duration and Convexity of a Portfolio

Let P be the price of the portfolio and let P_i denote the price of security i in the portfolio. Also, let D and D_i denote the duration of the portfolio and of an individual security i. By the definition of duration, the duration of the portfolio is

$$D = - \frac{1}{P} \frac{dP}{dy}$$

Since $P = \sum P_i$, this duration can be rewritten as follows:

$$D = - \frac{1}{P} \frac{d\left(\sum_i P^i\right)}{dy}$$

It is a fact from the calculus that the derivative of a sum equals the sum of the derivatives. Therefore,

$$D = - \frac{1}{P} \sum_i \frac{dP_i}{dy}$$

Multiplying dP_i/dy by P_i/P_i, since one can always multiply a term by 1, and recalling that $D_i = -\{1/P_i\}\, dP_i/dy$, gives that

$$D = \frac{1}{P} \sum_i P_i D_i$$

Finally, bringing P into the summation,

$$D = \sum_i \frac{P_i}{P} D_i$$

Since the second derivative of a sum also equals the sum of second derivatives, the same proof applies to convexity. Letting C and C_i be the convexity of the portfolio and of an individual security, the analogous result is that

$$C = \sum_i \frac{P_i}{P} C_i$$

Chapter 12
Macaulay and Modified Duration

As mentioned in the Introduction to Part Three, the sensitivity measures developed in this Chapter require restrictive assumptions and are applicable only to securities with fixed cash flows. Nevertheless, these measures help develop intuition that will be useful in understanding the price sensitivity of more complex securities. Furthermore, since this approach has received a great deal of attention and is used quite often, every fixed income professional should be familiar with the results of this section.

DERIVATIONS AND DEFINITIONS

Chapter 2 showed that a bond can be priced by discounting its cash flows by the appropriate spot rates. So, using the notation of that chapter, the price of $100 face value of the Treasury's 5 7/8s due February 15, 2004, as of February 15, 1994, is

$$P = 2.9375 \sum_{t=1}^{20} \left[1 + \frac{\hat{r}(t/2)}{2} \right] + 100 \left(1 + \frac{\hat{r}(10)}{2} \right)^{-20}$$

Note that t counts the number of semiannual periods. For a 10-year bond, t starts at 1 and ends at 20, which is 20 semiannual periods or 10 years. Also note that $\hat{r}(t/2)$ gives the spot rate applicable for a cash flow to be received in t semi-annual periods or $t/2$ years.

For the purposes of developing a simple model of price sensitivity, the above equation is quite complicated. It is not easy to answer the question of how price changes when the interest rate changes when there are not one but 20 different interest rates. The modern solution to this problem was outlined in Part Two: One must create a model of the term structure which describes how all rates change when any particular rate changes or, in a multi-factor model, when several rates change. This, in fact, has been the approach of this Chapter up to this point.

The older and more common approach, however, is to simplify the previously stated pricing equation by making the assumptions of a *flat term structure* and of *parallel shifts*. A flat term structure means that all cash flows can be discounted by the same rate, r. Parallel shifts mean that interest rates of all terms move up or down by the same amount, so they move in parallel.[47] Put another way, this approach assumes that a flat term-structure prevails both before and after any interest rate changes. Under the flat term-structure assumption, the pricing equation for the 5 ^{7}/₈s due February 15, 2004, becomes

$$
P = 2.9375 \sum_{t=1}^{20} \left(1 + \frac{r}{2}\right)^{-t} + 100 \left(1 + \frac{r}{2}\right)^{-20}
$$

Recall that yield-to-maturity is the one rate that, when used to discount a bond's cash flows, generates the bond's price. Viewing the above price expression in light of this definition, a good choice for r is, in fact, the bond's yield-to-maturity. Part One showed that each cash flow is properly discounted at its own rate. But here, for simplicity, the analysis requires using only one discount rate. Part Two showed that term structures of volatility mattered, since rates of different terms tend to move by different amounts. But, again, in the interest of simplicity, the duration measures discussed in this Chapter assume parallel shifts.

It will be useful to develop a more general pricing equation consistent with the simplifying assumptions of this Chapter. Consider a fixed income security maturing in T years with a fixed semiannual cash flow of $c(t/2)$ in t semiannual periods

---

[47]The reader will recall from Part Two that, in a one-factor model, specifying the evolution of the short-term rate, in combination with arbitrage arguments, completely determines the evolution of all other rates. Parallel shifts, therefore, as an independent specification of the evolution of other rates, are not consistent with the absence of arbitrage opportunities.

or $t/2$ years.[48] Cash flows are "fixed" by this formulation because the cash-flow schedule is completely set in advance. In particular, the cash flows do not depend in any way on the level of interest rates. The pricing equation for this fixed income security is

$$P = \sum_{t=1}^{2T} c\left(\frac{t}{2}\right)\left(1+\frac{r}{2}\right)^{-t}$$

Under this simplified pricing model, one can indeed ask how prices change when the interest rate changes. Due to the flat term-structure assumption there is only one interest rate before rates change. And, due to the parallel shift assumption, there is only one interest rate after rates change. Taking the derivative of price with respect to this one rate r reveals that

$$\frac{dP}{dr} = -\sum_{t=1}^{2T}\left(\frac{t}{2}\right)c\left(\frac{t}{2}\right)\left(1+\frac{r}{2}\right)^{-t-1}$$

Multiplying both sides by $-1/P$ and rearranging terms gives the following equation:

$$-\frac{1}{P}\frac{dP}{dr} = \frac{\displaystyle\sum_{t=1}^{2T}\left(\frac{t}{2}\right)c\left(\frac{t}{2}\right)\left(1+\frac{r}{2}\right)^{-t}}{P\left(1+\frac{r}{2}\right)}$$

The left-hand side of this equation is the definition of duration given in Chapter 11. The right-hand side is a simple expression for duration made possible by the assumptions of a flat term structure and parallel shifts. And it is this particular expression that is known as *modified duration* and written, for ease of reference, as D_{mod}:

$$D_{mod} = \frac{\displaystyle\sum_{t=1}^{2T}\left(\frac{t}{2}\right)c\left(\frac{t}{2}\right)\left(1+\frac{r}{2}\right)^{-t}}{P\left(1+\frac{r}{2}\right)}$$

[48]For a standard bond, $c(t/2)$ will be the coupon payment for $t = 1, \ldots, 2T - 1$, while $c(2T)$ will be the coupon plus principal payments.

It is easy to remember this expression if one pauses to think about each term in the expression. Each of the terms of the form $c(t/2)(1+r/2)^{-t}$ equals the present value of the bond's cash flow in $t/2$ years. These present value terms multiplied by $t/2$, the time, in years, at which the cash flow is received, can be called time-weighted present values. Therefore, in words, modified duration can be described as the sum of the time-weighted present value of the cash flows divided by $P(1+r/2)$.

Macaulay duration, written D_{Mac}, is a simple transformation of modified duration:

$$D_{Mac} = \left(1 + \frac{r}{2}\right) D_{mod}$$

Substituting the previously derived expression for D_{mod} into the above equation,

$$D_{Mac} = \frac{1}{P}\left[\sum_{t=1}^{2T}\left(\frac{t}{2}\right)c\left(\frac{t}{2}\right)\left(1+\frac{r}{2}\right)^{-t}\right]$$

In words, Macaulay duration is the sum of the time-weighted present values divided by price.

Recalling that $D_{mod} = [1/P]dP/dr$, Macaulay duration can also be written as follows:

$$D_{Mac} = -\left(1+\frac{r}{2}\right)\frac{1}{P}\frac{dP}{dr}$$

$$= -\frac{dP/P}{dr/(1+r/2)}$$

So Macaulay duration can also be described as the percentage change in price for a percentage change in the interest rate.[49]

---

[49]More precisely, Macaulay duration is the percentage change in price for two times the percentage change in $1 + r/2$. This can be seen simply by noting that the percentage change in $1+r/2$ is $\{dr/2\}/(1+r/2)$.

Since modified and Macaulay duration measure the same thing, one measure is not strictly preferable to the other. For estimating price changes, however, modified duration is easier to use. Consider a bond selling for $100 with a modified duration of 5 at a yield of 8 percent and a Macaulay duration, therefore, of 5(1+ .08/2) = 5.2. To estimate the effect of a 10 basis-point increase in yield on price using modified duration, simply multiply the interest rate change of 10 basis points by duration to obtain that price which will decrease by about 5 x .001 = .5 percent. From a price of $100 this means a drop of about $.50. Given a Macaulay duration, however, the calculation is more complicated. An increase in the interest rate from 8 percent to 8.1 percent is a percentage increase of .001/(1+.08/2) = .0961538%. Multiplying this by the Macaulay duration of 5.2 gives the price change of .5 percent and dollar price change of $.50. Despite the disadvantage in computation, Macaulay duration has the advantage of being easily interpreted. This advantage will be discussed later in the chapter.

Invoking the assumptions of a flat term structure and parallel shifts also allows for the derivation of a simple expression for the convexity of a fixed income security with fixed cash flows. Taking the second derivative of the pricing equation reveals that

$$\frac{d^2P}{dr^2} = \sum_{t=1}^{2T} \frac{t}{2} \frac{t+1}{2} c \left(\frac{t}{2}\right)\left(1+\frac{r}{2}\right)^{-t-2}$$

Dividing both sides by price and rearranging terms,

$$\frac{1}{P}\frac{d^2P}{dr^2} = \frac{\displaystyle\sum_{t=1}^{2T} \frac{t}{2} \left(\frac{t}{2}+.5\right) c \left(\frac{t}{2}\right)\left(1+\frac{r}{2}\right)^{-t}}{P\left(1+\frac{r}{2}\right)^2}$$

The left-hand side of this expression is the definition of convexity presented in Chapter 11. The right-hand side can be remembered as weighted present values divided by $P(1 + r/2)^2$. The weights in this case are $(t/2)(t/2 +.5)$. Since t denotes a number of semiannual periods, the weight is the years to the cash flow times the years plus .5.

AN EXAMPLE

Table 12.1 illustrates the calculation of Macaulay duration, modified duration, and convexity for the 5 7/8s due February 15, 2004. The first column lists the terms, in years, of the bond's cash flows. In terms of the previous section, this column lists successive values for $t/2$. The second column lists the cash flow at each term. For this simple security the cash flows are, of course, quite simple: half the coupon at each date before maturity and 100 plus half the coupon at maturity. The third column lists the present value of each of these cash flows, where the discounting is done at the bond's yield-to-maturity of 5.87 percent. So, for example, the present value of the coupon of $5.875/2 = 2.9375$ payable in four years is

$$\frac{2.9375}{\left(1 + \frac{.0587}{2}\right)^8} = 2.3306$$

The fourth column of the table weights each of the present values by the term, in years, at which it is received. Continuing with the example of the coupon payable in four years, its weighted present value is simply 4×2.3306, or about 9.32.

By definition, summing the present values obtained when discounting is done at the bond's yield-to-maturity gives the bond's price. In this case, according to the table, P = 100.04. Now, recall that Macaulay duration is the sum of the weighted present values divided by price. Therefore, summing the entries of the fourth column and dividing by the price gives the Macaulay duration of 7.70. Modified duration can be obtained simply by dividing Macaulay duration by $1+r/2$. In this case,

$$D_{\text{mod}} = \frac{7.70}{1 + \frac{.0587}{2}} = 7.48$$

Table 12.1 also computes the bond's convexity. To do this, each present value is weighted by the number of years times the number of years plus .5. For the case of the coupon to be received in four years, the present value of 2.3306 is multiplied by $4 \times 4.5 = 18$ to give a weighted present value of 41.95. Adding these weighted present values listed in the fifth column and dividing the result by the bond's price gives a convexity of about 69.37.

These calculations can as easily be made for any particular yield-to-maturity. Figures 12.1 and 12.2 graph the price-yield and duration-yield curves for the 5 7/8s due February 15, 2004. These are important graphs to keep in mind because all fixed income securities with fixed cash flows will have these basic

Table 12.1   The Calculation of Macaulay Duration, Modified Duration, and Convexity

Term	Cash Flow	Present Value	Time-Weighted Present Value	Weighted Present Value for Convexity
.5	2.9375	2.8537	1.4269	1.4269
1	2.9375	2.7724	2.7724	4.1586
1.5	2.9375	2.6933	4.0400	8.0800
2	2.9375	2.6165	5.2331	13.0826
2.5	2.9375	2.5419	6.3548	19.0644
3	2.9375	2.4694	7.4083	25.9292
3.5	2.9375	2.3990	8.3966	33.5864
4	2.9375	2.3306	9.3225	41.9513
4.5	2.9375	2.2642	10.1888	50.9440
5	2.9375	2.1996	10.9981	60.4895
5.5	2.9375	2.1369	11.7529	70.5177
6	2.9375	2.0760	12.4558	80.9628
6.5	2.9375	2.0168	13.1091	91.7634
7	2.9375	1.9593	13.7149	102.8618
7.5	2.9375	1.9034	14.2756	114.2045
8	2.9375	1.8491	14.7931	125.7412
8.5	2.9375	1.7964	15.2694	137.4254
9	2.9375	1.7452	15.7067	149.2137
9.5	2.9375	1.6954	16.1066	161.0657
10	102.9375	57.7181	577.1813	6060.4035

Price = 100.0374
Macaulay Duration = 7.7022
Modified Duration = 7.4826
Convexity = 69.3695

shapes. Prices may be higher or lower, and the curves may be flatter or steeper, but the following two facts will always characterize securities with fixed cash flows: The price-yield curve will be downward sloping and positively convex. Equivalently, the duration will always be positive and will always decrease as rates increase. Note that while the duration-yield curve looks like a line, it is, in fact, a curve.

The shapes in Figures 12.1 and 12.2 were derived under the flat term-structure and parallel shifts assumption. It turns out, however, that these shapes emerge for securities with fixed cash flows using any reasonable model of the term structure. Therefore, the reader should commit these graphs to memory as a benchmark against which to study the price behavior of more complex securities like those analyzed in Part Four.

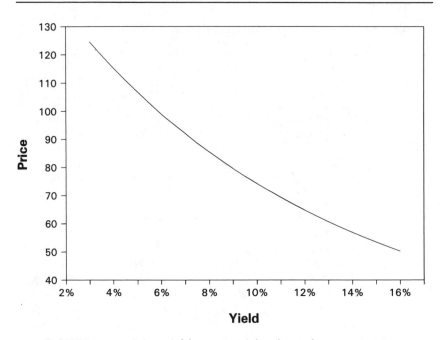

Yield

FIGURE 12.1   Price-yield curve: 5 7/8s due February 15, 2004.

DURATION: ANALYSIS AND INTUITION

The advantage of the simplifying assumptions made in this Chapter is that they allow for simple expressions of duration which, in turn, can be used to develop better intuition about price sensitivity in general. Table 12.2 presents three particularly useful special cases, namely zeros, perpetuities,[50] and par bonds. For the interested reader, these results are proved in Appendix 12A.

The first special case is that the Macaulay duration of a T-year zero-coupon bond equals T, its years to maturity. The Macaulay duration of a six-month zero is simply .5 while that of a 10-year zero is simply 10. Longer maturity zeros have larger durations and, hence, greater price sensitivities. This makes intuitive sense. An interest rate change will affect the price of a six-month zero through one period of discounting. On the other hand, the same interest rate change will be compounded 20 times in its effect on the price of a 10-year zero.

The fact that the Macaulay duration of zeros equals years to maturity allows for a convenient interpretation of the Macaulay duration of any other bond. In the previous section, for example, it was calculated that the Macaulay duration of the

[50]Perpetuities make coupon payments forever. They have no maturity nor do they ever repay principal.

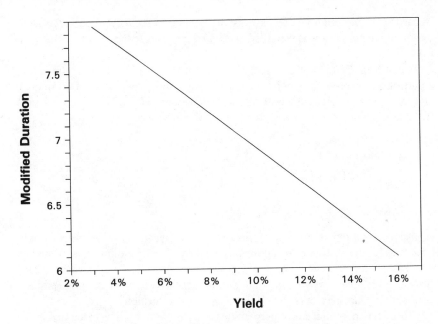

FIGURE 12.2   Duration-yield curve: 5 7/8s due February 15, 2004.

5 7/8s due February 15, 2004 is 7.7022. But D_{Mac} of a zero-coupon bond maturing in 7.7022 years is also 7.7022. Therefore, one can say that the 5 7/8s have a first order price sensitivity equivalent to that of a zero-coupon bond with a maturity of 7.7022 years. Put another way, the price sensitivity of zeros can be taken as a benchmark against which to judge the sensitivity of other bonds.

This special case of zeros also allows for additional insight into the expression for Macaulay duration, repeated here for easy reference:

$$D_{Mac} = \sum_{t=1}^{2T} \left(\frac{t}{2}\right) \frac{c\left(\frac{t}{2}\right)\left(1+\frac{r}{2}\right)^{-t}}{P}$$

Table 12.2   Durations for Special Cases

Security	Macaulay Duration	Modified Duration
Zero Coupon Bonds	T	$T/(1+r/2)$
Perpetuities	$(1+r/2)/r$	$1/r$
Par Bonds	$[(1+r/2)/r] \times [1-(1+r/2)^{-2T}]$	$[1-(1+r/2)^{-2T}]/r$

In particular, one can now explain why the fraction of security value contributed by a particular cash flow is weighted exactly by the years to the receipt of that cash flow.

Recall from Part One that a security with fixed cash flows may be viewed as a portfolio of zero-coupon bonds. So, a security making payments of c(.5), c(1), and so on, is equivalent to a portfolio with c(.5) face value of .5-year zeros, c(1) face value of 1-year zeros, and so on. Therefore, the term

$$\frac{c\left(\dfrac{t}{2}\right)\left(1+\dfrac{r}{2}\right)^{-t}}{P}$$

represents the fraction of the portfolio's value in t/2-year zeros. But, as learned in Chapter 11, the duration of this portfolio must equal the duration of each component zero, that is, t/2, weighted by these very fractions. In short, the years to cash flow receipts appear as weights in duration because each cash flow resembles a zero with a Macaulay duration equal to its years to receipt.

The next two special cases, perpetuities and par bonds, will be discussed in the context of Figure 12.3. This figure graphs Macaulay duration as a function of bond maturity for several special cases.

Since the Macaulay duration of a zero-coupon bond equals its years-to-maturity, the duration of zeros in Figure 12.3 is given by the 45-degree line. In words, increasing the maturity of zeros adds to duration in a 1-to-1 fashion.

The Macaulay duration of a par bond is also graphed in Figure 12.3 when its yield is 9 percent. Using the formula in Table 12.2, the duration when T = 0 is 0 and the duration of a perpetuity, corresponding to the case T = ∞ is (1+r/2)/r. Furthermore, it can be shown that a par bond's duration always increases as maturity increases. These three facts are enough to describe the par bond duration curve in the figure. In this case, therefore, one can trust one's intuition that the longer the bond the greater its price sensitivity.

Figure 12.3 also graphs duration curves for bonds with coupon rates of 2 percent and 16 percent when they too yield 9 percent. The former curve is labelled "Deep Discount Bonds" while the latter is labelled "Premium Bonds." A number of insights emerge from these two curves.

The premium bond curve is below the par bond curve, which is below the discount bond curve, which, in turn, is below the zero-coupon curve. This observation illustrates the fact that duration decreases as coupon levels increase. The intuition behind this fact is that higher coupon bonds have more of their value paid earlier. Therefore, they are, in effect, shorter bonds and have lower durations. Alternatively, the portfolio of zeros replicating relatively high coupon bonds

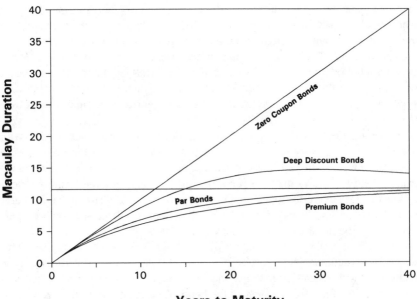

Years to Maturity

FIGURE 12.3 Duration and maturity.

has a relatively low duration because it consists of relatively many shorter-term zeros.

The unlabelled, horizontal line in the figure indicates the Macaulay duration of a perpetuity when the yield is 9 percent. Using Table 12.2, this duration equals $(1+.09/2)/.09 = 11.61$. Even though a perpetuity makes coupon payments forever, its duration is not that large. Intuitively, payments to be received in very many years are worth very little today. Therefore, even though these payments by themselves have large durations, they have little effect on the duration of the perpetuity.

While perpetuities are not traded in the United States, they serve as a useful limiting case for other coupon bonds. As the maturity of any coupon bond increases, it behaves more and more like a perpetuity. Intuitively, its principal payment becomes less and less valuable today. As a result, its coupon payments determine most of its price behavior, as in the case of a perpetuity. This effect appears in Figure 12.3. The duration curves for deep discount bonds, par bonds, and premium bonds all approach the perpetuity duration level of 11.61 as their maturities increase.

This last observation reveals a little-known fact about duration. The duration of discount bonds can fall as maturity increases. The deep discount curve in the figure rises above the duration of a perpetuity but will eventually fall back to that level. The phenomenon of decreasing duration as maturity increases only happens when bonds are selling at a deep discount and when they have long maturities. In the figure, the maximum duration is at about 30 years, declining only for maturities greater than that. Therefore, this has not been observed much in practice. However, with the relatively recent issuance of 50- and 100-year bonds, rising interest rates may make this currently obscure case more relevant. Portfolio managers may find themselves holding bonds that become more sensitive to rate moves as they mature!

There are two ways to explain why durations may sometimes decline with maturity. First, for very low coupons, deep discount bonds will initially behave like zero coupons. In fact, the coupon can be set low enough so that the deep discount curve follows the zero curve for a large maturity range. And if it does follow the zero curve for long enough, then its duration will rise above the duration of a perpetuity. Eventually, however, all coupon bonds must resemble a perpetuity and the duration must fall back to that duration level.

The second explanation is that for discount bonds the principal payment represents a particularly large portion of the bond's total value. When maturity is relatively short, extending maturity increases the duration of the principal payment and, therefore, the duration of the bond. When maturity is relatively long, however, extending maturity may reduce the value of the principal sufficiently that, even though its duration increases, the duration of the bond as a whole decreases. This does not happen for higher coupon bonds because the principal is not as dominant in the pricing of long maturities.

While not shown in Figure 12.3, increasing yield lowers duration. The intuition behind this fact is that increasing yield lowers the present value of all payments, but lowers the present value of the longer payments most. But if the values of these longer payments fall most, and therefore constitute less of a bond's value, the duration of the bond will fall. Conversely, decreasing the yield of a bond will increase its duration.

CONVEXITY: ANALYSIS AND INTUITION

The definition of convexity in the special case of this Chapter was previously given as

$$C = \frac{\sum_{t=1}^{2T} \left(\frac{t}{2}\right)\left(\frac{t}{2}+.5\right)c\left(\frac{t}{2}\right)\left(1+\frac{r}{2}\right)^{-t}}{P\left(1+\frac{r}{2}\right)^{2}}$$

For the special case of zero-coupon bonds, the only term that is not zero is that of t = 2T, giving that

$$C = \frac{T(T+.5)\left(1+\frac{r}{2}\right)^{-2T}}{P\left(1+\frac{r}{2}\right)^{2}}$$

But since, for a T-year zero, P = $(1 + r/2)^{-2T}$, this reduces further to

$$C = \frac{T(T+.5)}{\left(1+\frac{r}{2}\right)^{2}}$$

From this expression it is clear that longer maturity zeros (those with larger T) have greater convexity. In fact, convexity increases with the square of maturity. In any case, the price-yield curves of longer maturity zeros will be more curved than those of shorter maturity bonds. Since coupon bonds are portfolios of zeros, longer maturity coupon bonds usually have greater convexities than shorter maturity coupon bonds. This is illustrated in Figure 12.4, which graphs the price of the 5 7/8s due February 15, 2004, along with the price of the 6 1/4s due August 15, 2023. The 10-year bond's curve is much straighter than that of the 29.5-year bond.

(As in the case of duration, however, it is not always true that longer bonds have greater convexities. It may be that increasing maturity decreases the value of the principal payment by enough to lower the convexity of the bond.)

The intuition behind how duration is affected by coupon level and yield also applies to convexity. Lower coupons imply higher convexities. Lower coupons mean that more of the bond's value is in its later payments. But, since these later payments have higher convexities, the lower coupon bond has a higher convexity. Lower yields also increase convexity. As argued in the case of duration, lower yields increase all present values, but increase the present value of the later payments most. But, since these later payments have higher convexities, the convexity of the bond increases too.

The simple expression for the convexity of a zero allows for an analysis of *barbelling*. Barbelling refers to the practice of buying a portfolio consisting of long-maturity and short-maturity bonds constructed to achieve the same duration as that of an intermediate-maturity bond. An asset-liability manager, for example,

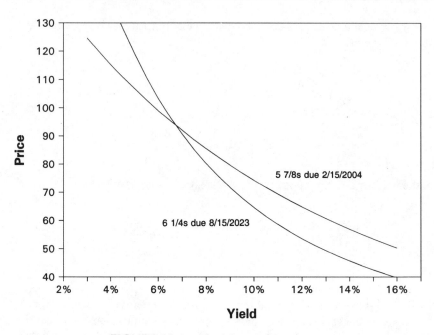

FIGURE 12.4 Maturity and convexity.

might need to purchase a portfolio of assets with a duration of 9. He could do so by purchasing several intermediate issues with durations all approximately equal to 9. Alternatively, he could purchase 2- and 30-year securities, which, as a portfolio, has a duration of 9. The former choice is often called a *bullet portfolio,* while the latter is called a barbell portfolio.

While bullet and barbell portfolios may be constructed to have the same duration, barbell portfolios will have greater convexities. To understand why this is true, consider an example with only zero-coupon bonds. At a yield of 6 percent, the convexity of a 10-year zero-coupon bond is 9 x 9.5/(1.03)^2 = 80.59. A barbell portfolio with 75 percent of its value in 2-year zeros and 25 percent of its value in 30-year zeros will have a duration of .75 x 2 + .25 x 30 = 9. Its convexity, however, will be

$$\frac{.75(2 \times 2.5) + .25(30 \times 30.5)}{1.03^2} = 219.15$$

which is substantially greater than the convexity of the 9-year zero. Basically, because convexity increases with the square of maturity, the increased convexity from the 30-year zeros more than makes up for the decreased convexity due to the

2-year zero. Of course, just because the barbell portfolio has a higher convexity than the bullet portfolio does not mean that it is superior to the bullet portfolio. As discussed in Chapter 11, the barbell portfolio will experience a lower return if rates do not change at all.

APPENDIX 12A

Special Cases of Duration

ZERO-COUPON BONDS

The general expression for Macaulay duration is

$$D_{Mac} = \frac{1}{P} \sum_{t=1}^{2T} \left(\frac{t}{2}\right) c \left(\frac{t}{2}\right) \left(1+\frac{r}{2}\right)^{-t}$$

For a T-year zero-coupon bond this expression simplifies. First, without loss of generality, c(T)=100 and all other cash flows are zero. In words, the only cash flow of a zero-coupon bond is its principal payment at maturity. Using this fact, the duration becomes

$$D_{Mac} = \frac{100\,T\left(1+\dfrac{r}{2}\right)^{-2T}}{P}$$

Second, the price of a T-year zero-coupon bond, when the one discount rate is r, equals $100/(1 + r/2)^{2T}$. Substituting this price in for P in the previous expressions shows that

$$D_{Mac} = T$$

To obtain modified duration, simply divide by $(1 + r/2)$ to get that

$$D_{mod} = \frac{T}{1+\dfrac{r}{2}}$$

PERPETUITIES

The price of a perpetuity paying a semiannual coupon of c when the discount rate is r is given by

$$P = \frac{c}{2} \sum_{t=1}^{\infty} \left(1 + \frac{r}{2}\right)^{-t} = \frac{c}{r}$$

where the equality follows by applying the formula in footnote 11 on page 32. Taking the derivative with respect to r shows that

$$\frac{dP}{dy} = -\frac{c}{r^2}$$

Multiplying by −1/P to obtain modified duration,

$$D_{mod} = \frac{-1}{P} \frac{dP}{dy} = \left(-\frac{r}{c}\right)\left(-\frac{c}{r^2}\right) = \frac{1}{r}$$

Finally, multiplying this expression by (1+r/2) gives the result that

$$D_{Mac} = \frac{1 + \frac{r}{2}}{r}$$

PAR BONDS

As recorded in Chapter 3, the price of a bond with a face value of $1, an annual coupon rate of c, and a maturity of T years is

$$P = \frac{c}{r}\left[1 - \left(1 + \frac{r}{2}\right)^{-2T}\right] + \left(1 + \frac{r}{2}\right)^{-2T}$$

Differentiating with respect to r gives that

$$\frac{dP}{dr} = T\left(1+\frac{r}{2}\right)^{-2T-1}\left(\frac{c}{r}-1\right) - \frac{c}{r^2}\left[1-\left(1+\frac{r}{2}\right)^{-2T}\right]$$

For par bonds, c = r. Substituting this coupon rate for r gives

$$\frac{dP}{dr}\bigg|_{c=r} = -\frac{1}{r}\left[1-\left(1+\frac{r}{2}\right)^{-2T}\right]$$

Furthermore, for par bonds, P=1. Therefore,

$$D_{mod} = -\frac{1}{P}\frac{dP}{dr} = \frac{1}{r}\left[1-\left(1+\frac{r}{2}\right)^{-2T}\right]$$

Finally, multiplying by (1+r/2) shows that

$$D_{Mac} = \frac{1+\frac{r}{2}}{r}\left[1-\left(1+\frac{r}{2}\right)^{-2T}\right]$$

Chapter 13
Key Rate Durations

MULTI-FACTOR MODELS AND DURATION

A major weakness of the analysis in Chapters 10 through 12 is that movements in the entire term structure can be described by one factor. Whether in a simple model of parallel shifts or in a more sophisticated term-structure model, the movement in the 6-month rate is assumed to predict perfectly the movement in the 10-year rate and in the 30-year rate.

The one-factor nature of the analysis presents a danger for hedging or asset-liability management. Consider an extension of the barbell example from Chapter 12. Assume that the term structure is flat at 6 percent and, with the $10,000 proceeds from assuming a 9-year zero liability, an asset-liability manager buys $7,500 of 2-year zeros and $2,500 of 30-year zeros. If rates move as the model assumes, the manager is fine. For example, say that all rates fall to 5.9 percent. The modified durations of the 2-, 10-, and 30-year zeros are 1.94, 8.74, and 29.13, respectively. Therefore, the value of the liabilities will rise by 8.74 x .001 = .874 percent to about $10,087. At the same time, the value of the 2-year zeros will rise by 1.94 x .001 = .194 percent to $7,514.55, and the value of the 30-year zeros will rise by 29.13 x .001 = 2.913 percent to $2,572.83, for a new asset total of about $10,087. Thus, as planned, the manager has immunized his portfolio against interest rate changes.

But what if the 30-year rate increases and the rest of the curve stays the same? Or, what if the 10-year rate decreases and the rest of the curve stays the same? In these cases the value of assets will fall below the value of the liabilities. In short, immunizing with a model that assumes parallel shifts or some other strong relationship between yields of different maturities will fail to protect against changes in the shape of the yield curve, whether against flattening, steepening, or other twists.

The general solution to this shortcoming is to construct a model with more than one factor. Say, for example, a short-term rate and a long-term rate were taken as factors. One would then compute a sensitivity, or a duration, with respect to each of the two factors. Asset-liability management (or hedging) would then be done with respect to both durations. In other words, asset durations with respect to the short-term rate and with respect to the long-term rate would be set equal to the corresponding liability durations. This procedure would protect a portfolio against movements in either end of the curve, whether or not these movements occur simultaneously. Of course, the portfolio might be subject to gains or losses from moves in the middle of the curve without corresponding moves on the ends.

Before describing sensitivity measures in a multi-factor model, consider the following review of the necessary calculations in a one-factor model.

Step 1: Compute the price of the security in question using the current term structure.

Step 2: Change the short-term rate by some small amount, say 10 basis points.

Step 3: Using the term-structure model, compute the new term structure that results from that short-term rate change.[51]

Step 4: Compute the security's new price under the perturbed term structure.

Step 5: Use the two prices and the change in the short-term rate, or in any other rate, to estimate duration.

In a multi-factor model, steps two through five have to be performed for each factor. If the factors are a short-term and a long-term rate, for example, the short-term rate is perturbed, the term structure adjusted as a consequence of that move, a new price computed, and a duration with respect to the short-term rate computed. Then the process is repeated for the long-term rate. The final result is two

---

[51]Variations of this methodology are used but, in the author's opinion, are less correct. One variation is to change the initial term structure in some way, recompute the binomial tree rates so that it matches the new term structure, and then obtain a new security price. The problem with this approach is that the perturbed term structure, which represents a scenario of change in rates, is completely independent of the term-structure model. So, for example, one might assume a parallel shift in the term structure, which is absolutely ruled out by the arbitrage arguments used to create the model. In addition, a good term-structure model captures the feature that rates of different terms have different volatilities, e.g., the short-term rate tends to move by more than the long-term rate. But specifying a term-structure perturbation outside the model does not utilize this volatility information in the calculation of durations.

Another variation is to move every rate in the tree up or down by a certain number of basis points and, with this new tree, compute the new security price. This method, while computationally quick and simple, is difficult to describe and understand in terms of term-structure movements.

The only problem with the approach described in the text is that it does rely heavily on the model. If the model's specification of how one rate moves relative to another is not very good, then it might be better to specify term-structure moves independently, that is, outside the model.

duration numbers, each reflecting the security's price sensitivity to its respective factor.

There are several different approaches to building multi-factor models for use in deriving measures of price sensitivity.[52] For illustrative purposes, the next section focuses on one such technique, namely, Ho's Key Rate Durations.

KEY RATE DURATIONS[53]

The key rate duration approach is not a true term-structure model in that it does not completely specify how rates evolve over time. Put another way, it is not a pricing model. The approach is meant as a method of computing durations with respect to several key rates given any particular pricing model.

The first step is to select several key rates or factors. In his article, Ho suggests taking one factor for each on-the-run Treasury security, but, for expository purposes, this introductory description will focus on three key rates: the 6-month rate, the 10-year rate, and the 30-year rate.

The next step is to describe how other rates change when the key rates change. Term-structure models can get quite complex in this regard, attempting to capture the observed correlations between rates and their respective volatilities. The key rate model's approach is more modest in this regard, assuming a very simple relationship between key rates and other rates. The rule is that a key rate's effect on other rates declines linearly, reaching zero at the adjacent key rates.

As an example, say that the 10-year rate increases by 10 basis points. Since there are 20 years between the 10-year rate and the right neighboring key rate, the 30-year rate, the effect of the change in the 10-year rate falls off at a rate of $10/20 = .5$ basis points per year. So, the 10-basis-point increase in the 10-year rate causes the 11-year rate to increase by $10 - .5 = 9.5$ basis points, the 12-year rate to increase by $10 - 2 \times .5 = 9$ basis points, and so on. Of course, rates in six-month intervals can be similarly computed by the rule that the effect falls off at a rate of .25 basis points per semiannual period. The 30-year rate, which is the neighboring key rate, and all rates beyond 30 years are unaffected by the change in the 10-year rate.

The 10-year rate move also affects rates of term less than 10 years. Since there are $10 - .5 = 9.5$ years between the 6-month key rate and the 10-year key rate, the 10-basis-point increase in the 10-year rate falls off by $10/9.5 = 1.0526$ basis points per year. So, the 10-basis point increase in the 10-year rate increases the 9-year rate by $10 - 1.0526 = 8.9474$ basis points, the 8.5-year rate by $10 - 1.5 \times 1.0526 = 8.4211$ basis points, and so on.

---

[52]See Litterman and Scheinkman (1988), for example.
[53]A more detailed description of this technique can be found in Ho (1992).

The effects of changes in the 6-month rate and in the 30-year rate are computed similarly. Since these are the leftmost and rightmost key rates, however, only the effects to the right of the 6-month rate and to the left of the 30-year rate need be considered. Figure 13.1 summarizes the effect of a 10-basis-point move in each of the three key rates on surrounding rates. The vertical, 10-basis-point lines represent moves in the key rates. The other dashed lines represent the increase in basis points on surrounding rates. These are added to the original value of those rates to obtain their values after the interest rate shift.

Table 13.1 illustrates the calculation of key rate durations in a particularly simple context, $100 face value of a 6.5 percent, 30-year coupon bond and the same key rates just discussed: 6 months, 10 years, and 30 years. The first column gives the term of all the bond's cash flows. The second column gives the initial spot rate curve, generated in Chapter 4. The third column gives the present value of the bond's cash flows under this initial term structure. The price of the bond, of course,

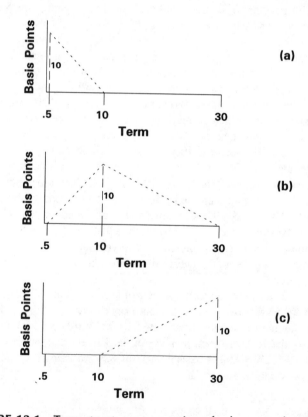

FIGURE 13.1   Term structure assumptions for key rate durations.

Table 13.1 Key Rate Duration Calculations for a Coupon Bond

Coupon = 0.065
Maturity = 30
Price: 100.7180   100.6326   100.2480   99.9946
Key Rate Durations: 0.8480   4.6661   7.1822

Term	Spot Rate Curve	Present Values	6-Mo. Key Rate Shift	Present Values	10-Yr. Key Rate Shift	Present Values	30-Yr. Key Rate Shift	Present Values
0.5	3.949703%	3.1871	4.049703%	3.1855	3.949703%	3.1871	3.949703%	3.1871
1	4.119650%	3.1201	4.214387%	3.1172	4.124913%	3.1200	4.119650%	3.1201
1.5	4.285251%	3.0497	4.374725%	3.0457	4.295777%	3.0493	4.285251%	3.0497
2	4.446382%	2.9764	4.530593%	2.9715	4.462171%	2.9754	4.446382%	2.9764
2.5	4.602845%	2.9005	4.681792%	2.8949	4.623898%	2.8990	4.602845%	2.9005
3	4.754365%	2.8227	4.828049%	2.8166	4.780681%	2.8205	4.754365%	2.8227
3.5	4.900582%	2.7434	4.969003%	2.7370	4.932161%	2.7405	4.900582%	2.7434
4	5.041047%	2.6632	5.104205%	2.6566	5.077889%	2.6593	5.041047%	2.6632
4.5	5.175212%	2.5824	5.233107%	2.5759	5.217317%	2.5777	5.175212%	2.5824
5	5.302425%	2.5017	5.355057%	2.4953	5.349793%	2.4960	5.302425%	2.5017
5.5	5.421918%	2.4216	5.469286%	2.4154	5.474550%	2.4148	5.421918%	2.4216
6	5.532800%	2.3424	5.574905%	2.3367	5.590695%	2.3345	5.532800%	2.3424
6.5	5.634052%	2.2648	5.670894%	2.2596	5.697210%	2.2558	5.634052%	2.2648
7	5.725246%	2.1892	5.756825%	2.1845	5.793667%	2.1790	5.725246%	2.1892
7.5	5.807978%	2.1154	5.834294%	2.1114	5.881662%	2.1041	5.807978%	2.1154
8	5.883825%	2.0437	5.904878%	2.0403	5.962772%	2.0312	5.883825%	2.0437
8.5	5.953988%	1.9738	5.969777%	1.9712	6.038199%	1.9601	5.953988%	1.9738
9	6.019394%	1.9058	6.029920%	1.9040	6.108868%	1.8910	6.019394%	1.9058
9.5	6.080771%	1.8397	6.086034%	1.8388	6.175508%	1.8237	6.080771%	1.8397
10	6.138694%	1.7754	6.138694%	1.7754	6.238694%	1.7582	6.138694%	1.7754

Table 13.1 (continued)

10.5	6.193625%	1.7129	6.193625%	1.7129	6.291125%	1.6960	6.196125%	1.7125
11	6.245932%	1.6522	6.245932%	1.6522	6.340932%	1.6356	6.250932%	1.6513
11.5	6.295914%	1.5933	6.295914%	1.5933	6.388414%	1.5769	6.303414%	1.5919
12	6.343814%	1.5361	6.343814%	1.5361	6.433814%	1.5201	6.353814%	1.5343
12.5	6.389829%	1.4806	6.389829%	1.4806	6.477329%	1.4650	6.402329%	1.4783
13	6.434115%	1.4267	6.434115%	1.4267	6.519115%	1.4116	6.449115%	1.4240
13.5	6.476800%	1.3746	6.476800%	1.3746	6.559300%	1.3598	6.494300%	1.3714
14	6.517956%	1.3240	6.517956%	1.3240	6.597956%	1.3098	6.537956%	1.3205
14.5	6.557599%	1.2751	6.557599%	1.2751	6.635099%	1.2613	6.580099%	1.2711
15	6.595721%	1.2278	6.595721%	1.2278	6.670721%	1.2145	6.620721%	1.2234
15.5	6.632292%	1.1821	6.632292%	1.1821	6.704792%	1.1694	6.659792%	1.1773
16	6.667270%	1.1380	6.667270%	1.1380	6.737270%	1.1258	6.697270%	1.1327
16.5	6.700590%	1.0955	6.700590%	1.0955	6.768090%	1.0837	6.733090%	1.0898
17	6.732175%	1.0545	6.732175%	1.0545	6.797175%	1.0432	6.767175%	1.0484
17.5	6.761929%	1.0150	6.761929%	1.0150	6.824429%	1.0043	6.799429%	1.0086
18	6.789743%	0.9771	6.789743%	0.9771	6.849743%	0.9669	6.829743%	0.9703
18.5	6.815493%	0.9406	6.815493%	0.9406	6.872993%	0.9310	6.857993%	0.9335
19	6.839039%	0.9057	6.839039%	0.9057	6.894039%	0.8966	6.884039%	0.8983
19.5	6.860227%	0.8723	6.860227%	0.8723	6.912727%	0.8637	6.907727%	0.8645
20	6.878891%	0.8403	6.878891%	0.8403	6.928891%	0.8322	6.928891%	0.8322
20.5	6.894851%	0.8098	6.894851%	0.8098	6.942351%	0.8022	6.947351%	0.8014
21	6.907916%	0.7807	6.907916%	0.7807	6.952916%	0.7736	6.962916%	0.7721
21.5	6.917937%	0.7531	6.917937%	0.7531	6.960437%	0.7465	6.975437%	0.7442
22	6.924810%	0.7269	6.924810%	0.7269	6.964810%	0.7207	6.984810%	0.7176
22.5	6.928427%	0.7020	6.928427%	0.7020	6.965927%	0.6963	6.990927%	0.6925
23	6.928684%	0.6784	6.928684%	0.6784	6.963684%	0.6732	6.993684%	0.6687
23.5	6.925474%	0.6562	6.925474%	0.6562	6.957974%	0.6514	6.992974%	0.6462
24	6.918696%	0.6352	6.918696%	0.6352	6.948696%	0.6308	6.988696%	0.6250

24.5	6.908254%	0.6155	6.908254%	0.6155	6.935754%	0.6115	6.980754%	0.6050
25	6.894060%	0.5970	6.894060%	0.5970	6.919060%	0.5934	6.969060%	0.5863
25.5	6.876033%	0.5797	6.876033%	0.5797	6.898533%	0.5765	6.953533%	0.5687
26	6.854109%	0.5635	6.854109%	0.5635	6.874109%	0.5607	6.934109%	0.5523
26.5	6.828236%	0.5485	6.828236%	0.5485	6.845736%	0.5460	6.910736%	0.5370
27	6.798378%	0.5345	6.798378%	0.5345	6.813378%	0.5324	6.883378%	0.5228
27.5	6.764519%	0.5216	6.764519%	0.5216	6.777019%	0.5199	6.852019%	0.5096
28	6.726663%	0.5098	6.726663%	0.5098	6.736663%	0.5084	6.816663%	0.4975
28.5	6.684838%	0.4989	6.684838%	0.4989	6.692338%	0.4979	6.777338%	0.4863
29	6.639091%	0.4890	6.639091%	0.4890	6.644091%	0.4883	6.734091%	0.4761
29.5	6.589498%	0.4800	6.589498%	0.4800	6.591998%	0.4797	6.686998%	0.4668
30	6.536155%	14.9942	6.536155%	14.9942	6.536155%	14.9942	6.636155%	14.5650

is given by the sum of the entries in the third column which comes to approximately $100.7180.

The second column records the term structure of spot rates after a 10-basis-point shift in the six-month key rate. Note that the six-month rate, as the key rate, increases by exactly 10 basis points. Rates between 6 months and 10 years change by less than 10 basis points, with the effect falling linearly as the distance from 6 months increases. The 1-year rate, for example, increases by about 9.5 basis points while the 9-year rate increases by a little over 1 basis point. Rates of term greater than 10 years, since they are past the 10-year key rate, do not change at all.

The third column gives the present value of the bond's cash flows under the new, shifted term structure and the sum gives the price of $100.6326. In other words, if the six-month key rate increases by 10 basis points, but no other key rate changes, the price of the bond will fall from $100.7180 to $100.6326. The estimate for the six-month key rate duration, therefore, is

$$-\frac{\dfrac{100.6326 - 100.7180}{100.7180}}{.001} = .848$$

This process is repeated for the other key rates. The 10-year rate is assumed to shift up by 10 basis points, affecting all rates from 6-months to 30-years. Then, the new bond price of 100.2480 implies a 10-year key rate duration of

$$-\frac{\dfrac{100.2480 - 100.7180}{100.7180}}{.001} = 4.666$$

(Note that the new price is always compared with the price from the original term structure. This ensures that the estimated duration measures the change in price for a shift in only one key rate.) Finally, the same procedure with respect to a change in the 30-year key rate, which changes rates of term longer than 10 years, gives a key rate duration of 7.1822.

As one would expect, the coupon bond, whose value is largely determined by the value of its principal payment, has a 30-year key rate duration that is large relative to the other key rate durations. Put another way, this coupon bond's price will be only slightly affected by changes in short-term rates, moderately affected by changes in intermediate rates, and substantially affected by changes in long-term rates.

Conceptually, the sum of the key rate durations is comparable to modified duration because the combined effect of a 10-basis-point shift in all key rates is, in fact, a parallel shift. To illustrate this last point, consider changes in the 5-year rate recorded in Table 13.1. A 10-basis-point shift in the 6-month key rate, the 10-year key rate, and the 30-year key rate raises the 5-year rate by about 5.26, 4.74, and 0 basis points, respectively. Thus, the simultaneous 10-basis-point shift in all key rates raises the 5-year rate by 10 basis points as well: 5.26 + 4.74 + 0 = 10. The reader can easily verify that this argument holds not only for the 5-year rate but also for any rate.

The sum of key rate durations is not exactly equal to modified duration because key rate durations use the initial term structure as a starting point whereas modified duration assumes a flat term structure. But the intuition behind the comparability of the sum of key rates and modified duration is quite useful. Key rate durations can be thought of as a decomposition of modified duration into sensitivities to different parts of the yield curve. In the coupon bond example, a modified duration of about 12.70 is shown to be composed of .848 exposure to short-term rate risk, 4.666 to intermediate-term rate risk, and 7.182 to long-term rate risk. The implication for hedging or immunization is that one should not simply compare the modified duration of 12.70 to the other leg of a transaction. Rather, one should compare risks with respect to each segment of the yield curve.

Bar graphs of key rate durations, as a function of term, can be useful for un-

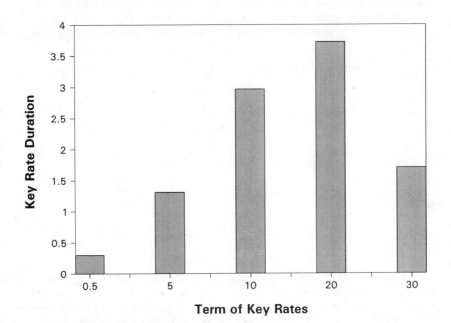

FIGURE 13.2   Key rate duration of a non-prepayable mortgage.

derstanding a security's sensitivity to changes in the shape of the term structure. To illustrate this point, Figure 13.2 analyzes a 30-year, non-prepayable mortgage using five key rates at 6 months, 5 years, 10 years, 20 years, and 30 years. Note that the price sensitivity of the mortgage initially increases with the term of the key rate but then decreases.

The initial increase of key rate durations is due to the fact that longer-term cash flows have greater durations than shorter-term cash flows. Changes in the 5-year rate mostly affect the value of payments with terms and durations of about 5 years, while changes in the 10-year rate mostly affect payments with terms and durations of about 10 years. Therefore, the price sensitivity due to movements in the 10-year rate will tend to exceed that due to those in the 5-year rate. On the other hand, a typical mortgage's cash flows are level, that is, the same from one period to the next. Therefore, the present value of these payments declines with term. So, while longer payments do have greater durations, they also contribute less to the total value of the mortgage. This explains why the 30-year key rate duration of the mortgage is less than that of the 10- and 20-year key rates. Thirty-year payments, by themselves, do have greater durations than earlier payments, by themselves. But, the 30-year payments contribute so little to mortgage value relative to these earlier payments that the effect of the 30-year key rate on mortgage value is less than the effect of the 10- and 20-year rates.[54]

It is often related that mortgage-backed securities, although they are long-term securities, tend to follow intermediate rates more closely than they follow long-term rates. The explanation for this common wisdom is evident from the analysis of Figure 13.2 already given. It is in analyzing issues of this sort that bar graphs of key rate durations are particularly useful.

---

[54]Since the modified duration of a zero-coupon bond is about equal to its years to maturity, the duration effect is linear in term. Discounting, however, which raises one plus the interest rate to the term of the payment, makes the present value effect exponential in term. For shorter terms, therefore, the duration effect dominates and key rate durations increase with term. For longer terms, however, the present value effect dominates and key rate durations decrease with term.

Part Four
Selected Applications

Chapter 14
Forward and Futures Contracts

Spot contracts are agreements to buy and sell some asset today, meaning that the cash and the asset change hands today. By contrast, forward and futures contracts are agreements to trade an asset on some particular future date. The price at which the asset will be traded on that date is fixed today, but the exchange of cash for the asset takes place in the future. In practice, futures contracts are extremely useful for speculating on the direction of rates and for hedging against interest rate risk. This usefulness stems from the great liquidity of many interest rate futures contracts relative to that of individual assets and from the relatively small amount of capital needed to establish a futures position relative to a spot position of equivalent size.

THE PRICING OF FORWARD CONTRACTS

A *forward contract* is an agreement to buy or sell a security in the future at a price specified at the time of the agreement. The *forward price* refers to that agreed-upon future price and the *expiration date, delivery date,* or *maturity date* refers to the time of the future purchase or sale. Like bond price quotations, the forward price does not include accrued interest. The actual amount paid for the security, therefore, is the agreed upon forward price plus accrued interest as of the contract's maturity date. The *underlying security* is the security that will be bought or sold on the expiration date. Finally, the *buyer* of the contract, who is *long* the forward, agrees to buy the underlying security on the expiration date from the *seller* of the contract, who is *short* the forward. For example, on February 15, 1994, one might buy the following forward contract:

Delivery Date: 8/15/94
Underlying Security: $100 par value of the 4 3/8s due 8/15/96
Forward Price: $101.24

When a forward contract is first negotiated, the forward price is set such that the future buyer and the future seller are willing to enter into the agreement without any exchange of money up front. In other words, at the time of the agreement, the *value* of the forward contract is zero. Over time, however, the value of the forward contract will rise or fall in a manner to be described later. For now, however, simply note that the value of the forward contract is not the same concept as the forward price. The value of the forward contract denotes how much one would pay or receive for entering into the forward contract. The forward price is the price at which the forward purchase or sale will be conducted.

The discussion now turns to the determination of forward prices. At what price would the value of a forward contract to buy or sell the 4 3/8s due August 15, 1996, on August 15, 1994, be equal to zero? For the purposes of answering this question, use the discount function derived as of February 15, 1994, given originally in Table 1.2 and reproduced in Table 14.1 for convenience. Using this discount function, the price of the 4 3/8s is 99.47.

An arbitrage argument can be made to determine the forward price. Let f be the quoted forward price and let S' be the currently unknown spot price of the 4 3/8s bond on the expiration date six months from now. An investor who is long the contract will, at expiration, be required to purchase a bond worth S' for a price of f. Therefore, the value of his position in six months is S' − f.

Table 14.1 Discount Factors from Bond Prices Given in Table 1.2

t	d(t)
.5	.9824773
1	.9621478
1.5	.9398588
2.0	.9158669
2.5	.8920414

Now, instead of purchasing the forward contract, assume that the investor does the following:

borrows fd(.5)
buys $100 face amount of the 4 3/8s for $99.47

These transactions result in a cash outflow of

$99.47 − fd(.5)

today. In six months, the investor has to pay f dollars to settle his loan obligation but still has the bond. Therefore, the value of his position in six months is S' − f, exactly as if he had bought the forward contract. In other words, the transactions just given replicate the forward contract.

To prevent arbitrage, it must be the case that the value of the forward contract equals the value of its replicating portfolio. At the time of the agreement, the value of the forward contract is zero, by definition, and the value of the replicating portfolio is $99.47 − fd(.5). Therefore,

0 = $99.47 − fd(.5)

or

$$f = \frac{\$99.47}{d(.5)} = \$101.24$$

In words, the forward price equals the future value of the current price of the underlying asset, where the future value is computed to the expiration date of the contract.

The arbitrage argument becomes more complicated when the underlying asset makes payments between now and the expiration date. Consider, for example, a forward contract on the 4 3/8s for delivery in one year. Buying the forward contract still produces a payoff of S' − f on the expiration date. But buying the bond entitles the buyer to a coupon payment in six months. Thus, borrowing the present value of the forward price and buying the bond does not replicate the long position in the forward contract. The arbitrage argument, therefore, needs to be modified.

Say the investor executes these trades:

borrows fd(1) for 1 year
borrows 2.19d(.5) for 6 months
buys $100 face value of the 4 3/8s for $99.47

Note that 2.19d(.5) = .5 x (4 3/8)d(.5), the present value of the next coupon payment.

In six months, the investor collects the coupon of 2.19 and uses that money to pay off his six-month loan obligation. In one year he has a bond worth S' but must pay f to meet his one-year loan obligation. Thus, his position generates no cash flows until one year from now at which time it is worth S' – f. Therefore, this set of transactions does replicate the forward contract. The no-arbitrage condition then requires that the value of the replicating portfolio equal the value of the forward contract. Mathematically,

$$fd(1) + 2.19d(.5) - \$99.47 = 0$$

Solving for f,

$$f = \frac{\$99.47 - 2.19d(.5)}{d(1)} = 101.15$$

In words, the forward price equals the future value of the underlying security minus the present value of its cash flows before expiration.

By similar arguments, one can derive a more general formula for the forward price. Let T be the delivery date, in years. Let f be the quoted forward price and let AI(T) be the accrued interest on the underlying security as of the delivery date. Let S be the spot or current quoted price of the underlying security and let AI(0) be the accrued interest as of the contract initiation date. Finally, let D be the present value of all the underlying security's cash flows from today until the expiration date of the futures contract. Then, the quoted forward price, f, is given by the equation

$$f + AI(T) = \frac{S + AI(0) - D}{d(T)}$$

where d(T) is, as usual, the present value of $1 to be received in T years.

Intuitively, the forward pricing formula can be explained as follows. A forward contract obligates the buyer to purchase a security in T years. The present value of the security purchased at that time is S + AI(0) – D, the current value of the security minus any payments made before the forward purchase and, therefore, not received by the forward buyer. Hence, if one had to pay for forward delivery of the security today, a fair price would be S + AI(0) – D. But, in a forward contract, one does not pay until the delivery date. So, the fair forward price is the future value of S + AI(0) – D in T-years, or [S + AI(0) – D]/d(T).

As the delivery date approaches, the forward price approaches the spot price. In terms of the pricing equation, T = 0 implies that (1) D = 0 (there are no payments between now and an imminent expiration); (2) AI(T) = AI(0); and (3) d(T) = d(0) = 1. Therefore, f = S. The intuition behind this result is straightforward: The forward price of an agreement to buy or sell a security today should simply be the security's current price.

As an example of a case in which accrued interest must be included in the forward price calculation, consider a forward contract traded on February 14, 1994, that expires on August 15, 1994, written on the Treasury's 10 1/8s due November 15, 1994, and is currently quoted at 104 5/8. Using the discount values in Table 14.1 and the additional fact that d(.25) = .9924, the following values can be generated:

$$S = 104\frac{5}{8}$$

$$AI(0) = \left(\frac{3}{12}\right)\left(10\frac{1}{8}\right) = 2.53$$

(Represents accrued interest from 11/15/93 to 2/15/94.)

$$D = .5 \times 10\frac{1}{8} \times d(.25) = 5.02$$

$$AI(T) = \left(\frac{3}{12}\right)\left(10\frac{1}{8}\right) = 2.53$$

(Represents accrued interest from 5/15/94 to 8/15/94.)

Applying the forward pricing equation with these values,

$$f + 2.53 = \frac{104\frac{5}{8} + 2.53 - 5.02}{.9825}$$

or

f = 101.42

Until this point the discussion has centered on the forward price rather than on the value of the forward contract. Recall that the forward price is set such that the value of the forward contract at initiation is zero. Alternatively, the forward price is set such that both buyer and seller are willing to enter into the forward agreement without exchanging any cash today. It is important to note, however, that the value of a particular forward contract will rise or fall after the initial agreement.

On the delivery date, a long position in a forward contract pays $S' + AI(T) - f - AI(T) = S' - f$. Clearly, the value of the forward contract rises or falls together with the spot price of the underlying asset. If the spot price has risen since the initiation of the forward contract, it turned out well to have committed to purchase the asset for the relatively low price of f. Similarly, it did not turn out well to have committed to sell the asset for the relatively low price of f. In other words, the forward contract has become an asset to the purchaser and a liability to the seller. Mathematically, the value of a long position in the forward contract has become positive. If, at any time before delivery, the buyer and seller decide to cancel their agreement, the seller will have to pay the buyer this positive value.

If the spot price has fallen since the initiation of the forward contract, the conclusions of the previous paragraph can be reversed. The buyer regrets having committed to purchase the asset at a fixed price while the seller is glad to have committed to sell the asset at that relatively high price. Also, the value of a long position in the forward contract is negative and the buyer will have to pay the seller to cancel the agreement.

IDENTIFYING THE UNDERLYING SECURITY

In many cases the underlying security of a forward contract is readily identifiable and the forward pricing equation may be readily applied. In some cases, however, identifying the underlying security requires some extra thought. One example of this is the T-bill futures contract.[55] At this point in the text it is convenient to discuss the forward equivalent of this contract. The distinguishing features of futures contracts will be discussed in the next section.

A T-bill forward contract would be a commitment to buy or sell a T-bill of a particular maturity at some future date for some prespecified forward price. Consider, for example, a contract to buy $100 face value of a six-month T-bill in one year for f. What is the underlying security of this forward contract?

[55]The Eurodollar futures contract has replaced the T-bill futures contract as the most popular tool for short-term risk management. The text avoids Eurodollar futures since Eurodollar rates contain a default premium, an important subject not covered in this book.

The answer is not a six-month T-bill. Say that one tried to replicate this forward contract by borrowing the present value of the forward price and simultaneously buying a six-month T-bill. One year later, when the forward contract expires, it will be worth S' – f, where S' is the price of a six-month T-bill one year from now. But, one year from now, the supposed replicating portfolio will no longer contain a six-month T-bill! The six-month T-bill bought when the portfolio was constructed will have matured. Consequently, the described portfolio does not replicate the forward contract.

Consider, however, borrowing the present value of the forward price, fd(1), and buying a 1.5-year zero-coupon bond for S. In one year, when the contract expires, the 1.5-year zero will have become a six-month zero, the equivalent of a six-month T-bill, worth S'. The total value of the portfolio, therefore, would be S' – f, matching the expiration value of the forward contract. By arbitrage arguments, then, the initial value of the forward contract must equal the current value of the replicating portfolio. Mathematically,

$$0 = fd(1) - S$$

or

$$f = \frac{S}{d(1)}$$

This expression is a special case of the forward pricing formula given in the previous section with the following remarks. First, the underlying security is a 1.5-year zero, that is, a security that, at the expiration date, will have become the security to be bought or sold through the contract. Second, since zero-coupon bonds make no coupon payments, $D = 0$. To conclude, since the price of $100 face value of a 1.5-year zero is $100d(1.5)$, the forward price for a six-month T-bill for one-year delivery is $100d(1.5)/d(1)$ or $97.68.

MARKING-TO-MARKET AND THE PRICING OF FUTURES CONTRACTS

As described previouly, changes in the value of a forward contract are settled at the delivery date or, if desired, at the time of canceling the forward agreement. A futures contract differs from a forward contract in that changes in the value of a futures contract are settled daily in a process known as *marking-to-market*.

Table 14.2 Treasury Bond Futures Prices

Date	Futures Price	Daily Change in Buyer's Position	Cumulative Change in Buyer's Position
2/15/94	112:24		
2/16/94	112:19	-$156.25	-$156.25
2/17/94	111:19	-$1,000	-$1,156.25
2/18/94	110:23	-$875	-$2,031.25
2/22/94	111:5	+$437.50	-$1,593.75
2/23/94	110:14	-$718.75	-$2,312.50
2/24/94	109:18	-$875	-$3,187.50

Source of Futures Prices: Bloomberg

To explain this procedure, the second column of Table 14.2 lists prices for the September 1994 T-Bond futures contract from February 15, 1994, to February 24, 1994. Each contract is written on $100,000 face value of T-bonds. (The following section will more fully describe the structure of the T-bond futures contract.)

On February 15, 1994, the T-bond futures price is 112 24/32. As in the case of forwards, this is the price at which both buyers and sellers are willing to enter into futures contracts with no side payments. In other words, the value of a futures contract at the current futures price is zero. The next day, however, the futures price falls to 112 19/32. The futures buyer has lost money: On the 15th he committed to buy T-bonds in September for 112 24/32, but investors on the 16th can costlessly commit to buy the same bonds on the same future date for only 112 19/32. As a result of this loss in value, two transactions take place. First, the buyer pays the seller the fall in the contract's settlement value, that is, $100,000 x (112 24/32% – 112 19/32%) = $156.25. Second, the buyer and seller are automatically rolled over into new September futures contracts with the new futures price of 112 19/32. By definition, the value of being in a futures contract on the 16th with a futures price of 112 19/32 is zero. But, the seller is ahead and the buyer is behind by the mark-to-market payment of $156.25.

This discussion reveals a critical difference between forward and futures contracts. After their initiation, forward contracts generally have positive or negative values before final settlement at maturity. Futures contracts, however, after their daily marking-to-market, have zero value. This difference may very well explain the historical predominance of futures contracts over forward contracts. With a forward contract, the gains to one side can become quite substantial before the counterparty need make any payments. Therefore, there is a relatively large risk that the losing party will disappear or become insolvent and fail to make good on his obligations. With a futures contract, however, the winning party has at most one day of winnings at risk. If the counterparty fails to make his required payment, the winner sacrifices a relatively small sum and enters into a contract with someone else. In modern times, a futures exchange, with solid credit, is the official counterparty for all contracts. This arrangement minimizes such defaults and makes it unnecessary for buyers to examine the credit quality of sellers and *vice versa*.

Returning to the T-bond futures prices, on February 17, 1994, the futures price falls again, dropping to 111 19/32. As a result of this decline, the buyer must pay the seller $100,000(112 19/32% − 111 19/32%) = $1,000. Continuing in this fashion, one can describe the February 24, 1994, positions of buyers and sellers who opened their positions on February 15, 1994. At the end of trading on the 24th everyone is in a futures contract with a futures price of 109 18/32. The buyers are down their cumulative marking-to-market payments of $100,000(112 24/32% − 109 18/32%) = $3,187.50 per contract and sellers are up by exactly that amount. The third and fourth columns of Table 14.2 list the daily and cumulative change in the value of the buyer's position at each date.

Extending this discussion to the delivery date reveals another critical difference between futures and forward contracts. Assume that the futures price on the delivery date is 108. Buyers lose a total of $100,000(112 24/32 − 108%) = $4,750 per contract. Were this a forward contract, for which the whole loss is realized on the expiration date, the total loss would be the same $4,750. With a futures contract, however, the loss is spread out over the life of the contract; buyers experience some winning days and some losing days, but wind up with the same total loss.

This effect of marking-to-market makes futures contracts more difficult to price than forward contracts. The difficulty can be explained as follows. When a futures position wins over its lifetime, it pays small sums each day. Winnings may be reinvested while losses have to be financed, either by borrowing or by withdrawing funds from interest-bearing accounts. The final value of a position, therefore, depends on the evolution of interest rates over the life of the contract. Therefore, one needs a term-structure model to compute fair futures prices.

The next section will illustrate how to compute futures prices with a term-structure model. The discussion now turns to a more qualitative question. Let f_{for} be the forward price and f_{fut} the futures price of contracts written on the same bond and expiring on the same date. Will f_{for} be greater than, equal to, or less than f_{fut}?

If bond prices rise over the lives of these contracts, then futures contracts will be preferred. Since futures pay winnings as they occur, they will be preferred to forwards, which postpone the payment of all winnings until delivery. On the other hand, if bond prices fall over the lives of the contracts, forwards will be preferred: When one is losing money, one wants to make good on the losses with as great a delay as possible. Since, at the start, one does not know whether bond prices will rise or fall, one might conclude that neither futures nor forwards are *ex ante* preferred. But that conclusion is false.

When bond prices rise and futures contracts are preferred, interest rates are falling. Hence, while winners in futures enjoy the reinvestment of their winnings, they must reinvest at relatively low rates. On the other hand, when bond prices fall and futures contracts are not preferred, interest rates are rising. Hence, losers in futures must finance their losses at relatively high rates. Taken together, these observations lead to the conclusion that the advantage of reinvesting futures gains is not as great as the disadvantage of having to finance futures losses. Alternatively, investors will assume long positions in futures only if $f_{fut} < f_{for}$. In short, the effect of marking-to-market is to lower the futures price relative to the forward price.[56]

The previous discussion indicates that, despite the similarities between forward and futures contracts, it is not correct to use the forward pricing equation given earlier to find futures prices. Having said that, it should also be said that, for short-term contracts, the difference between futures and forward prices will be relatively small. This is so because the value of reinvesting winnings and the cost of financing losses are relatively unimportant when the contract expires relatively soon. The extreme case of this is quite obvious: The forward price of a one-day forward contract will equal the futures price.

TERM-STRUCTURE MODELS AND FUTURES PRICES

Say that someone has chosen a term-structure model of the type discussed in Part Two. The choice will result in a risk-neutral tree of short-term rates. From this tree one can construct a price tree for the asset underlying the futures contract. Then, using the fact that the futures price equals the spot price at expiration, one can construct the tree of futures prices, starting from the expiration date and moving backwards in time to the present.

Say that, having constructed the price tree for the underlying asset, two adjacent node values for the spot price at the expiration of the futures contract are S^u and S^d. Since these are also the futures prices at expiration, this branch of the futures tree will be

where f indicates the futures price on the day before expiration, to be determined.

---

[56] A rigorous proof of this point can be found in Cox, Ingersoll, and Ross (1981). Readers should not conclude that this is a general proposition about all futures and forwards: It applies particularly to contracts on bonds. For contracts on other assets the correlation between futures prices and interest rates is not as clear.

Say that the one-day discount factor, available from the interest rate tree, is d(1/365). The futures price is the price such that buyers and sellers are willing to enter into futures contracts without exchanging cash. What f satisfies this condition?

In the up-state, the payoff to buyers of the futures contract is $S^u - f$, namely the mark-to-market on the last day of the contract. Similarly, the payoff to buyers in the down-state is $S^d - f$. Assuming, for simplicity, that the risk-neutral probabilities are .5 for both the up- and down-states, the value of these payoffs is

$$d\left(\frac{1}{365}\right)\left[.5\left(S^u - f\right) + .5\left(S^d - f\right)\right]$$

But, the value of entering into a futures contract at any time must be zero. Hence,

$$d\left(\frac{1}{365}\right)\left[.5\left(S^u - f\right) + .5\left(S^d - f\right)\right] = 0$$

Solving for f, this equation becomes

$$f = .5\, S^u + .5 S^d$$

In words, the futures price equals the expected value of the spot price using the risk-neutral probabilities.

The argument just made will be true for any node in the futures price tree. If the next day's two possible values for the futures price are f^u and f^d and the appropriate one-day discount factor is d(1/365), then the futures price at the current node must satisfy the equation

$$d\left(\frac{1}{365}\right)\left[.5\left(f^u - f\right) + .5\left(f^d - f\right)\right] = 0$$

giving the similar condition

$$f = .5 f^u + .5 f^d$$

Since this reasoning applies over the entire tree, the following conclusion emerges. The futures price today equals the expected spot price at delivery where the expectation is computed using the risk-neutral interest rate process. This fact makes it quite simple to calculate fair futures prices given a term-structure model.

DELIVERY OPTIONS AND THE CHEAPEST TO DELIVER

The description of futures contracts in the last two sections does not yet match the complexity of traded futures contracts. The underlying security of traded contracts is seldom a single, particular bond. The reason for this is that market participants are always concerned about the possibility of a *squeeze*. If there were really a contract requiring the purchase or sale of the Treasury's 7 1/2s due November 15, 2016, then a syndicate of investors might find it worthwhile to purchase a large fraction of the supply of those bonds and simultaneously go long many futures contracts. At the expiration date, those who sold futures contracts would have to scramble to find the 7 1/2s in order to fulfill their commitment to sell them. At that point the syndicate would sell the 7 1/2s to these desperate shorts for a price far exceeding the present value of the bonds.

In order to avoid such squeezes, futures contracts usually allow for delivery of several different securities. The T-bill contract traded on the International Monetary Market of the Chicago Mercantile Exchange, for example, allows for the delivery of 89-, 90-, or 91-day T-bills. And, in a further attempt to prevent squeezes, expiration dates coincide with both the new issuance of 91-day bills and with the 13-week to maturity point of Treasury bills that were originally sold as 1-year bills.

The T-bond contract, traded on the Chicago Board of Trade, takes this logic a step further. The underlying security of the contract is fictitious, that is, an 8 percent 20-year Treasury bond. At expiration, the seller of the contract can deliver any Treasury bond with at least 15 years to maturity or first call date. Of course, not all deliverable bonds are worth the same amount. Therefore, the exchange publishes *conversion factors* that determine the value of the delivered bond relative to the fictitious underlying security. A conversion factor of 1.2, for example, means that the delivered bond is worth 1.2 times the worth of the hypothetical 8 percent 20-year bond. Therefore, a seller who delivers a bond with that conversion factor receives not the futures price plus accrued interest but 1.2 times the futures price plus accrued interest.

To continue this discussion, define the following variables *at the time of delivery*. Let the futures price be f. Let the price of bond i, eligible for delivery, be its quoted price S'_i plus its accrued interest AI_i. Also, let the conversion factor for bond i be CF_i. Someone short the futures contract could purchase the bond for

$$S'_i + AI_i$$

and deliver it through the futures contract for

$$CF_i \times f' + AI_i$$

Therefore, the total cost of delivery using bond i is

$$S'_i + AI_i - (CF_i \times f' + AI_i) = S'_i - CF_i \times f'$$

If conversion factors were set perfectly, one unit of any delivered bond i would be worth exactly CF_i of the underlying security. Mathematically $S_i = f' \times CF_i$—for all bonds eligible for delivery. But this implies that the cost of delivering any security, $S'_i - f' \times CF_i$, equals zero. In other words, if conversion factors perfectly capture the value differences across eligible bonds, sellers would have no preference to deliver any one bond rather than any other.

But it is difficult to set conversion factors exactly. The price of the Treasury's 11 1/4s due February 15, 2015, relative to the price of a fictitious 8 percent 20-year bond depends on one's estimation of the term structure. Worse yet, the price of the 11 3/4s due February 15, 2014, that are callable in 2009, depends on one's choice of term-structure models. Rather than face the extremely difficult task of specifying the calculation of discount factors and of term-structure models, markets have adopted simple rules for calculating conversion factors. As a result, conversion factors are not perfect. They do not accurately reflect the value of each deliverable bond relative to the fictitious underlying security.

Before developing this last point further, the calculation of conversion factors for the T-bond futures contract will be presented. For the September 1994 T-bond contract, the 11 3/4s due November 15, 2014, will be used as an example. The procedure is as follows:

Step 1: Determine the time from the delivery month to call or, if not callable, maturity. The 11 3/4s are first callable in November 2009. The time from September 1994 to November 2009 is 15 years and 2 months.

Step 2: Round the time-to-call or maturity down to the nearest quarter. In this case the rounded time is 15 years.

Step 3: Calculate the price of $1 face value of the bond assuming a yield-to-maturity of 8 percent, and a time to maturity equal to the result of step 2. Recalling the formula from Chapter 3

$$P = (c/y)(1 - (1 + y/2)^{-2T}) + (1 + y/2)^{-2T}$$

where c is the coupon rate, y is the yield, and T is the years to maturity, the "price" of the 11 3/4s is

$$(.1175/.08)(1 - (1.04)^{-30}) + (1.04)^{-30} = 1.3242$$

This is the conversion factor for the 11 3/4s.[57] The logic behind this choice of a conversion factor is as follows. When yields are flat at 8 percent, the price of $1 face value of the fictitious 8 percent bond is $1. And step 3 showed that, under the same yield assumption, the price of $1 face value of the 11 3/4s is $1.3242. Therefore, if one delivers the 11 3/4s instead of the underlying bond, namely the fictitious 8s, one is entitled to 1.3242 times the future price.

Before proceeding, it should be noted that conversion factors need not be calculated by each investor. The futures exchange publishes a list of conversion factors for each deliverable bond and each futures contract. Figure 14.1 reproduces such a list appearing on Bloomberg screens.[58] The column labelled USU4 is for the September 1994 contract. The other columns, USZ4, USH5, USM5, USU5, and USZ5 are for the December 1994, March 1995, June 1995, September 1995, and December 1995 contracts, respectively.

The procedure used to compute conversion factors is far from the correct way of discounting cash flows described in Part One. Therefore, as mentioned before, conversion factors do not truly relate the value of all deliverable bonds and it is not true that, at delivery, $S'_i = f' \times CF_i$ for all eligible bonds. Consequently, the cost

---

[57]This step is slightly more complicated if rounding maturity to the nearest quarter does not give an even number of semiannual periods. In that case the procedure can be illustrated by the 10 5/8s due August 15, 2015. From the delivery month of September 1994, the maturity of this bond is 20 years and 11 months. Rounding down to the nearest quarter gives 20 years and 9 months. One quarter from now, when the bond will have 20 years and 6 months, or 41 semiannual periods to maturity, it will have a price of

$$(10\ 5/8\%/8\%)(1 - 1.04^{-41}) + 1.04^{-41} = 1.2624$$

and will make a semiannual coupon payment of .5 x .10265. Discounting these values back one quarter to get price plus accrued as of the delivery date gives

$$(1.2624 + .5 \times 10\ 5/8\%)/1.04^{1/2} = 1.29$$

As a present value of future cash flows, this 1.29 includes accrued interest as of the delivery date (see Chapter 4). Since futures prices are quoted without accrued interest, subtract the accrued interest to get the "price" of $1 face value of the 10 5/8s, that is, the conversion factor:

$$1.29 - 3/12\ 10\ 5/8\% = 1.2634$$

[58]I would like to thank Sanjiv Gupta and Bloomberg for providing this and other Bloomberg exhibits.

	C pn or M ty order M		A sc. or D ec. order A			
Bonds/Futr's	U8U4	U824	U8H5	U8N5	U8U5	U825
T 11 $\frac{3}{4}$ 11/14	1.3242	n.a.	n.a.	n.a.	n.a.	n.a.
T 11 $\frac{1}{4}$ 02/15	1.3230	1.3216	1.3197	1.3182	1.3162	1.3147
T 10 $\frac{5}{8}$ 08/15	1.2634	1.2624	1.2608	1.2598	1.2582	1.2570
T 9 $\frac{7}{8}$ 11/15	1.1892	1.1881	1.1874	1.1863	1.1856	1.1843
T 9 $\frac{1}{4}$ 02/16	1.1265	1.1262	1.1253	1.1250	1.1241	1.1237
T 7 $\frac{1}{4}$ 05/16	.9236	.9238	.9243	.9245	.9250	.9252
T 7 $\frac{1}{2}$ 11/16	.9486	.9487	.9491	.9491	.9495	.9496
T 8 $\frac{3}{4}$ 05/17	1.0777	1.0772	1.0771	1.0765	1.0764	1.0758
T 8 $\frac{7}{8}$ 08/17	1.0908	1.0907	1.0901	1.0899	1.0893	1.0891
T 9 $\frac{1}{8}$ 05/18	1.1184	1.1177	1.1175	1.1168	1.1166	1.1158
T 9 11/18	1.1060	1.1054	1.1052	1.1046	1.1044	1.1038
T 8 $\frac{7}{8}$ 02/19	1.0928	1.0927	1.0922	1.0921	1.0915	1.0914
T 8 $\frac{1}{8}$ 08/19	1.0132	1.0133	1.0131	1.0132	1.0130	1.0132
T 8 $\frac{1}{2}$ 02/20	1.0537	1.0537	1.0533	1.0534	1.0530	1.0530
T 8 $\frac{3}{4}$ 05/20	1.0811	1.0806	1.0806	1.0801	1.0800	1.0795
T 8 $\frac{3}{4}$ 08/20	1.0811	1.0811	1.0806	1.0806	1.0801	1.0800
T 7 $\frac{7}{8}$ 02/21	.9862	.9864	.9863	.9865	.9863	.9866
T 8 $\frac{1}{8}$ 05/21	1.0137	1.0134	1.0136	1.0134	1.0135	1.0133
T 8 $\frac{1}{8}$ 08/21	1.0135	1.0137	1.0134	1.0136	1.0134	1.0135
T 8 11/21	1.0000	.9998	1.0000	.9998	1.0000	.9998

Bloomberg-all rights protected.   Frankfurt:69-920410 Hong Kong:521-3000 London:71-330-7500 New York:212-318-2000
Princeton:609-279-3000   Singapore:226-3000   Sydney:2-241-1133   Tokyo:3-3201-8900   Washington DC:202-434-1800
G137-11-0 21-Jul-94 18:42:39

FIGURE 14.1   Conversion factors.

of delivery, $S'_i - CF_i \times f'$, is not the same for all bonds. Finally, then, there will be one bond that is *cheapest to deliver* in that it will have the lowest cost of delivery across all bonds.

Given the prices of various Treasury bonds, along with the conversion factors in Figure 14.1, one can compute the cost of delivery for each bond assuming that delivery takes place today, at the current futures price of 112 24/32. Consider, for example, the cost of delivering the 11 3/4s due November 15, 2014. The current ask price of this bond is 153.41 and its conversion factor is 1.3242. So, the cost of delivery is 153.41 − 112 24/32(1.3242) = 4.10. This calculation is done for several eligible bonds in Table 14.3.

Of the bonds listed in the table, the cheapest to deliver are the 11 3/4s due November 2016. While there is no simple rule for determining which bonds will

Table 14.3   Cost of Delivery through the September 1994 T-Bond Futures Contract for Various Treasury Bonds. Current futures price is 112 24/32

Coupon	Maturity	First Call	Conv. Factor	Ask Price	Yield	Cost of Delivery
11 3/4%	11/2014	11/2009	1.3242	153.41	6.34	4.10
9%	11/2018		1.1060	128.94	6.61	4.24
8 3/4%	8/2020		1.0811	126.66	6.61	4.76
7.625%	11/2022		.9583	113.50	6.57	5.45
6.25%	8/2023		.8040	97.41	6.45	6.75

be cheaper to deliver before performing the calculations already described, there is some intuition behind the resulting delivery costs.

The first effect is the slope of the term structure. The conversion factor calculations assume that all bonds yield 8 percent. If the yield curve is upward sloping, however, then the cash flows of long-term bonds are discounted at too low a yield relative to the cash flows of short-term bonds. Therefore, long-term bonds are valued at relatively inflated prices, making them cheaper to deliver. Conversely, if the term structure is downward-sloping, short-term bond cash flows are discounted at a relatively low yield and valued relatively highly. In this case, short-term bonds will tend to be cheaper to deliver. On February 15, 1994, the long end of the term structure was not terribly steep, so this effect on the cheapest to deliver is not overwhelming. (Recall Figure 2.1.)

The second effect is the level of yields. Pretend, for the moment, that the true term structure is flat at a yield above 8 percent. Then the conversion factor calculations, which assume an 8 percent yield, overvalue all bonds. Furthermore, for a given discrepancy between the true yield and 8 percent, this overvaluation is most severe for bonds with the greatest price sensitivities, namely those with long durations. Therefore, long maturity and low coupon bonds will tend to be cheapest to deliver when rates are above 8 percent. Now pretend that the true term structure is flat at a yield below 8 percent. The conversion factors undervalue all bonds in this case, but the undervaluation is least severe for short-duration bonds. Therefore, shorter maturities and higher coupon bonds will tend to be cheapest to deliver when rates are below 8 percent. (These "shorter maturities," of course, are all eligible for delivery, so they are callable or mature in 15 years or more.) The effect of yield levels does seem to be quite important in Table 14.3. With yields between 6.34 percent and 6.61 percent, short maturity and high coupon bonds, like the 11 3/4s due November 20, 2014, tend to be relatively cheap to deliver.

The third effect has to do with callability. Given that rates are low relative to 11 3/4 percent coupon rate, it is likely that the bond will be called and that its maturity date will turn out to be November 15, 2009, as assumed by the conversion factor calculation. But, because the Treasury may not call the bonds if rates rise substantially before November 15, 2009, the assumption of a definite call overvalues the callable bond. (See Chapter 17 for a more detailed explanation of this point.) This effect, therefore, further lowers the delivery cost of the 11 3/4s.

The fourth effect arises because some bonds sell differently than others. The 6 1/4s due August 15, 2023, which is the on-the-run 30-year bond, is particularly liquid and, as a result, sells for a relatively high price. This will make the bond particularly unattractive to deliver through the futures contract.

All market participants can compute the cost of delivery for each bond and determine the cheapest to deliver. It follows that sellers will plan to deliver that cheapest-to-deliver bond. Furthermore, buyers know that sellers plan to do this.

As a result, the futures contract will be priced based on the cheapest-to-deliver bond. In other words, the cheapest-to-deliver bond becomes the underlying security for the futures contract. This description is an oversimplification because the cheapest-to-deliver bond can change over the life of the futures contract. The most sophisticated models, therefore, will take into account the possibility of changes in the identity of the cheapest-to-deliver bond.

If one's first reaction to the calculation of conversion factors was that they were horribly inaccurate estimates of value and that it was amazing that exchanges actually used them, their use can now be justified. It is best to lay down relatively simple rules for financial contracts and let the marketplace adjust price accordingly. Rather than make an extremely complicated model to determine relative values of eligible bonds, make simple, even if inaccurate, rules. The market will then use its collection of models to determine the cheapest to deliver and, in turn, the appropriate futures price. This market convention is analogous to the accrued interest convention discussed in Chapter 4. The most important consideration is a rule that is simple and easy to use. The market price of bonds will correct any inaccuracies resulting from that simplification.

Given that the cheapest-to-deliver bond can be thought of as the underlying security, it may seem that the squeeze problem can emerge again. Can a group of investors profit by going long the futures contract and simultaneously buying a large supply of the cheapest-to-deliver bond? Not really. In the case of there being only one eligible bond, the syndicate of investors can demand relatively high prices for that deliverable bond because the alternative to not buying is failing to deliver. In the case of a cheapest-to-deliver, however, the syndicate can only demand a premium equal to the difference between the cost of delivering the cheapest-to-deliver and the cost of delivering the next cheapest-to-deliver. And, in practice, these costs may not be far enough apart to justify the expense of generating the squeeze. In addition, there is always the risk that the cheapest-to-deliver will change and that the position will not generate any premium.

One additional complexity of futures contracts will be mentioned in this section. Until now it has been assumed that there is one particular delivery date. In practice this may not be the case. In the T-bond futures contract, for example, trading stops on a particular date, so that the final futures price is fixed, but the seller can deliver on any day in the month of expiration.

The considerations entering into the timing decision are as follows. First, since the futures price is fixed, there is no price risk in advancing or delaying delivery. Second, the buyer has to pay accrued interest as of the delivery date. Therefore, when the futures price is fixed, the seller can borrow money, buy the bond to be delivered, and earn interest on the bond to the delivery date. If short-term borrowing rates are less than the yield on the bond, delaying delivery will tend to be profitable. This situation is most likely, of course, when the term structure is upward-sloping. Third, since the price at which the bond will be sold is fixed, there is a desire to obtain those funds as soon as possible. This consideration tilts the decision to early delivery.

CONCLUSION

While delivery considerations have played an important part in the discussion of futures contracts, it should be mentioned that almost all financial futures contracts do not end in delivery. Buyers sell before delivery, canceling their obligations, and sellers buy before delivery, canceling their obligations. This happens for the same reason that futures contracts are so popular in the first place: The transaction costs of futures is often low relative to those in the underlying bond markets. Therefore, it is cheaper for a buyer to close his futures position than to take delivery and sell the bond. Similarly, it is cheaper for a seller to close his position than to purchase the bond and sell it through the contract.

The fact that financial futures do not typically end in delivery should not be misinterpreted. First, this in no way affects the usefulness of futures for speculating or hedging. Since positions are marked-to-market, stepping out of a position slightly before expiration has approximately the same payoff structure as staying in the position and taking or making delivery. Second, this fact does not mean that the cheapest-to-deliver calculations just presented are not important. Even if no one actually delivers, futures prices would still be set by cheapest-to-deliver considerations. If that were not the case, futures prices would not be set correctly relative to their final payoffs and arbitrage opportunities would be available in which some parties would change their behavior and decide to make delivery.

While this chapter has not focused on hedging, it should be apparent how the material presented here can be used in a hedging context. The basic idea behind hedging is to set the net PVBP (see Part Three) of a portfolio equal to zero. The challenge of using futures in a hedge is to calculate accurately the PVBP of a futures contract. The pricing considerations discussed in this unit, along with a particular term-structure model, can be used for such a calculation. Then, equipped with the PVBPs of the futures contract and of the asset to be hedged, it is a very simple exercise to figure out how many contracts one needs to buy or sell to achieve a net PVBP of zero.[59]

There are many simple, widely used rules of thumb which give fast and reasonable solutions to the problem of determining hedges with futures contracts. Given the complexity of futures contracts, however, readers are encouraged to determine hedge positions carefully and more exactly. This chapter and Part Two should prove useful starting points for this purpose.

---

[59]For a more detailed treatment, see Duffie (1989).

Chapter 15
Floaters and Inverse Floaters

Floating rate notes make coupon payments that increase with the level of interest rates, while *inverse floaters* make coupon payments that decrease with the level of interest rates. It is generally true that securities whose cash flows change with the level of interest rates are more difficult to price than securities with fixed cash flows. More precisely, pricing variable cash flows usually requires a term-structure model like those developed in Part Two. As it turns out, however, many floating rate bonds are an exception to this rule. Despite the fact that their cash flows are not fixed, they are as easy to price as securities with fixed cash flows. The first section of this chapter demonstrates this fact. The second section discusses a simplified form of an inverse floater under restrictive assumptions about interest rate movements in order to build intuition about more realistic inverse floating structures.

THE PRICE AND DURATION OF FLOATERS

Consider a 3-year floating rate note that makes semiannual coupons equal to .5 of the six-month rate prevailing at the beginning of the coupon period. If $100 of this bond were issued on February 15, 1994, when the six-month rate is 3.57 percent, then the first coupon, payable on August 15, 1994, would be set at $100 x 3.57%/2 = $1.79. Six months from now, on August 15, 1994, the second coupon, payable on February 15, 1995, would be set, and so forth. At maturity, on February 15, 1997, the note pays the coupon set on August 15, 1996, and the $100 principal value.

This floating rate note can be priced by starting at the maturity date and working backwards to today. Let the six-month spot rate on August 15, 1996, be r. Then, the note's payment at maturity is

$$100 + 100\frac{r}{2} = 100\left(1 + \frac{r}{2}\right)$$

To price the note on August 15, 1996, discount this cash flow by the prevailing six-month rate, r.

$$\frac{100\left(1 + \frac{r}{2}\right)}{1 + \frac{r}{2}} = 100$$

The price of the floating rate note on August 15, 1996, is par because it earns a six-month coupon rate exactly equal to the six-month spot rate.

Knowing that the price of the note on August 15, 1996, is 100, it can be priced six months earlier, that is, on February 15, 1996. Redefine r to be the six-month spot rate as of February 15, 1996. In that case, the value of the bond on August 15, 1996, is its price, just deduced to be 100, plus the coupon payment of 100r/2, for a total of 100(1+r/2). The price on February 15, 1996, is the present value of that sum, or 100. Once again, the price of the floater is par. Continuing with this line of reasoning, it can be concluded that the price of a floating rate note on each and every coupon date is equal to par.

Given the price of the floater on coupon dates, it is easy to price the floater between coupon dates. Say that the coupon rate has already been set at r, that three months have elapsed since the last reset date, and that the current three-month discount factor is d(.25). Invoking the previous argument, the value of the floater in three months will be 100(1+r/2). The value today is simply the present value of that quantity, or 100(1+r/2)d(.5).

This discussion reveals that any time after a coupon reset a floater will make its next coupon on the following reset date and be worth par just after that. Hence, a floater is exactly equivalent to a bond with one coupon payment remaining and with maturity equal to the time until the next coupon reset. It follows immediately that the Macaulay duration of a floater equals the time until its next reset date. With semiannual resets, a 3-year floater, a 10-year floater, and a 50-year floater (if such things existed) all have Macaulay durations of .5.

While this book does not discuss credit risk, it should be noted that the reasoning of this section must be modified if credit risk is present. With the possiblility of default it is no longer true that the floating rate note will equal par at all reset dates.

A PRIMER ON INVERSE FLOATERS

Consider a 3-year inverse floater that pays semiannual coupons at a rate equal to 12 percent minus the six-month rate prevailing at the beginning of the coupon period. Assume, for the purposes of this section, that the six-month rate will not, over the life of the note, rise above 12 percent so that the coupon of this inverse floater is always positive. This is a simplified description of an inverse floater and a restrictive assumption about future interest rates. But, for the purpose of gaining intuition about inverse floaters, this structure is quite instructive.

Say that $100 of the inverse floater just described is purchased on February 15, 1994, when the six-month rate is 3.57 percent. The first coupon, payable on August 15, 1994, will be $100(.12 - .0357)/2 = 4.22$. If, on August 15, 1994, the six-month rate has risen to 3.70 percent, then the second coupon, payable on February 15, 1995, will be $100(.12 - .0370)/2 = 4.15$. Therefore, the coupons of the inverse floater fall as interest rates increase.

To price this inverse floater one need only recognize the following fact: A portfolio of $50 face value of the floater described in the previous section and $50 face value of the inverse floater described here is equivalent to $100 face value of 6 percent coupon bonds. If the six-month rate is r, then the next coupon of the floater is $50r/2$ and the next coupon of the inverse floater is $50(.12 - r)/2$. The sum of these two cash flows is $50 \times .12/2 = 100 \times .06/2 = 3$, exactly the same payment made by a 6 percent coupon bond. At maturity, the principal cash flows from both the floater and inverse floater are 50, so the sum is 100, again matching the corresponding cash flow from the 6 percent coupon bond.

The price of the 6 percent bond is easily determined from the term structure. On February 15, 1994, a 6 percent 3-year bond would have sold for about 103.34. Since February 15, 1994, is a coupon date for the floater, the price of the floater on that date is par. Or, the price of $50 face value of the floater is $50. Then, given the relationship among the prices of the 6 percent coupon bond, the floater, and the inverse floater developed in the previous paragraph, the price of $50 face value of the inverse floater is

$$\$103.34 - \$50 = \$53.34$$

Equivalently, the price of $100 face value of the inverse floater is $106.68.

The duration of the inverse floater can be determined similarly. The Macaulay duration of the 3-year 6 percent coupon bond is about 2.81 and the Macaulay duration of the floater is .5. Let D_{IV} be the Macaulay duration of the inverse floater. Then, viewing the 6 percent bond as a portfolio containing $50 face value of both the floater and inverse floater, the results in Part Three about the duration of a portfolio imply that

$$2.81 = \frac{\$50}{\$103.34} \times .5 + \frac{\$53.34}{\$103.34} \times D_{IV}$$

Solving reveals that $D_{IV} = 4.98$

This duration value is very revealing. A 3-year inverse floater has a Macaulay duration of 4.98, substantially larger than that of the 3-year 6 percent coupon bond. It is this property of inverse floaters that has caught some investors off guard. The duration of inverse floaters will exceed the duration of fixed coupon bonds with similar maturities.

There are two ways to explain the relatively large duration of the inverse floater. The first is a technical explanation. The duration of the 6 percent coupon bond will be a weighted average of the durations of the floater and the inverse floater. But the duration of the floater is quite short, equal to the time until the next reset date. Hence, the weighted average can equal the duration of the 6 percent coupon bond only if the duration of the inverse floater exceeds the duration of the 6 percent coupon bond.

The second, more intuitive explanation for the inverse floater's long duration is the following. As rates increase, the inverse floater loses value from two sources. First, like any fixed income security, increasing the discount rate lowers the present value of the cash flows. Second, as rates increase, the cash flows from the inverse floater decline. This second effect makes the inverse floater's price decline more rapidly than do fixed coupon securities of similar maturity. The argument works in reverse as well. When rates decline, the inverse floater gains from a lower discounting rate and from an increase in its cash flows, once again increasing its price sensitivity relative to similar maturity bonds.

Chapter 16
Interest Rate Swaps

DESCRIPTION

From nonexistence in the early 1980s, swaps have grown into a very large and liquid market. Part of the appeal of swaps is their simplicity relative to other interest rate derivative products. Consider the following swap agreement. Over the next two years, party A agrees to pay 4.40 percent of $1,000,000 to party B, on a semi-annual basis. In return, party B agrees, over the same two years, to make semiannual payments to party A at the prevailing six-month T-bill rate, on that same $1,000,000. No cash is exchanged at the time of the agreement. Thus, the parties agree to exchange, or *swap*, interest payments. The $1,000,000 is called the *notional* principal amount because the swap agreement does not provide, at any time, for payments of that $1,000,000. That figure enters into the agreement only for the purpose of calculating interest payments. Party A, the fixed rate payer, is said to have bought, or to be *long* the swap. Party B, the floating rate payer, is said to have sold, or to be *short* the swap. Finally, the fixed rate in the agreement, 4.40 percent in this example, is called the *swap rate*.

For illustrative purposes, say that the six-month T-bill rate, expressed as a spot rate, turns out to take on the values given in Table 16.1.

In this interest rate scenario, the cash flows of the swap from each party are given in Table 16.2. Party A makes its fixed payment of $1,000,000 x 4.40%/2 = $22,000 every six months over the next two years. Party B's payments depend on the spot rate. The current six-month spot rate is 3.50 percent, so the first payment, six months from now, is $1,000,000 x 3.50%/2 = $17,500. In six months, the rate turns out to be 3.60 percent, so the payment in one year is $1,000,000 x 3.60%/2 = $18,000, and so on. Note, once again, that the parties never exchange the $1,000,000.

Table 16.1   Hypothetical Future Six-month T-bill Rates, or Spot Rates

Date	6-month Spot Rate
2/15/94	3.50%
8/15/94	3.60%
2/15/95	4.00%
8/15/95	3.80%

Given the particular path of rates given in Table 16.2, party B clearly gains from having agreed to the swap while party A clearly loses. It need not have turned out that way, however. Had the six-month rate risen above 4.40 percent over the next 1.5 years, the swap might have proved profitable for party A and unprofitable for party B.

PRICE AND PRICE SENSITIVITY

Consistent with the rest of this book, this section begins by assuming that both parties will definitely make their promised payments, so that there is no credit risk. This assumption will be revisited, however, in the next section.

While swap counterparties never agree to swap notional amounts, it will be convenient for pricing purposes to assume that they do so. This does not affect the cash flows of the agreement: Assuming that A pays $1,000,000 to B on February 15, 1997, and that B pays $1,000,000 to A on February 15, 1997, has a zero net effect. But, this assumption allows for the following characterization of the swap. The buyer of the swap sells a fixed rate note to the seller of the swap and simultaneously buys a floating rate note from him. In the particular example given here, A sells a 4.40 percent 2-year note to B and buys a 2-year floating rate note from B.

This characterization of swaps immediately suggests a pricing methodology. Let P_{fix} and P_{float} be the prices of the two notes. The value of the swap, from the

Table 16.2   Payments in the Sample Swap Agreement
(It is assumed that realized 6-month rates are as listed in Table 16.1.)

Date	Payment of A to B	Payment of B to A
8/15/95	$22,000	$17,500
2/15/96	$22,000	$18,000
8/15/96	$22,000	$20,000
2/15/97	$22,000	$19,000

buyer's perspective, is simply $P_{float} - P_{fix}$. Similarly, the value of the swap, from the seller's perspective, is $P_{fix} - P_{float}$.

Chapter 15 showed that, on reset dates, the price of a floating rate note is par. Therefore, for the value of the swap to be zero at initiation, so that parties will enter into the agreement without any immediate exchange of cash, the value of the fixed rate note must also be par. It follows immediately that the swap rate must equal the coupon on a par bond with maturity equal to the length of the swap. In this example, the swap rate of 4.40 percent must be the coupon on a 2-year par bond.

While the value of a swap at the time of initiation is zero, its value will change over time. Because fixed rate notes have longer durations than floating rate notes, rising interest rates tend to lower the value of the fixed rate note more than the value of the floating rate note, thus raising the value of the swap to the buyer and lowering the value to the seller. Similarly, falling interest rates tend to lower the value to the buyer and raise the value to the seller.

Because there is such a simple expression for the value of a swap to the buyer, $P_{float} - P_{fix}$, there is an equally simple expression for the price sensitivity of a swap. Let $PVBP_{float}$ and $PVBP_{fix}$ be the PVBPs of the floating rate and fixed rate notes. Then, recalling from Chapter 11 that the PVBP of a portfolio is simply the sum of the PVBPs of the component parts, a portfolio long one floating rate bond and short one fixed rate bond, that is, a long position in a swap, has a sensitivity of $PVBP_{swap}$, where

$$PVBP_{swap} = PVBP_{float} - PVBP_{fix}$$

It is also possible to express the duration of a swap as a weighted average of the duration of component parts. Letting D_{float}, D_{fix}, and D_{swap} be the durations of the floating rate note, the fixed rate note, and a long swap position, the durations are related by the following equation:

$$D_{swap} = \frac{P_{float}}{P_{float} - P_{fix}} D_{float} - \frac{P_{fix}}{P_{float} - P_{fix}} D_{fix}$$

The difficulty with this expression, however, is that at the time of initiation the value of the swap is zero, so the right-hand side of the above equation is undefined. This is not surprising: Duration measures percentage changes in price. But a percentage change in price cannot be defined if the starting price is zero.

While most swaps are an exchange of the floating rate *flat*, that is without any spread, against the fixed rate, some swaps provide for a spread off the floating rate. This twist does not complicate pricing very much. The cash flows of a two-year floating rate note paying the six-month rate plus 10 basis points on a semiannual basis can be divided into two parts: a standard floating rate note and four semiannual payments of 5 basis points times the notional amount. In other words, a spread off the floating rate index gives rise to a fixed set of cash flows. Both of these parts, therefore, are easy to price. The floating rate note is priced as before, and the fixed cash flows from the spread component are discounted using the appropriate discount factors.

CREDIT RISK AND SWAPS

The price and price sensitivity discussions in the previous section have to be adjusted in the presence of credit risk. In particular, it is no longer innocuous to assume that being long a swap is equivalent to being long a floating rate note and short a fixed rate note. The reason for this is that a swap subjects the parties to a default on the interest payments alone while notes subject purchasers to default on interest and principal.

Say that a company with far less than a AAA credit rating sells a two-year fixed rate note at 100 basis points over equivalent maturity treasuries. The company then wants to buy a swap, like the one in the main example of this section, from a AAA entity. It is tempting to reason that the company should pay 4.40% + 1.00% = 5.40% in exchange for receiving the AAA entity's floating rate payments. But this reasoning is incorrect. The 100 basis-point spread over treasuries takes into account the possibility that the company will default on its principal payment. The risk to the counterparty in the swap is much less, because the company can default only on its fixed rate interest payments.

In fact, the risk to the counterparty is even smaller than losing those fixed rate payments. Most swaps agreements have the provision that a payment default by one party absolves the other party from making payments. So, if the company does default on its fixed rate obligations, the AAA entity need not continue with its floating rate payments. The implication is that the only exposure of the AAA entity is the value of the swap. If rates have fallen since the initiation of the swap, then the swap will have positive value to the AAA entity and negative value to the company. If the company defaults, the AAA entity will lose that swap value. But even this is a bit of an exaggeration of the default risk facing the AAA entity: It can line up with other creditors to recover the lost swap value.

There is a clever, but flawed argument that appears to reduce the presence of credit risk even further. If rates have fallen and the company defaults, the AAA entity loses. But, if rates have risen, so that the value of the swap to the AAA entity is negative, a default by the company would benefit the AAA entity. Since most company defaults are unrelated to the level of interest rates, these effects offset each other and reduce the effect of credit risk on the pricing of swaps. The problem with this argument is that it assumes that the company cannot sell its swap to a third party. For when it can do so, it will sell a swap with positive value before it defaults while it will hold swaps with negative value. This behavior clearly subjects the AAA entity to the risk of losing positive swap value in the event of default.

It has been argued here that the credit risk of swaps is much smaller than that of regular notes, because only the value of the swap is subject to loss. But there are swap agreements that mitigate even that loss. Some agreements require that, in the event of a credit downgrade of one of the counterparties, the swap be settled at current market value. In other words, if the swap is worth $5,000 to the AAA entity and the company experiences a credit downgrade, the company must pay $5,000 to the AAA entity and close the swap agreement. Since the vast majority of defaults are preceded by credit downgrades, this provision provides a great deal of protection to the AAA entity.

The example of a swap between a AAA entity and a company is representative of much swap activity. Corporate users of swaps had expressed great reluctance in bearing credit risk when entering into swap agreements. In response, financial institutions have set up AAA subsidiaries from which to conduct their swap activities. As a result, corporations can often analyze their swaps without reference to credit risk.

To summarize, this section argues that the nature of swap cash flows and the provisions of swap agreements greatly reduce the importance of credit risk. Furthermore, corporations can minimize their exposure by dealing only with AAA subsidiaries. These remarks have important policy implications. Citing the notional amount of swaps outstanding greatly inflates the perceived amount of credit risk in the market. The credit exposure on a swap with $1,000,000 of notional principal is not at all comparable with the credit exposure on $1,000,000 of traditional notes.

LIBOR AS THE FLOATING RATE INDEX

The analysis so far has assumed that the floating rate used to determine the floating rate payment is the six-month Treasury spot rate. This is not usually the case. The most common floating rate index is LIBOR, the London Interbank Offer Rate, which is not a *risk-free* rate, that is, not a rate on a default-free loan. In fact, LIBOR is the rate most appropriate for borrowers with a rating of AA. Therefore, LIBOR rates exceed corresponding maturity Treasury rates.

Returning to the assumption that there is no credit risk among the swap counterparties, a swap of six-month LIBOR for the yield on a 2-year Treasury would have positive value to the receiver of the floating rate, that is, to the buyer of the swap. Because the counterparties will definitely make their payments, the fictional 2-year fixed rate note embedded in the swap is worth par. The fictional 2-year floating rate note, however, that pays a rate above the six-month spot rate, is worth more than par.

As mentioned earlier, market convention dictates that, when initiated, swaps have zero value. For this to be true when LIBOR is swapped against a fixed rate, the fixed rate, that is, the swap rate, must exceed the yield on an equal maturity par Treasury. By how much the swap rate must exceed Treasury rates depends on the perception of how much credit risk is built into LIBOR. Figure 16.1 shows a Bloomberg screen of swap rates and Treasury yields as of February 15, 1994. As expected, swap rates exceed the Treasury rates.

As can be seen from the graph and the spread exhibit below the graph, spreads over Treasuries increase with maturity. The basic intuition behind this phenomenon is that the advantage of receiving an above-market rate increases with maturity. Receiving the premium of LIBOR above the risk-free rate for five years is worth more than receiving that premium for two years. Hence, the payer of a fixed rate in a 5-year swap is willing to pay a greater spread over Treasuries than is the fixed-rate payer in a 2-year swap.

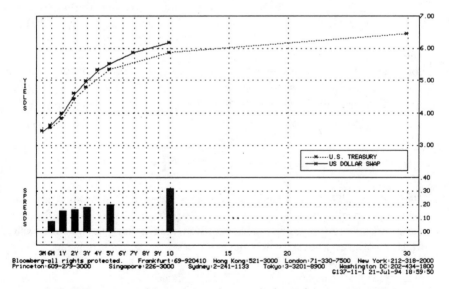

FIGURE 16.1   Yield curves and spreads for February 15, 1994.

ZERO SUM GAMES AND THE SWAPS MARKET

In an effort to explain the phenomenal growth of the swaps market, and in an effort to sell particular swap deals, it has often been claimed that it is possible for all parties in a swap to gain, in a present-value sense, from participating in the swap. The purpose of this section is to examine this claim and to discuss why, even when the claim is not true, swaps should be very popular financial tools.

The following example of an early interest rate swap will help focus the discussion.[60] In 1983, B.F. Goodrich, a BBB-credit, had determined to sell intermediate-term fixed rate debt to finance its operations. At the same time, Rabobank, a AAA Dutch banking group, had determined to sell floating rate debt to match its floating rate assets. Table 16.3 indicates selected market rates available to various credits at that time.

Rabobank could have borrowed through floating rate debt at LIBOR + .25 percent directly. B.F. Goodrich could have borrowed through fixed rate debt at 12.50 percent. Instead, the following occurred:

1. Rabobank sold 8-year fixed rate debt at 10.70 percent.
2. B.F. Goodrich sold 8-year floating rate debt at LIBOR + .5 percent.
3. Rabobank sold a swap to Morgan Guaranty, a AAA bank, to receive 10.70 percent and pay LIBOR.
4. B.F. Goodrich bought a swap from Morgan Guaranty to pay 10.70 percent and receive LIBOR.
5. B.F. Goodrich paid undisclosed fees to Morgan Guaranty.

Figure 16.2 diagrammatically depicts this swap agreement.

The combination of Rabobank's fixed rate borrowing and its short swap position synthetically created floating rate debt. Its total payments of 10.70 percent +

Table 16.3   Market Rates at the Time of the B.F. Goodrich-Rabobank Swap

Security	Rate
3-Month T-Bills	8.07%
3-Month LIBOR	8.75%
7–10 Year AAA Floating Rate Notes	LIBOR + .25%
7–10 Year AAA Fixed Rate Notes	10.70
7–10 Year BBB- Fixed Rate Notes	12.50

All note rates are expressed on a semiannual basis.
Source: Harvard Business School Case 9-284-080.

[60]This example is discussed in Harvard Business School Case 9-284-080. Readers are referred there for a detailed description of the transaction.

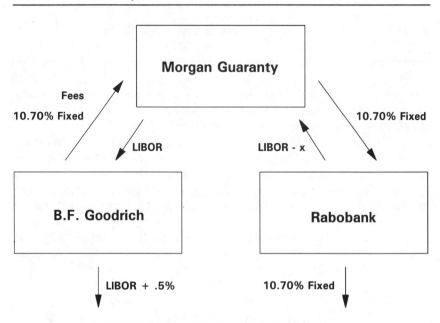

FIGURE 16.2   The B.F. Goodrich-Rabobank swap.

LIBOR minus its receipts of 10.70 percent left it with payments of LIBOR. The net result is floating rate debt at below the LIBOR + .25 percent it would have had to pay from direct borrowing in the floating rate markets.

The combination of B.F. Goodrich's floating rate borrowing and its long swap position synthetically created fixed rate debt. Its total payments of LIBOR + .5 percent + 10.70 percent minus its receipts of LIBOR left it with payments of 11.2 percent. This is equivalent to fixed rate debt at below the 12.50 percent it would have had to pay from direct borrowing in the fixed rate debt markets. So long as the fees it paid were not too big, the transaction seems to be an improvement on what it could have done on its own.

Both swap parties seem to be better off. Furthermore, the intermediary seems to be better off as well. It receives 10.70 percent from B.F. Goodrich which it immediately pays to Rabobank. It receives LIBOR from Rabobank which it immediately pays to B.F. Goodrich. And, it collects its fees.

The question now is whether all parties were truly better off after the transactions and, if so, where did that extra value come from?

It is easy to argue that Rabobank benefitted from the transaction. Its fixed rate borrowing from the market was done at a fair rate. Its swap with Morgan Guaranty, however, was done at advantageous terms. Ignoring default risk for these two AAA entities, Rabobank effectively bought a 10.70 percent fixed rate note from Morgan Guaranty, which was worth par according to Table 16.3. Also, it effectively sold a floating rate note worth less than par: The fair rate would have been LIBOR + .25 percent, according to the table, but it paid only LIBOR. Thus, Rabobank seems to have gained in a present-value sense.

The swap between Morgan Guaranty and B.F. Goodrich is a bit more complicated. Clearly, 10.70 percent is too little for a BBB to pay for 7–10 year fixed rate debt. But, following the discussion in the previous section, it is not clear what the fair rate should be. (The answer is not 12.50 percent, for example, which is the BBB- rate inclusive of the risk of principal default.) While the below-market fixed rate favors B.F. Goodrich, Morgan Guaranty is also paying a below-market rate, LIBOR instead of LIBOR + .25 percent. Then there are the fees.

While valuation principles do not reveal the value of the swap between B.F. Goodrich and Morgan Guaranty, it is not unreasonable to assume that Morgan Guaranty would at least break even on the complete deal.[61] But, having reasoned that Rabobank unambiguously wins from its swap, Morgan Guaranty can only break even, in a present-value sense, if B.F. Goodrich loses in a present-value sense.

Finally, one can ask why B.F. Goodrich would engage in the swap if it loses from it in a present-value sense. The answer lies in an, as yet, unexamined part of the complete transaction. B.F. Goodrich, a BBB- credit, managed to sell eight-year floating rate debt at a rate of LIBOR + .5 percent. Considering that AAA credits have to pay LIBOR + .25 percent, B.F. Goodrich, somehow, borrowed at a remarkably advantageous rate. So, B.F. Goodrich was willing to take a loss on its swap in order to complete the entire transaction at a gain. Presumably, the present-value of borrowing at LIBOR + .5 percent more than compensated for present-value losses of the swap. Put another way, B.F. Goodrich shared the gains of its borrowing at LIBOR + .5 percent with Rabobank and Morgan Guaranty in order to transform its excellent floating rate financing opportunity into fixed rate financing.

Was everyone better off in a present-value sense? Well, all the named players were. It seems hard to escape the conclusion, however, that the purchasers of B.F. Goodrich's floating rate debt should have gotten a better rate for the credit risk that they were assuming.

B.F. Goodrich's floating rate borrowing was exceptional. But it is not likely that the enormous swap market has been built and continues to grow on opportunities of this sort. It is more likely that swaps and their accompanying transactions do not offer any present-value gains but are nevertheless desirable.

Consider the situation of a savings and loan that borrows short-term through

---

[61]It is possible that Morgan Guaranty would accept losses here to further other business arrangements with the two counterparties. The author, however, prefers the explanation in the text.

deposits and lends long-term through mortgages. Since the duration of mortgages exceeds the duration of short-term deposits, the S&L is subject to the risk that interest rates will increase and that its assets will fall in value by more than the fall in the value of its liabilities. One solution is to buy a swap. Paying fixed and receiving floating, in combination with receiving a fixed rate from mortgages and paying a floating rate to depositors, leaves the S&L with a portfolio much more protected against the risk of rising rates. Note that there need be no present-value gain in buying the swap. The S&L would gain solely from the point of view of risk management.

The S&L in the above example could, of course, sell all of its mortgages and purchase short-term securities with the proceeds. But this is likely to be a considerably more expensive plan than the execution of a swap. As mentioned in the context of futures, an important advantage of derivatives is their relative liquidity. Trading a generic swap or futures contract that is of interest to very many market participants will cost less than trading a particular bond or mortgage with particular features and credit characteristics.

An example of selling swaps to advantage might be that of a corporation whose debt, in the view of management, has become too long. It could sell a swap, receiving fixed and paying floating, thus effectively reducing the duration of its debt. The company could, of course, accomplish the same thing in the cash market. It could purchase its own bonds in the market or through a tender offer. But, once again, cash transactions are likely to be much more expensive than derivatives trades. And, should management's view or the company's situation change again, it will be much easier to undo the swap than to buy back old short-term debt and issue new long-term debt.

Chapter 17
The Options Embedded in Corporate Bonds

Corporate bonds often have one or many *embedded options*. Bond options are called "embedded" when they cannot be separated from their underlying securities. This is usually the case for corporate callable bonds. These bonds allow the issuer to *call*, or repurchase, its bonds at some prespecified set of *call prices*. But, these options cannot be traded separately. *Sinking fund provisions* in corporate bonds also constitute a set of embedded options, even though this equivalence is less widely understood.

Section 1 of this chapter describes typical corporate call provisions. Section 2 illustrates, through a simple example, how a term structure model can be used to price callable bonds. Section 3 graphically analyzes a more realistic example to develop intuition about the pricing of call provisions. Section 4 introduces sinking fund provisions, describes their pricing in some simple cases, and discusses the great complexity they add to corporate bond pricing.

THE CALL PROVISION

In March 1993, Limited Inc. issued 7.5 percent bonds due on March 15, 2023. The bonds were *call protected* for the first 10 years, sometimes written "NC10" and read "non-call 10," meaning that Limited had no option on these bonds over the next 10 years. As of March 15, 2003, however, Limited has the right to *call* these bonds, that is, to repurchase them from investors, at prices given in Table 17.1.

Table 17.1   Call Prices for the Limited 7 1/2s due March 15, 2023

Date	Call Price
3/15/2003	103.16
3/15/2004	102.85
3/15/2005	102.53
3/15/2006	102.21
3/15/2007	101.90
3/15/2008	101.58
3/15/2009	101.26
3/15/2010	100.95
3/15/2011	100.63
3/15/2012	100.32
3/15/2013	100.00

The first row of the table indicates that Limited has the right to call the bond issue for $103.16 per $100 face value at any time from March 15, 2003, to March 15, 2004. After that time, the call price drops: from March 15, 2004, to March 15, 2005, the bonds may be called for 102.85 percent of par. The last row of the table states that from March 15, 2013, and beyond, Limited may call the bonds at par. By the way, if Limited calls the bonds between coupon dates, it must pay accrued interest in addition to the scheduled call price. The logic here is that as time passes the interest is earned. A call provision does not give the issuer the right to retroactively decide not to pay interest already earned.

This call provision is fairly typical of those in the corporate bond market. The call price starts at some premium above par and then declines, year by year, to par. Once the call price hits par, it stays there until maturity. The decline in the call price from year to year, by the way, is usually linear, falling from year to year by the same amount. The fall in the call price of the Limited's bonds is about $.32 per year.

In the rest of this section, the price behavior of callable bonds will be discussed in detail. The basic idea is as follows. Like most corporate bonds, the Limited's bonds pay a fixed coupon every six months, in this case at 7.5 percent. If interest rates rise after the bonds are sold, the issuer wins in the sense that it is then borrowing at a relatively low rate of interest. For example, if long-term corporate rates rise to 8 percent, new corporate borrowers have to borrow at 8 percent while the Limited continues to borrow at 7.5 percent. On the other hand, if rates fall after the sale of the issue, say to 7 percent, investors in the bonds win. The call provision, however, by allowing the issuer to purchase bonds at some fixed set of prices, caps the amount by which investors can profit from a rate decline.

Imagine that another bond issue which pays a coupon of 7.5 percent is due on March 15, 2003, but is not callable. Say that rates as of March 15, 2003, are well below 7.5 percent and that this noncallable bond sells for 110. The Limited's bond, even though it has the same coupon and maturity, will not sell for 110. Most likely, Limited will decide to call the bonds and, anticipating this choice, the market price of the bonds will approximately equal the call price of 103.16. If, on the other hand, rates on March 15, 2003 turn out to be well above 7.5 percent, and the noncallable bond sells for 95, the Limited will not call its bond and the bond will not be worth 103.16 at that date. To summarize, the call feature caps investor gains when rates fall, but does not put a floor under losses when rates rise.

There is an important relationship between the value of a callable bond and the value of an otherwise identical noncallable bond. The phrase "otherwise identical" means that, except for the call features, every feature of the noncallable bond is identical to that of the callable bond. Let P_C and P_{NC} be the prices of the callable and otherwise identical noncallable bond, respectively. Let C be the value of the issuer's option to call the bond. Then,

$$P_C = P_{NC} - C$$

The value of the option is subtracted from the value of the noncallable bond because the issuer has the option. Hence, the call feature reduces the value of the noncallable bond to investors by exactly the value of the embedded option.

It is important to understand that this relationship is not just a definition. It is a strong prediction of relative pricing based on arbitrage arguments. Assume, for example, that $P_C < P_{NC} - C$. An arbitrageur could execute the following trades:

Purchase the callable bond for P_C
Purchase the option on the bond for C [62]
Sell the noncallable bond for P_{NC}

The cash flow from these transactions is $P_{NC} - C - P_C$, which, by assumption, is positive.

If rates subsequently fall and the company eventually exercises its call option, the arbitrageur will deliver his callable bond to the company in exchange for the call price. At the same time, the arbitrageur will exercise his call option, buy the bond with the call price received from the company, and use the bond purchased through the call to cover his short position. In this rate scenario, therefore, the arbitrageur has no net cash flows in the future. On the other hand, if rates rise so

---

[62]Since the option is embedded, it does not trade. Therefore, statements in the text about buying or selling the option should be taken to mean buying or selling portfolio of other securities that replicate the option under consideration.

that the issuer never calls its bond, the arbitrageur's option will expire worthless. Furthermore, at maturity, he will deliver his callable bond, with its expired call option, to cover his short position. In this scenario too, the arbitrageur neither makes nor receives any payment after the position is established. The analysis of these two scenarios proves that the original revenue from the transactions constitutes a riskless arbitrage profit. Ruling out the existence of such profits, the key to arbitrage pricing, leads to the conclusion that the original pricing relationship cannot occur and, therefore, that $P_C \leq P_{NC} - C$. Making a similar argument to show that it is impossible for P_C to strictly exceed $P_{NC} - C$ leaves the result that $P_C = P_{NC} - C$.

While conceptually important, the above relationship does not, by itself, help to price the callable bond. While the noncallable bond can be priced by the methods of Part One, neither the callable bond nor the value of the option can be so priced. The role of the next section, therefore, is to apply the techniques of Part Two to price the embedded option and the callable bond.

Most call provisions allow the issuer to call an issue "in whole or in part" and "at any time," so long as the holders are given some advance notice, usually 30 days. By the way, when calling an issue in part, bonds to be called are selected randomly from all outstanding bonds. Some call provisions, however, do differ from these typical features. Occasionally the issuer may be required to redeem an entire issue or no bonds at all. Other call provisions may permit the issuer to call bonds only on coupon payment dates.

A provision related to callability, namely, *refundability*, is rarely included in new issues but still exists in many less recent issues. As an example, consider the Eaton Corp.'s 8 1/2s due January 15, 2017. They were callable quite soon after their issuance in 1987, but are "not callable . . . prior to January 15, 1997, as part of, or in anticipation of, any refunding operation by the application, directly or indirectly, of the proceeds of indebtedness for money borrowed which shall have an interest cost of less than 8.626 percent per annum." This provides for 10 years of protection from refunding, written "NR-10" for "non-refundable 10." It means that the issuer can call the bonds if it has the cash, but cannot sell new debt at lower interest rates to finance its call. The idea behind preserving callability in the early years while sacrificing refundability is to provide flexibility to the company without buying an expensive interest rate option. Flexibility here means the opportunity to remove debt for any management objective not related to interest rates, for example, improving the balance sheet, removing restrictive covenants, getting rid of excess cash, lowering debt service, and so on. In theory, investors would not demand much in extra interest to sell a nonrefundable call because these refunding events are as likely to occur after rates have risen (when bondholders like calls) as after rates have fallen (when bondholders dislike calls).

As it turned out, however, companies were extremely creative in getting around nonrefundability provisions. Examples of this behavior include using money from asset sales or from the sale of non-debt securities to call their premium debt. The most egregious method of circumventing the intention of nonrefundability provisions were the transactions that came to be known as "gun-to-the-head" tender offers. To explain these transactions, imagine that a company has $100,000,000 face value of an outstanding debt issue that sells for 110 percent of par. Also imagine that the bonds are callable but not refundable at 102 and that the issuer has $50,000,000 in cash. The company then makes a tender offer to buy the bonds for 105, financed by the sale of new debt, and announces its intention to use its $50,000,000 in cash to call any bonds that are not tendered at the call price of 102. Even though the tender price of 105 is well below the market price of 110, investors may tender anyway. A small investor is afraid that if he doesn't sell for 105 but enough other investors do, the company will have enough money to call his bonds at the lower price of 102. It may certainly be argued that selling debt to finance the tender at the same time as threatening a call is essentially a refunding. But an argument is just that. In any case, the ability of corporations to circumvent the nonrefundability provision has virtually eliminated the use of that provision.

PRICING CALLABLE BONDS WITH A TERM-STRUCTURE MODEL

This section will consider the following simple example. Assume that a term-structure model of the type discussed in Part Two has been settled upon. From this model one derives the following risk-neutral tree, with probabilities of up and down moves equal to .5, for the evolution of the six-month rate in six-month time steps:

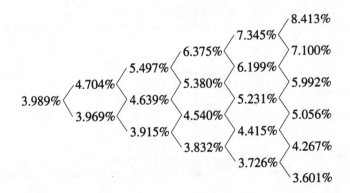

The goal here will be to price a three-year, 7 percent coupon bond callable in one year at 103, in 1.5 years at 102, in two or 2.5 years at 101, and at maturity, of course, at 100. The first step is to construct the tree for the price of the security underlying the option, namely a three-year, 7 percent coupon noncallable bond. The resulting tree, to be discussed at present, is given below.

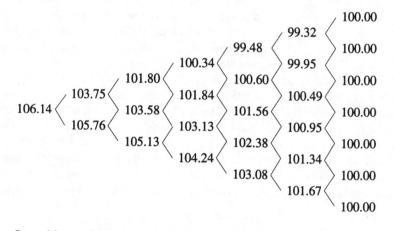

In problems of this sort, it is most convenient to express prices as *ex-coupon prices*. In other words, each price represents the bond's price right after a coupon date. So, for example, the bond's value on date 6 is recorded as 100, instead of 103.5, because the coupon has already been paid.[63]

The construction of this tree starts at date 6 where the terminal value is known to be par, ex-coupon. Then date 5 prices, 2.5 years from the present, can be calculated. Consider state 5 on this date, corresponding to a six-month interest rate of 8.413 percent. From the perspective of this state, the bond's value at the end of the next six months will be 100 + 3.5 in the up-state and 100 + 3.5 in the down-state. Note that the coupon has to be added to the ex-coupon price in the tree to get the total value in the future. Since a risk-neutral pricing tree is being used, the value of the bond in state 5 is

$$\frac{.5 \times 103.5 + .5 \times 103.5}{1 + \dfrac{.08413}{2}} = 99.32$$

Continuing in this fashion gives all possible bond prices on date 5.

Having calculated these prices, bond prices on date 4 can be calculated. Consider state 4, this time corresponding to a six-month rate of 7.345 percent. The two possible future values here are 99.32 + 3.5 = 102.82 and 99.95 + 3.5 = 103.45. So the price of the bond in this state is

$$\frac{.5 \times 102.82 + .5 \times 103.45}{1 + \dfrac{.07345}{2}} = 99.48$$

This technique is used over and over again, for all states and all dates. The ex-coupon price at each date equals the sum of the expected value and the coupon payment discounted by the short-term rate.

Equipped with the price of the noncallable bond, the price of the option on that bond can be computed. The following tree gives the resulting option values.

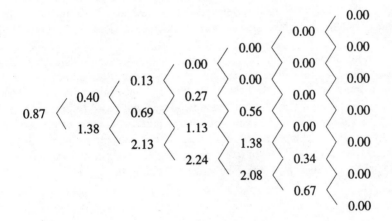

At maturity, the option is worth zero: The right to call a bond for 100 when it matures—which can be redeemed at 100 in any case—is not worth anything. At any time before maturity, however, calculating the value of the option is more complex.

The issuer, who is the option holder, has two choices whenever the option may be exercised. It can exercise the option or it can hold the option for another period. Since it owns the option, it will choose the strategy that maximizes the value of the option. With this objective, the valuation proceeds as follows:

1. Calculate the value of holding the option for another period. Call that value V_H.
2. Calculate the value of exercising the option immediately. Call that value V_E.

3. If $V_H > V_E$, the issuer will hold the option for another period and the option is worth V_H. If $V_E > V_H$, the issuer will exercise immediately and the option is worth V_E. Summarizing, the value of the option is worth the maximum of V_H and V_E, written as

$$\text{Max } (V_H, V_E)$$

On date 5, the option will definitely become worthless over the next six months. Therefore, V_H as of this date is zero. In states 2 through 5 the corresponding noncallable bond prices are all less than 101. Therefore, V_E is also equal to zero or, in the language of options, the option is *out-of-the-money*. Thus, the value of the option in these four states is zero.

In the states 0 and 1, however, the option may be profitably exercised; it is *in-the-money*. The noncallable bond prices in these states are 101.34 and 101.67, so the value of immediate exercise is .34 and .67. Since this exceeds the value of holding, which is zero, the options will be exercised and be worth .34 and .67.

Given option values for all states on date 5, option values on date 4 can be calculated. States 3 and 4 are easy: The option will be worthless at the end of the next six months, so $V_H = 0$. And since the option is out-of-the-money, $V_E = 0$. Therefore, the value of the option in these two states must also be zero.

State 2 is also quite easy. The value of holding is zero, but the option is worth 101.5623 - 101 = .5623 if exercised immediately. Thus, the option value is .5623.

In state 1, corresponding to an interest rate of 4.415 percent, the value of the option is not immediately evident. The value of holding the option is

$$V_H = \frac{.5 \times 0 + .5 \times .34}{1 + \dfrac{.04415}{2}} = .17$$

But, the value of exercising immediately, V_E, is 102.38 − 101 = 1.38. The value of the option, therefore, is $\max(V_E, V_H) = 1.38$ and the optimal policy is to call the bond at this node.

At this point in the discussion a general rule for these calculations can be recorded. Let B be the value of the bond at a particular node, let r be the six-month rate corresponding to that node, let K be the relevant call price, let the values of the option in up-and-down states be V^u and V^d, and let V be the value of the option at the node of interest. Then,

$$V_H = \frac{.5V^u + .5V^d}{1 + \dfrac{r}{2}}$$

$$V_E = \max(0, B-K)$$

and

$$V = \max(V_H, V_E)$$

Working backwards in time and applying this rule at each node will produce the option value tree previously given.

It is important to point out that just because an option is in-the-money does not mean that it should be exercised. Consider state 1 on date 2. The noncallable bond price is 103.58 and the relevant call price is 103, so $V_E = .58$. The value of holding, on the other hand, is

$$V_H = \frac{.5 \times .27 + .5 \times 1.13}{1 + \dfrac{.04639}{2}} = .69$$

Since $V_H > V_E$, it is optimal to hold the option over the next 6 months and the option value equals the value of holding, .69.

As explained in the stock option pricing literature, there are two forces leading call option holders to delay exercise and one force leading holders to exercise. The forces for delay are as follows. First, while the underlying security price may go up or down, call option holders are awarded asymmetrically: They win if prices rise but do not lose more than their initial investment if prices fall. This asymmetry favors letting the option ride. Second, holding everything else constant, there is a time value of money incentive to delay payment of the exercise price and, therefore, to delay exercise of the option. The force for early exercise is dividends or, in the bond context, coupon payments. The earlier the option is exercised to buy the bond, the sooner interest is earned. Put another way, a call option shares in the price appreciation of the underlying security but not in any dividend or interest payments.

In the bond context, there is often an additional incentive to delay exercise. Since the call prices of embedded bond options usually decline with maturity, it may pay to wait and exercise at lower call prices. In the example of the text, the relatively rapid decline of the call price from 103 after one year to 102 after 1.5 years is a contributor to the decision not to call in state 1 on date 2.

In summary, the optimal call strategy is a complex blend of the considerations just listed. There are no short cuts to substitute for building a risk-neutral pricing tree and calculating the optimal policy at each node.

Having completed the option price tree, the price tree for the callable bond is obtained by subtracting the option value at each node from the price of the noncallable bond at each node. In particular, the price of the callable bond today is 106.14 − .87 = 105.26. The following tree shows callable bond prices at each node. The row above the tree lists the call prices applicable on each date. Note how easy it is to read off the nodes at which calls are optimal. Anytime the callable bond price equals the exercise price, the optimal policy is to call.

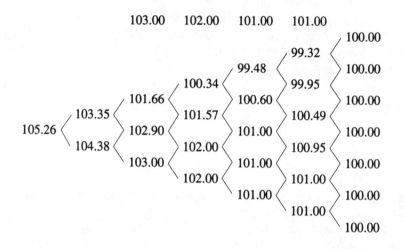

For practical purposes, the job is done. There is something to be learned, however, from seeing this pricing problem solved by directly building a tree for the price of a callable bond.

Starting at maturity, the price of the callable bond will be par in all states. Stepping back six months, the issuer of the bond, who owns the call option, has two possible choices. First, it can leave the bond outstanding for the next six months. Second, it can call the bond. Taking state 5 as an example, if it leaves the bond outstanding, the bond is worth

$$\frac{.5 \times 103.5 + .5 \times 103.5}{1 + \frac{.08413}{2}} = 99.32$$

If, on the other hand, it calls the bond for its call price of 101, the bond is worth 101. Since the bond represents a liability to the issuer, it seeks to minimize the value of the bond. Therefore, it will select the lower value of the two choices. In state 5 it will choose not to exercise the call and the bond will be worth the value that emerges given that decision, 99.32.

A GRAPHICAL ANALYSIS OF CALLABLE BONDS

While the analysis of the previous section illustrates how to price callable bonds, it provides little insight about the price behavior of callable bonds. This section graphically explores the intuition behind this price behavior. All prices and durations were computed using the original Salomon Brothers model described in Chapter 8 and a smoothed February 15, 1994, term structure.

This section will consider a 9 percent, 16-year bond callable at par in three years. To study its price behavior, consider two reference bonds. The first is a 9 percent, 16-year noncallable bond. The second is a 9 percent, 3-year bond.[64] The dashed and dotted curves in Figure 17.1 graph the price-yield curve of these reference bonds as a function of the 10-year par yield. (Recall that in a one-factor model the choice of the horizontal-axis rate is arbitrary.) When rates are particularly low, the 16-year bond is worth more than the 3-year bond because it earns above-market interest for a longer time. Conversely, when rates are particularly high, the 3-year bond is worth more because it earns below-market interest for a shorter time. Also, the 16-year bond's price-yield curve is the steeper of the two curves, because its duration is greater.

The solid line in the figure shows how the price-yield curve of a callable bond relates to the curves of the two reference bonds. In particular, the following facts detail the relationship between the callable and reference bonds. These facts, by themselves, dictate the qualitative features of the callable bond's price-yield curve. In other words, Figure 17.1 would appear qualitatively the same no matter what term-structure model had been used.

Fact 1: The price of the callable bond will always be below the price of the 3-year bond.

---

[64]If the call price of the callable bond were 102 instead of 100, the 3-year reference bond would change. If would be a bond that paid $4.50 every six months, like the callable bond being priced, but it would pay 102 instead of 100 at maturity. While admittedly an odd structure, this reference bond has fixed cash flows and, as such, can easily be priced. Moreover, the bond must be structured in this way for the analysis of this section to hold for call prices greater than 100. See, in particular, Fact 1 in the list given in the text proper.

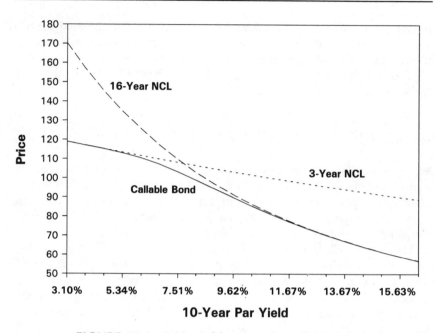

FIGURE 17.1   Price-yield curve of a callable bond.

Fact 2: The price of the callable bond will always be below the price of the 16-year bond.

Fact 3: As rates increase, the price of the callable bond approaches the price of the 16-year bond.

Fact 4: As rates decrease, the price of the callable bond approaches the price of the 3-year bond.

The intuition behind Fact 1 is as follows. From now until three years from now, the callable bond and the noncallable bond make exactly the same payments, that is, $4.50 every six months. However, three years from now, the 3-year bond will be worth par while the callable bond will be worth par or less: It will be worth par if the issuer decides to call but less than par if the issuer decides not to call. Now, if the cash flows from both the 3-year and callable bonds are the same for the next three years, but the 3-year bond is worth as much or more than the callable bond in three years, then the 3-year bond must be worth more today as well. This last bit of reasoning invokes the rule that, if security A provides cash flows equal to or larger than those of security B at every future date, the price of security A must exceed the price of security B.

Fact 2 follows immediately from the fact that the price of an option is always positive. Since the price of the callable bond equals the price of the 16-year bond minus the price of the option, the price of the callable bond must be less than the price of the 16-year bond. In fact, the difference between the 16-year noncallable curve and the callable bond curve equals the price of the embedded option.

When rates are high and bond prices low, the option to call the bond at par is worth very little. More loosely, when rates are high the likelihood of the bond being called in three years is quite low. But, this being the case, the callable bond's price and price behavior will resemble that of the 16-year noncallable bond. This explains Fact 3.

When rates are low and bond prices high, the option to call the bond is very valuable. The probability that the bond will be called in three years is high. But, this being the case, the callable bond's price and price behavior will resemble that of the 3-year reference bond. This explains Fact 4.

Aside from appreciating the general shape of callable price-yield curves, Figure 17.1 has two other messages. First, while bonds with fixed cash flows are always characterized by positive convexity, callable bonds have a region of negative convexity. For very high rates, where the callable bond mimics a 16-year noncallable, and for very low rates, where the callable bond mimics a 3-year noncallable, the callable bond's price-yield curve is positively convex. But, for intermediate rates, around the point at which the two reference bond prices cross, the curvature of the callable bond's price curve changes from convex to concave. The intuition behind this convexity change will be discussed shortly.

The second message from Figure 17.1 concerns the notion of *yield-to-call*. As defined in Chapter 3, yield-to-maturity is the one rate that, when all of a bond's cash flows are discounted at that rate, gives the market price. Part One raised some issues of caution with respect to the use of yield-to-maturity, but its use in the context of callable bonds is particularly troublesome. Since the bond may not be outstanding until maturity, the cash flows in the yield-to-maturity definition may never be realized. It is in response to this conceptual difficulty that some have turned to yield-to-call.

To calculate the yield-to-call of a bond, assume that the bond will definitely be called at some future date. The yield-to-call calculation usually assumes that the call will take place on the first call date. In principle, however, one could assume that the call takes place at any date at which the bond is callable. To distinguish between all the possible assumptions one could specify yield-to-first-call, yield-to-first par-call, yield-to-November 15, 1998, call, and so on. In any case, the assumption of a particular call scenario gives a specific set of cash flows. The yield-to-call of the bond is the one rate that, when used to discount these cash flows, gives the bond's price.

As an example, consider the 9 percent, 16-year bonds analyzed in this section when the 10-year par yield is 5.93 percent and the price is 111.10. Assuming that the bond will be called in three years, its cash flows are $4.50 every six months for the next three years and the call price of 100 in three years.[65] The yield-to-call, y_c, therefore, would be defined by the following equation:

$$
111.10 = 4.50 \left[\frac{1}{1+\frac{y_c}{2}} + \frac{1}{\left(1+\frac{y_c}{2}\right)^2} + \ldots + \frac{1}{\left(1+\frac{y_c}{2}\right)^6} \right] + \frac{100}{\left(1+\frac{y_c}{2}\right)^6}
$$

Solving for y gives a yield-to-call of approximately 4.97 percent.

Some market participants believe that bonds can be priced on a yield-to-call basis when rates are low and on a yield-to-maturity basis when rates are high. In some sense they are right. When rates are extremely low and the callable bond behaves like the 3-year noncallable, the yield-to-call of callable bonds is as useful a concept as yield-to-maturity is in the context of noncallables. Similarly, when rates are extremely high and the callable bond behaves like the 16-year noncallable, the yield-to-maturity of a callable bond is as useful as in the noncallable case. But in the intermediate cases, that is, when the option value has to be determined, both the yield-to-call and yield-to-maturity are misleading.

First, price the callable bond on a yield-to-maturity basis when rates are moderately high. Since rates are relatively high, assume the bond will be outstanding until maturity. Then, under this assumption, discount the bond's cash flows using the 16-year yield (or, more accurately, the appropriate spot rates). Note that this procedure will produce the price-yield curve of the 16-year noncallable bond in Figure 17.1. But this curve is always above the price of the callable bond! So, pricing a callable bond on a yield-to-maturity basis will always overestimate the price of the callable bond. The intuition here is simply that the issuer has an option that it will use to its advantage. Assuming any fixed strategy on the part of the issuer, that is, any non-optimal strategy, will result in an overestimate of the value of bonds to holders.

Second, price the callable bond on a yield-to-call basis when rates are moderately low. This means assuming that the bond will be called in three years and discounting its cash flows by a 3-year rate. But this procedure gives the three-year curve in Figure 17.1, which always exceeds the price of the callable bond. So, pricing a callable bond on a yield-to-call basis will always overestimate the price of the callable bond. The intuition is the same as before. Since the issuer has the option, assuming non-optimal behavior overestimates the value to holders.

Since the assumptions behind yield-to-maturity and yield-to-call pricing are

[65]If the call price were 102 instead of 100 then the assumed principal flow in three years would be 102.

the extremes, some market participants believe that the resulting prices will bracket the true callable bond price. As the previous analysis shows, however, this is not the case. Both prices will exceed the price of the callable bond. Once again, there are no short cuts to substitute for building a term-structure model and pricing by arbitrage.

Figure 17.2 graphs the duration-yield curves of the two reference bonds and the callable bonds. The durations were calculated numerically, along the lines described in Part Three.

The 3-year duration-yield curve is below that of the 16-year because the former is a shorter bond. The 16-year duration-yield curve is steeper because longer bonds are generally more convex than shorter bonds. (See Chapter 12.)

When rates are very high the option to call the bond is worth very little and the callable bond behaves like the 16-year noncallable bond. Hence, as rates increase, the duration of the callable bond approaches the duration of the 16-year noncallable bond. However, since the callable bond may be called and, in that case, turn out to be a relatively short-term bond, the duration of the callable bond will be below that of the 16-year bond.

As rates fall, the callable bond will eventually behave like the 3-year reference bond. Since the callable bond may not be called and, in that case, turn out to be

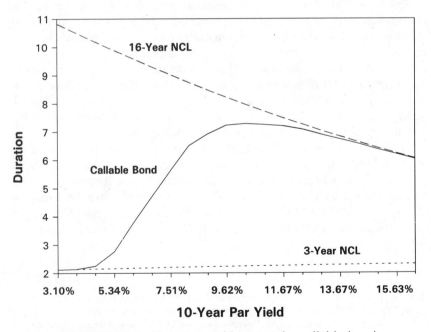

FIGURE 17.2   Duration-yield curve of a callable bond.

a relatively long-term bond, the duration of the callable bond will be above that of the 3-year bond.

Figure 17.2 shows that, as rates increase, the price sensitivity of the callable bond changes from resembling that of a short-term bond to resembling that of a long-term bond. This change requires that price sensitivity increase as rates increase. But that is exactly the definition of negative convexity. Also, this is the intuition behind the region of negative convexity apparent in Figure 17.1.

SINKING FUND BASICS

While not very widely understood or studied, sinking fund provisions appear in a large fraction of corporate bonds, particularly those of longer term. In January 1987, Eaton Corp. sold $100 million of 8.5 percent debenture due January 15, 2017. The bonds carried a sinking fund provision requiring the company to redeem $5 million in principal on or before every January 15 from January 15, 1998, to January 15, 2016.[66] So, unlike a nonsinking fund bond, the scheduled principal payments of a sinking fund bond are spread out over many years. As will be described in this section, however, the actual principal payments of the bond may be quite different.

Sinking fund provisions allow the issuer two methods of retiring the required principal amount. First, the issuer can purchase the required amount in the open market and deliver the bonds to the trustee for the issue. Second, the issuer can call the required amount at par. Since this almost always implies a call of only part of an issue, the particular bonds to be called are selected randomly. The second method of acquiring bonds reveals that while sinking fund provisions are worded as a requirement of the issuer, they actually confer a valuable series of interest rate call options. If rates are high at the time of a sinking fund requirement, so that the value of the outstanding bonds is low, the company will choose to satisfy its sinking fund requirement by market purchases. If, on the other hand, rates are low at the time of a sinking fund requirement, so that the value of the outstanding bonds is high, the company will choose to satisfy its requirement by par calls. Eaton Corp., for example, has 19 European options,[67] each to buy $5,000,000 principal amount of its bonds. The options mature on January 15, 1998, January 15, 1999, and so on, through January 15, 2016.

---

[66]Sinking funds got their name from provisions requiring that the company set aside funds for the eventual retirement of principal. After some abuses with respect to the safekeeping of these funds, however, these original sinking fund provisions were replaced by the kind described in the text. Almost all currently outstanding sinking fund bonds require periodic redemption of debentures.
[67]A European option is one that cannot be exercised before maturity.

To illustrate the pricing of a sinking fund provision, consider the following simple example: $30 million face value of a 7 percent, 3-year bond with the obligation to sink $10 million after one year and $10 million after two years. The risk-neutral interest rate process and the price process for a 7 percent noncallable, nonsinking fund bond are as set earlier in this chapter and repeated here for easy reference:

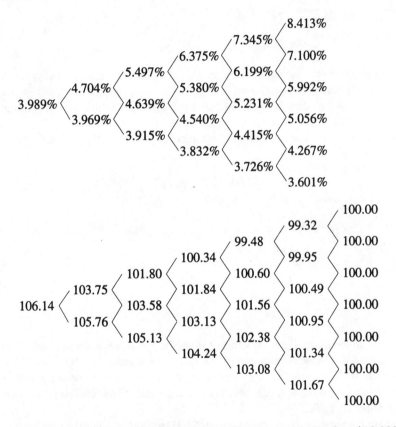

The key insight is that the issuer has one European option to buy $10,000,000 of the otherwise equivalent nonsinking fund bond at par on date 2 and another European option to buy $10,000,000 at par on date 4. To value the one-year option, construct the following tree:

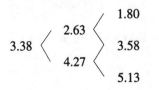

On date 2, the expiration date of the option, the option is worth its immediate exercise value. In state 2, for example, the option is worth $101.80 - 100 = 1.80$. On date 1, the option is worth its discounted expected value using the risk-neutral interest rate process. In state 1, for example, this value is

$$\frac{.5 \times 1.80 + .5 \times 3.58}{1 + \dfrac{.04704}{2}} = 2.63$$

Notice that, unlike the valuation of a standard call option, there is no need to check the value of immediate exercise on date 1: Since this option is European, it can only be exercised on date 2. Proceeding in this fashion shows that the value of the one-year European option today is 3.38.

The value of the two-year European option is valued similarly, giving the price tree below:

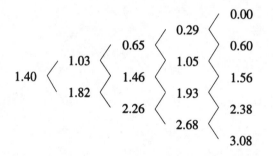

On date 4, the maturity date, the value of immediate exercise is determined. Note that at state 4 this value is zero because the value of the underlying bond, at 99.32, is less than the call price. For all other dates, calculate the value of the option at each state from discounted, risk-neutral expected values. The result is a two-year option value of 1.40.

The option values just computed are per $100 face value. Since they each cover $10,000,000 face value, the one- and two-year options are worth $338,190 and $139,960, respectively. Since $30 million of the underlying security is worth

$$\$30,000,000 \times 106.1362\% = \$31,840,860$$

the sinking fund bond value, equal to the value of the underlying security minus the value of the embedded options, is equal to

$31,840,860 - $338,190 - $139,960 = $31,362,710$

or, per $100 face value, $100 x $31,362,710/$30,000,000 = $104.54.

Another way to get this value from the value of the underlying security and the two options is to notice that each option gives the right to call 1/3 of the outstanding issue. Each of the options, therefore, can be thought of as the right to call 1/3 of a bond, worth 1/3 x 3.38 and 1/3 x 1.40 for the one- and two-year options respectively. Viewed this way, the value of each sinking fund bond is

$$106.14 - \frac{1}{3} \times 338 - \frac{1}{3} \times 1.40 = 104.54 ^{68}$$

In either case, the sinking fund provision lowers the value of an otherwise identical nonsinking fund bond from 106.14 to 104.54, or by 1.60. Thus all else equal, sinking fund provisions lower the value of corporate bonds. Therefore, thinking about sinking fund bonds only as an issuer requirement is somewhat misleading.

The pricing procedure just carried out can easily be repeated for a 4 percent instead of a 7 percent bond. The sinking fund provision in this case turns out to lower the value of the bond by less than .01. While in the previous case the sinking fund provision is worth 1.60, here it is nearly worthless. The explanation for this difference is simple. When the coupon is high relative to the level of interest rates, the underlying bond price is high and options to call at par are relatively valuable. When the coupon is low, however, the underlying bond price is low, and options to call at par are not very valuable.

Having pointed out that sinking fund provisions grant valuable options to the issuer, it should be pointed out that there is a circumstance in which sinking funds make the bonds more valuable to investors and represent a burden for the issuer. This circumstance is when the bonds are *accumulated*, that is, cornered by an investor or syndicate of investors.

Say that interest rates are relatively high and that the sinking fund bonds are

---

[68]This expression reveals that the pricing methodology assumes that investors are risk-neutral with respect to lottery risk. Even though 1/3 of the outstanding bonds will be called through the sinking fund, some investors will have more than 1/3 of their bonds called and others less. Despite this risk, the pricing model of the text indicates that they value sinking fund bonds using the true probability of 1/3 for pricing purposes. The explanation for this is that lottery risk is diversifiable. Holding a large portfolio of sinking fund bonds, for example, reduces the probability that an unexpectedly large or small fraction of an investor's bonds will be called through the sinking fund option. As in the capital asset pricing model, risk that disappears in a diversified portfolio is not priced because all investors hold diversified portfolios.

selling at a discount. The accumulator decides to buy all of the outstanding bonds. At the next sinking fund date the issuer will attempt to meet its sinking fund requirement through market purchases because prices are below 100. But, no one comes forward to sell. Eventually, the corporate treasurer gets a call from the accumulator offering to sell the bonds for par. Even though the bonds are worth less, in a present-value sense, the treasurer must agree. Failing to meet a sinking fund payment results in a default, like other breaches of the bond's indenture provisions. The accumulator cannot, of course, ask for more than par because the issuer can always call the required amount at par.

Valuing an accumulated sinking fund bond issue is simple. Consider the example presented above. If accumulated from the start, the bonds will be retired at par on each sinking fund date. If rates are high the accumulator will refuse to sell and the issuer will be forced to pay par. On the other hand, if rates are low, the issuer will choose to call the bonds at par. So the cash flows of the 7 percent accumulated sinking fund bond issue will be as follows:

Date 1: 7%/2 x $30,000,000 = $1,050,000
Date 2: 7%/2 x $30,000,000 + $10,000,000 = $11,050,000
Date 3: 7%/2 x $20,000,000 = $700,000
Date 4: 7%/2 x $20,000,000 + $10,000,000 = $10,700,000
Date 5: 7%/2 x $10,000,000 = $350,000
Date 6: 7%/2 x $10,000,000 + $10,000,000 = $10,350,000

Since $30,000,000 of bonds are outstanding between date 0 and date 2, the interest payments on dates 1 and 2 are calculated for all $30,000,000. On date 2, $10,000,000 worth of bonds are redeemed or bought at par. Therefore, the interest payments on dates 3 and 4 are based on $20,000,000 principal amount, and so forth. The resulting cash flows are fixed and, therefore, can be valued by discounting at the current discount factors. From the smoothed term structure of Chapter 4, these are

d(.5)   =.980445
d(1)   =.959640
d(1.5) =.937743
d(2)   =.914912
d(2.5) =.891302
d(3)   =.867073

so the value of the accumulated issue is

.980445 x $1,050,000 + .959640 x $11,050,000 +
.937743 x $700,000 + .914912 x $10,700,000 +
.891302 x $350,000 + .867073 x $10,350,000 = $31,365,629

or $100 x $31,365,629/$30,000,000 = $104.55 per $100 face value. Note that this is only slightly above the value of the nonaccumulated, or *competitively-held*, value of 104.54.

The reason that accumulation is worth only 104.55 − 104.54 = .01 is that the 7 percent bonds pay an above-market coupon and, as such, are likely to be called to meet sinking fund requirements. These calls would take place whether the issue were accumulated or not. In this case, therefore, accumulation has value only in the relatively unlikely event that the bonds become worth less than par and the issuer is forced to pay par to meet its sinking fund requirement.[69] Accumulation is worth quite a bit, however, for the 4 percent bonds. Computing the value of an accumulated holding in this case shows that the accumulated value is 98.91, or 98.91 − 97.81 = 1.10 above the competitively-held price. This large difference is due to the fact that the 4 percent bond is a discount issue for which the issuer will be forced to pay par.

Issuers can defend themselves against accumulation by strategically repurchasing their own bonds, particularly when bond prices are low.[70]

THE PARTIAL CALL

It was mentioned in the first section of this chapter that call options usually grant the issuer the option to call a bond in whole or in part. From the analysis of optimal exercise policy in that section, however, it seems that it is never optimal to call a bond in part. If it is worth retiring $1 face value of a premium bond, it is worth retiring $100,000,000 of bonds. It may be, of course, that for some reason a corporation cannot obtain financing to call all of its outstanding debt and must settle for calling part of it. But, as this section shows, when a sinking fund and a standard call option are both included in a bond issue, there are situations in which it is, in fact, optimal to call only part of an issue. This is of more than theoretical interest. Almost all sinking fund bond issues do contain standard call options as well.

Consider $30,000,000 face value of a 6 percent, 3-year sinking fund bond issue

---

[69]The accumulator would, presumably, hedge his interest rate exposure. Doing so ensures that when bond prices fall he doesn't lose money from the general fall of bond prices, but does make money from the additional value of his accumulated position.

[70]For further discussion of this point, see Kalotay and Tuckman (1992).

callable at any time until maturity. The call prices are 103 over the next year, 102 over the following year, and 101 over the final year. How much of the issue, if any, should the issuer call today? The following trees provide the starting point of the analysis: the six-month rate tree and the value of the otherwise identical noncallable, nonsinking fund bond.

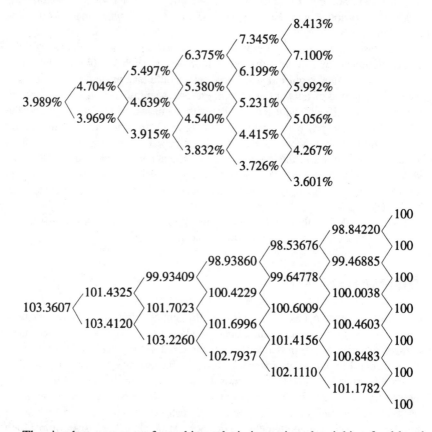

The simplest way to perform this analysis is to view the sinking fund bond issue as three separate issues. The first $10,000,000 will be retired in one year, the second in two years, and the third in three years. Each piece has a different total option value associated with it. The one-year piece may be called at 103 over the first year and may then be called at par through the sinking fund. The two-year piece may be called at 103 over the first year, at 102 over the second year, and then at par through the sinking fund. Finally, the three-year piece can be called at 103, then 102, then 101, and, at maturity, at par. The trees to follow calculate the total option value on each of the three pieces, beginning with the one-year piece. For ease of reference, the standard call price schedule is recorded above each tree.

```
103          103          102
                                   0
                      0.831611  <
     1.592181<                  > 1.702341
                      2.416264  <
                                   3.226008
```

At the end of the year the one-year piece can be called through the sinking fund at par. Therefore, the option value is the value of immediately exercising that option. There is no need to consider the standard call option on this date because its call price of 102 exceeds the sinking fund call price of 100. Put another way, the issuer will never call this $10,000,000 piece through the standard call option because it can call it through the sinking fund provision for less.

On date 1, the total value of the option on the one-year piece is determined as the maximum of the value of holding and of exercising immediately. The value of holding in state 0, for example, is

$$\frac{.5 \times 1.70 + .5 \times 3.23}{1 + \frac{.03969}{2}} = 2.42$$

The value of exercising immediately is $103.41 - 103 = .41$. Since the value of holding is larger, the standard call option is not exercised and the total option value is 2.42. Continuing in this fashion gives a total option value of 1.59 on the one-year piece today. Note that this is greater than the value of exercising the standard call immediately, $103.36 - 103 = .36$, so it is not optimal to call the one-year piece today.

The next tree gives the total option value on the two-year piece.

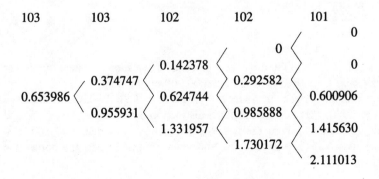

```
103        103        102        102        101
                                                    0
                                       0  <
                          0.142378  <        > 0
              0.374747  <            > 0.292582  <
  0.653986  <            > 0.624744  <            > 0.600906
              0.955931  <            > 0.985888  <
                          1.331957  <            > 1.415630
                                       1.730172  <
                                                    2.111013
```

On date 4 the issuer can use the sinking fund option so the option value equals the value of immediately exercising that option. Then, on date 3, the standard option at 102 is available. So, the option value on date 3 is the maximum of the value of holding the option and the value of exercising immediately at 102. Continuing backwards in this fashion, remembering to adjust the call price to 103 on dates 0 and 1, gives a total option value of .65. Like the option value on the one-year piece, this exceeds the value of exercising immediately of .36.

The next tree gives the value of the option on the three-year piece.

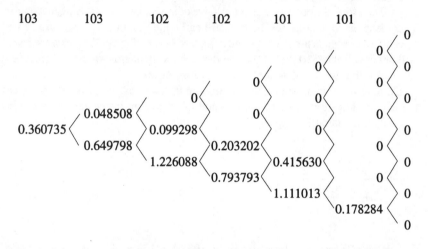

103   103   102   102   101   101

Notice that at maturity, on date 6, when the bond must be worth par, the option value is zero. There is no value in calling a bond worth par at a price greater than or equal to par. Stepping back through time, the valuation proceeds as in the standard call case, revealing an option value today of .36. This equals the value of exercising immediately while the value of holding today is only

$$\frac{.5 \times .05 + .5 \times .65}{1 + \dfrac{.03989}{2}} = .34$$

Thus, it is optimal to call the three-year piece today. In summary then, the issuer should call only $10,000,000 of the $30,000,000 outstanding.

Operationally, the issuer instructs the trustee to call $10,000,000 of the issue and pays $10,300,000 to do so. Since the distinction between the one-, two-, and three-year pieces exists only for the purposes of valuation, the particular $10,000,000 of called bonds is chosen at random. But when the trustee gets the bonds, the issuer instructs him to apply that $10,000,000 to the payment due at maturity. It is in this last step that the issuer has indeed called the three-year piece.

To understand the intuition behind the optimality of the partial call, it is useful to have computed the relevant option values and optimal strategies for several other bonds. Table 17.2 reports these values and strategies for 3-year callable, sinking fund bonds with coupon rates of 5.5 percent, 6 percent, 6.5 percent, and 7.5 percent.

The table shows that as the coupon rate increases, more and more of the issue is called. Furthermore, the later pieces are called first. The fact that more of higher coupon issues are called is quite simple to explain. The advantage of calling a bond, from the issuer's perspective, is to stop making interest payments at above-market rates. The disadvantage is having to pay a premium to call the bond and having to sacrifice any future option value. When the coupon rate increases, the balance tends to tip toward the advantage of saving the issuer from making above-market interest payments.

Why are the longer-term pieces called first? When deciding to call the three-year piece, the issuer asks whether avoiding above-market interest payments over the next three years is worth paying the premium and sacrificing future option value. When deciding to call the one-year piece, the issuer asks whether avoiding above-market interest payments over the next year is worth paying the premium and sacrificing future option value. Clearly, the period over which above-market rates are paid favors the decision to call the three-year piece over the one-year piece.

The previous paragraph focused on avoiding the payment of above-market rates of interest. But there is another factor favoring the call of the longer pieces over the shorter pieces. Calling the three-year piece sacrifices the future value of the standard call option. But calling the one-year piece sacrifices a call at par through the sinking fund at the end of the year. Put another way, if the issuer waits one year to call the one-year piece, it can be called at par instead of at 103. Waiting one year

Table 17.2 Option Values and Optimal Call Policies for Several Callable, Sinking Fund Bonds

	Option Values and Optimal Call Policies					
	1-Year Piece		2-Year Piece		3-Year Piece	
Coupon	Value	Policy	Value	Policy	Value	Policy
5.5%	.9123	No Call	.3496	No Call	.0663	No Call
6%	1.5921	No Call	.6539	No Call	.3607	Call
6.5%	2.4791	No Call	1.7485	Call	1.7485	Call
7.5%	4.5240	Call	4.5240	Call	4.5240	Call

to call the three-year piece allows a call through the standard call option at 102 instead of 103. Clearly, this effect also favors the call of the longer pieces first.

The valuation technique of dividing the issue up into a number of different pieces is useful in understanding the interaction between sinking fund provisions and the standard call option. But this technique cannot be used very often in practice. Sinking fund provisions most often provide "double-up" options, allowing the issuer to call twice the required sinking fund amount at par. This option creates an interaction between pieces that prevents the use of the separation technique.[71]

CONCLUSION

The discussion has so far avoided the question of why issuers include call and sinking fund provisions in their debt. If the provisions are priced fairly, so that the offering price properly takes the total option value of the bonds into account, then there is no present-value advantage for a corporation to include these provisions. At the same time, however, the issuer must monitor market levels to determine optimal call policy, the optimal use of sinking fund provisions, and the best ways to discourage accumulators.

Call and sinking fund provisions were first introduced when interest rates were much less volatile than they are today. Thus, the interest rate option component of these provisions was not as important as other considerations. These include the flexibilities provided by the call option, previously discussed, and the plan for an orderly retirement of debt established by a sinking fund. But, over time, as interest rate volatility increased, the embedded interest rate options came to dominate the field.

If this analysis is correct, issuers will gradually phase out these embedded options. There is, in fact, some evidence that they have begun to do so. But there are other arguments for the continued inclusion of these options. These include tax motivations[72] and the denial of the assumption that the market accurately prices embedded options. Time will tell.

---

[71]Readers interested in pursuing this point should read Jamshidian and Russell (1990).
[72]See Boyce and Kalotay (1979).

Chapter 18
Mortgage-Backed Securities

A *mortgage* is a loan secured by property. Until the 1970s, banks made mortgage loans and held them until maturity, collecting principal and interest payments until the mortgages were paid off. This *primary market* was the only mortgage market. During the 1970s, however, investment banks began to *securitize* mortgages, particularly home mortgages. Individual mortgage loans were pooled together and then sold off, in pieces, to investors. The growth of this *secondary market* substantially changed the mortgage business. Banks which might otherwise restrict their mortgage lending, because of limited capital or because of asset allocation decisions, can continue to make mortgage loans secure in the knowledge that these loans can be quickly and efficiently sold. At the same time, investors have a new security through which to lend their surplus funds.

BASIC MORTGAGE MATH

The most typical mortgage structure is a fixed rate, *level payment* mortgage. Say that, to buy a home, an individual borrows from a bank $100,000 secured by that home.[73] And, to pay back the loan, the individual must pay the bank $898.83 every month for fifteen years. The name "level payment mortgage" comes from the feature that the monthly payment of the loan is the same every month. The interest rate on the mortgage is defined as the yield-to-maturity of the mortgage. In this example, the interest rate on the mortgage, r, is defined such that

[73]Note that a mortgage is a special case of a leveraged buyout in that the loan made to buy the asset is secured by that same asset.

$$898.83 \sum_{t=1}^{180} \frac{1}{\left(1+\dfrac{r}{12}\right)^t} = 100,000$$

Solving for r by trial and error or a calculator reveals that r = 7 percent.

The intuition behind this definition of the mortgage rate is as follows. If the term structure were flat at r, then the left-hand side of the above equation would equal the present value of the mortgage's cash flows. The mortgage is a fair loan only if the present value of these flows equals the original amount given by the bank to the borrower. In short, under the assumption of a flat term structure, the above equation can be thought of as a fair pricing condition. Mortgage pricing without the flat term-structure assumption will soon be examined.

While this description started with a mortgage payment and solved for the mortgage rate of interest, the payment can also be derived from the rate. This latter calculation is, in fact, much easier. Let X be the unknown monthly payment and let the mortgage rate be 7 percent. Then, the equation relating X to the rate is

$$X \sum_{t=1}^{180} \frac{1}{\left(1+\dfrac{.07}{12}\right)^t} = 100,000$$

Solving for X using the techniques in Chapter 3,

$$X = \frac{100,000\left(\dfrac{.07}{12}\right)}{1 - \dfrac{1}{\left(1+\dfrac{.07}{12}\right)^{180}}} = 898.83$$

The rate of the mortgage can be used to divide the monthly payment into its interest and principal components. These accounting quantities are particularly useful for tax purposes since interest payments are deductible from income while principal payments are not. The interest component of the monthly payment is taken to be r/12 times the amount outstanding over the past month, where r is the rate on the mortgage. The principal payment is what's left over, namely, the difference between the fixed monthly payment and the interest component. Continuing with this example, the interest component of the first monthly payment is

$$\frac{.07}{12} \times \$100,000 = \$583.33$$

and the principal component, therefore, is

$$\$898.83 - \$583.33 = \$315.50$$

After the first monthly payment, which like all payments includes a principal component, the principal balance declines from \$100,000 to \$100,000 − \$315.50 = \$99,684.50. This result, in turn, allows for the calculation of interest and principal in the second monthly payment. The interest component equals .07/12 times the amount outstanding over the second month, namely \$99,684.50:

$$\frac{.07}{12} \times \$99,684.50 = \$581.49$$

And the principal component equals

$$\$898.83 - \$581.49 = \$317.34$$

Continuing in this fashion produces an *amortization table,* selected entries of which are given in Table 18.1. Particularly noticeable is the feature that early payments

Table 18.1   Selected Entries from a Mortgage Amortization Table
(The 15-year mortgage has a rate of 7% and a monthly payment of \$898.83.)

Months Remaining	Beginning Balance	Interest Payment	Principal Payment
179	100,000	583.33	315.49
178	99,684.50	581.49	317.34
177	99,367.16	579.64	319.19
141	86,622.02	505.30	393.53
105	70,908.20	413.63	485.20
69	51,534.23	300.62	598.21
33	27,647.57	161.28	737.55
2	2,665.33	15.55	883.28
1	1,782.05	10.40	888.43
0	893.62	5.21	893.62

are mostly interest while later payments are mostly principal. This can be understood by remembering the phrase "interest lives off principal." Interest at any time is due only on the then-outstanding principal amount. So, as principal is paid off, the amount of interest necessarily declines.

If a homeowner wants to know his principal balance, he can always work through the amortization table, as previously described. But there is an instructive shortcut. The present value of the remaining payments, when discounted at the mortgage rate, equals the principal outstanding. This is another fair pricing condition, under the assumption that the term structure is flat and that the interest rates have not changed since the origination of the mortgage.

To illustrate this shortcut, say that the homeowner wants to know the principal balance after six years. Since at that time there would be (15 – 6) x 12 = 108 months remaining, the present value of the remaining payments using the original discount rate of 7 percent is

$$898.83 \sum_{t=1}^{108} \frac{1}{1 + \left(\frac{.07}{12}\right)^t} = 71,870.31$$

The principal outstanding after six years, therefore, is $71,870.31.

As explained in Chapter 3, to price a fixed income security each cash flow must be discounted by the discount factor appropriate to that cash flow's maturity. Therefore, the true fair pricing condition of a $100,000 mortgage paying X per month for T months is

$$X \sum_{t=1}^{T} d(t) = \$100,000$$

Though often neglected in most discussions of mortgages, it is most useful to think of this equation as the starting point for mortgage pricing. The lender uses the discount factors or, equivalently, the term structure of interest rates, to determine the fair mortgage payment. It then computes the one mortgage interest rate as another way to quote this mortgage payment. This discussion is perfectly analogous to that concerning the yield-to-maturity of a coupon bond in Chapter 3. Bonds are priced using the term structure of interest rates and then those prices are quoted in terms of yield.

The fair pricing condition just given holds only at the time of the mortgage's origination. Over time the discount factors will change and the present value of the mortgage's cash flows will change. Mathematically, the present value of the mortgage with N months remaining to maturity is

$$X \sum_{t=1}^{N} \tilde{d}(t)$$

The monthly payment, X, is the same in this equation as in the previous one. But the discount function $\tilde{d}(t)$ reflects the time value of money in the current economic environment.

The present value of the mortgage after its origination may be greater than, equal to, or less than the principal outstanding. If rates have risen since origination, the mortgage payment level set in the past reflects relatively low rates of interest. Alternatively, the mortgage has become a below-market loan and the value of the mortgage will be less than the principal outstanding. This is perfectly analogous to the case of a coupon bond issued at par that now sells at a discount because rates have risen. If, on the other hand, rates have fallen since the origination of the mortgage, the mortgage has become an above-market loan and the value of the mortgage will exceed the principal outstanding.

It is important to note the difference between the discussion of the previous paragraph and the discussion of the mortgage rate. The present value of the mortgage using the original mortgage rate always equals the principal outstanding because, after origination, the original mortgage rate has nothing to do with the value of the mortgage. Given the fixed monthly payment, only rates reflecting current market conditions can be used to value the mortgage.

THE PREPAYMENT OPTION IN THEORY

One very important feature of mortgages was not mentioned in the previous section. Homeowners have the right to *prepay* mortgages. This means that a homeowner can pay the bank the principal outstanding and be freed from the obligation of making any further payments. In the example of the previous section, the mortgage balance at the end of six years is $71,870.31. In this case then, the prepayment option allows the borrower to pay the bank $71,870.31 and be free of any future payment obligations.

The prepayment option is most valuable when mortgage rates have fallen. In that case, as discussed in the previous section, the value of the mortgage exceeds the principal outstanding. Put another way, the value of the mortgage's future cash flows exceeds the principal outstanding. Therefore, it may be worthwhile for a borrower to pay the bank the principal outstanding and not make those future cash flows.

After some thought it becomes apparent that the prepayment option is very much like a call option on a bond. In the bond context, the issuer is the borrower and it has an option to call the bond at some set of call prices. Said another way, the issuer has the option to pay the call price and not make any future interest or principal payments. Similarly, the homeowner/borrower has the option to pay the outstanding principal amount and not make any more mortgage payments. Thus, the prepayment option is a call option with call prices equal to the principal amount outstanding. The calculation of these call prices provides another use for the amortization tables described in the previous section.

When pricing the embedded options in corporate bonds, practitioners find it reasonable to assume that the issuing corporation will optimally exercise its options. As will be discussed in the next section, this is not the case with homeowners and their option to prepay. Nevertheless, the first step in understanding the behavior of mortgage-backed securities is to understand how they would behave under the unrealistic assumption of optimal prepayments. Using this as a benchmark, the next section will explain the behavior of mortgage-backed securities under more realistic assumptions.

To illustrate mortgage pricing under the assumption of optimal prepayments, consider a 3-year, prepayable, semiannual payment mortgage with a principal amount of $100,000 and a mortgage rate of 4.64 percent. The text will soon explain why this particular mortgage rate was chosen.

Before beginning the pricing process, begin with the following risk-neutral six-month rate tree derived from the original Salomon Brothers model.

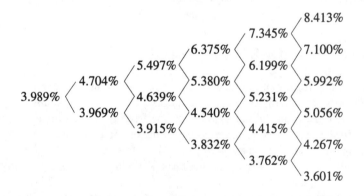

When pricing callable bonds, the first step was to compute the price tree for the underlying noncallable bond. Here, the first step in pricing a prepayable mortgage is to compute the price tree for the underlying nonprepayable mortgage. To compute this tree, compute that the semiannual mortgage payment is

$$\frac{100,000 \times \dfrac{.0464}{2}}{1 - \left(1 + \dfrac{.0464}{2}\right)^{-6}} = 18,045.86$$

Using this payment amount, one can construct the following tree for the price of the nonprepayable mortgage. The row above the tree gives the principal outstanding at each date after that date's payment has been made.

```
100000.00   84274.14   68183.45   51719.44   34873.48   17636.69   0.00
                                                                        0.00
                                                      17317.40
                                            34163.50           0.00
                                  50736.42           17427.19
                        67188.91           34452.08           0.00
              83638.37           51243.07           17520.93
100174.68            67930.47           34699.22           0.00
              84615.25           51677.45           17600.91
                        68566.70           34910.12           0.00
                                  52048.62           17668.89
                                            35089.92           0.00
                                                      17726.69
                                                                   0.00
```

As in the case of callable bonds, it is most convenient to use the ex-coupon mortgage prices, that is, the prices right after the mortgage payment on that date has been made. Hence, the value of the mortgage on the last date, right after the last mortgage payment, is zero.

The value of the mortgage at all other nodes of the tree is computed as follows. Let V^u and V^d be the possible values of the mortgage in the up and down states, respectively, and let r be the six-month rate at the node under consideration. Then, the value of the mortgage at that node is

$$\frac{.5V^u + .5V^d + 18,045.86}{1 + \dfrac{r}{2}}$$

In words, the value of the mortgage equals its risk-neutral expected value in six months plus the mortgage payment to be received in six months, all discounted at the current six-month rate. For example, the value of the mortgage on date 4, state 1 is

$$\frac{.5 \times 17,600.91 + .5 \times 17,668.89 + 18,045.86}{1 + \dfrac{.04415}{2}} = 34,910.12$$

The value of the nonprepayable mortgage today turns out to be $100,175. It is no accident that this value exceeds the $100,000 actually borrowed. When the homeowner took out his mortgage, he received not only $100,000, but also a prepayment option. Because this option has value, the homeowner had to assume obligations worth $100,175 in exchange for the $100,000 he took home in cash and the prepayment option.

Equipped with this price tree, one can compute the value of the prepayment option. As in the case of a bond option, the value of the option at each node is the maximum of the value of holding the option and the value of exercising immediately. The value of holding the option is determined in the same way as in the bond case. The value of immediate exercise, however, is somewhat different. The exercise price of the prepayment option at each date is the principal amount outstanding, given above in the price tree of the nonprepayable mortgage.

The following tree gives prepayment option prices at each node:

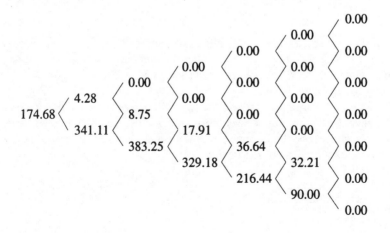

Since the pricing process is very similar to that in the callable bond context analyzed in Chapter 17, two examples of the creation of this tree should suffice.

Date 3, state 1: At this node the value of the mortgage is less than the principal outstanding, so the homeowner will certainly not prepay. More formally, the value of immediate exercise is zero. The value of the option, therefore, is just the value of holding the option over the next period:

$$17.91 = \frac{5 \times 0 + .5 \times 36.64}{1 + \dfrac{.0454}{2}}$$

Date 1, state 0: The value of immediate exercise is

Max (84,615.25 – 84,274.14,0) = 341.11

The value of holding the option is

$$\frac{.5 \times 8.75 + .5 \times 383.25}{1 + \dfrac{.03969}{2}} = 192.19$$

The optimal strategy is clearly to exercise immediately and prepay the mortgage. The result of this choice is a prepayment option worth 341.11 at this node.[74]

The value of the option today is about 175, as expected. The total value of the homeowner's new liability, 100,000, must equal the present value of future mortgage payments, 100,175, minus 175 in option value. In fact, subtracting the value of the option from the nonprepayable mortgage at each node gives the entire pricing tree for the prepayable mortgage:

---

[74]It turns out, in this simple example, that in every node for which the prepayment option is in-the-money, prepayment is optimal. This need not be the case, however. As in the call option case, when the value of immediate exercise is relatively small, one may forgo prepaying immediately to preserve a relatively high option value.

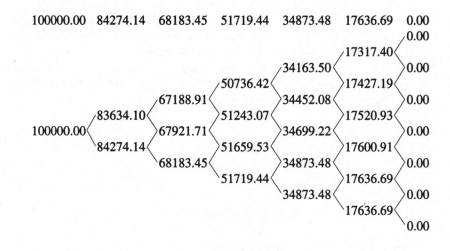

100000.00   84274.14   68183.45   51719.44   34873.48   17636.69   0.00

THE PREPAYMENT OPTION IN PRACTICE

If homeowners exercised their prepayment options with the same efficiency that characterizes corporate exercise of embedded options, the mortgage market would not be the analytically demanding market that it is. The fact is that many homeowners do not prepay when analysis along the lines of the previous section indicates that they should. Furthermore, some homeowners prepay when the analysis indicates that they shouldn't.

One reason that homeowner behavior does not match the behavior predicted in the previous section is that prepayments sometimes occur for reasons unrelated to interest rate movements. Examples include defaults, disasters, and sales of homes when mortgages are not *assumable*.

Defaults generate prepayments because mortgages, like many other loans and debt securities, become payable in full when the borrower fails to make a payment. If the borrower cannot pay off the outstanding principal amount, the home can be sold to raise some, if not all, of the necessary funds.

Disasters generate prepayments because, again, like other debt securities, mortgages are payable in full if the collateral is damaged or destroyed by fire, flood, earthquake, and so on. Without insurance, of course, it may be hard to recover the amount due.

The final example of noninterest-rate-related prepayments is the sale of a home without assumption of the mortgage. Mortgages may be assumable or *due-on-sale*. If a mortgage is assumable, someone who buys a home may take over the mortgage at the same rate of interest. If a mortgage is due-on-sale, the outstanding balance must be paid at the time the home is sold. Since people often decide to move without regard to the interest rate, the prepayments resulting from the working of due-on-sale clauses will not be very much related to the behavior of interest rates.

While mortgages with due-on-sale clauses can explain some prepayments that are not related to the level of interest rates, it is important to realize that prepayments of assumable mortgages will depend on the level of interest rates. If rates are very high relative to the mortgage rate on the home, the buyer and seller will find it worthwhile to have the buyer assume the mortgage. In fact, one would imagine that a home with a below-market, assumable mortgage would be worth more than an identical home without such a mortgage. On the other hand, if rates are very low relative to the existing mortgage rate, the buyer and seller will not find it worthwhile to assume the mortgage and the mortgage will be prepaid. In this case, however, one has to ask why the homeowner didn't prepay the mortgage earlier, when rates first reached their low levels. This brings the discussion to homeowners' *refinancing* decisions.

When interest rates are low relative to a homeowner's mortgage rate, it may pay to refinance the mortgage. This means that the homeowner asks his bank, or another bank, for a new mortgage loan sufficient to pay off the outstanding principal on the old mortgage. This is the most common interest-rate-related prepayment because many homeowners do not have the cash or do not want to liquidate enough financial assets to pay off the old mortgage without new borrowing. Nevertheless, the analysis of the refinancing decision is the same as the analysis of prepaying a mortgage discussed in the previous section. Whether the prepayment will be financed by borrowing through a new mortgage or by available cash does not, in itself, affect the prepayment decision. Said another way, if the new mortgage is a fair loan, it has zero value at the time of its origination. Therefore, the refinancing decision reduces to the decision of whether prepayment is optimal.

In practice, a homeowner would have to add one consideration to the analysis of the previous section before using it to make a refinancing decision. Banks charge fees when making mortgage loans; they are often called *points* since the fee usually takes the form of a number of percentage points on the amount borrowed. But this complication raises no conceptual difficulties. The points charged by the bank can simply be added to the outstanding principal to get the true cost of exercising the prepayment option. Using these total costs instead of the outstanding principal balance alone will lead to an optimal prepayment decision in the presence of points.

Despite the fact that optimal prepayment and refinancing decisions can be made using the analysis of the previous section, the fact is that homeowner refinancings are not accurately described by that analysis. So, not only are there prepayments that are unrelated to interest rate movements, but also prepayments motivated by refinancing considerations cannot be described by a term-structure model and the assumption of optimal exercise.

Just because refinancing behavior doesn't match that implied by a term-structure model does not mean that homeowners are not optimizing from their own perspective. Given their knowledge of where interest rates are, their financial sophistication, and their costs of becoming better informed about the refinancing decision, it may be optimal for many homeowners to delay refinancing until the gains to refinancing are extremely large. Needless to say, however, to the extent this consideration affects prepayments, accurate models of prepayments will be difficult and, consequently, so will the pricing of mortgage-backed securities.

There are two well-known empirical facts about prepayments which support the view that homeowner refinancings have a life of their own. First, refinancing activity lags interest rate moves. If rates fall, for example, it takes a while for refinancing activity to pick up. Some of this is due to the time it takes for banks to process new mortgage loans. But some of this is no doubt also due to the time it takes homeowners to learn about refinancing possibilities and to come to their decisions. Second, mortgage pools that have been heavily refinanced in the past respond more slowly to new drops in rates. This phenomenon has been called the *burn-out* effect. The simplest explanation behind this effect is that homeowners with the least cost of becoming informed about the refinancing decision tend to refinance at the first opportunity for profitably doing so. Those left in the pool did not deem it worthwhile the first time rates fell, so they are unlikely to prepay the second time unless rates fall much further.

In summary, because some prepayments do not depend on the level of interest rates and because other prepayments do not respond "optimally" to interest rate movements, the assumption of optimality used in the previous section will not do a good job of pricing mortgage-backed securities. The next section examines pricing techniques used specifically in the mortgage context.

MORTGAGE PRICING MODELS

The earliest approaches to pricing mortgage-backed securities can be called *static cash-flow models*. These models assumed that prepayments could be predicted as a function of their age. Typical assumptions are that the prepayment rate increases gradually as mortgages age, then levels off at some constant prepayment rate. Assumptions of this sort are motivated by empirical regularities, relating the average length of time a homeowner has been in a house to the likelihood of his prepaying the mortgage. (The Public Securities Association, or PSA, model is one such functional relationship.)

Another assumption in the same class is based on data provided by the Federal Housing Authority. This model uses past behavior of prepayments, as a function of age, to predict future prepayments. If, for example, the historical data show that

10-year-old mortgages prepay at .4 percent per month, it is assumed that newly issued mortgages will, 10 years from now, prepay at .4 percent per month.

One reason some people like these models is that they allow for a yield calculation. Since the assumed cash flows depend only on the age of the mortgage, one can write down all of the cash flows that a mortgage pool will generate over time. And, given a set of cash flows and a market price, one can easily compute a yield-to-maturity for the mortgage.

Despite this small advantage, there are two severe problems with this approach. First, the model is really not a pricing model at all. Yes, given a market price one can compute a yield. But a pricing model must provide a way to determine price. And static cash-flow models cannot be used to determine price because they do not specify what yield is appropriate for a mortgage. A 30-year bond yield, for example, is clearly not appropriate because the scheduled cash-flow pattern of a mortgage differs from that of a bond and, more importantly, because the cash flows of a mortgage are not really fixed. The fact that prepayments will change as interest rates change will affect the pricing of mortgages but is not captured at all in static cash-flow models.

The second, although not unrelated problem with static cash-flow models is that they provide misleading price-yield and duration-yield curves. Since these models assume that cash flows are fixed, the interest rate behavior of mortgages under this assumption will be qualitatively like the interest rate behavior of bonds with fixed cash flows. But, as indicated in previous sections and as to be explored more fully later, the price-yield and duration-yield curves of mortgages are more likely to resemble those of callable bonds. The prepayment option substantially alters the qualitative shape of the price-yield and duration-yield curves because mortgage cash flows, like those of callable bonds, are not fixed but, instead, depend on how interest rates evolve over time.

Another set of models may be called *implied models*. Recognizing the difficulties encountered by static cash-flow models, implied models have a more modest objective. They do not seek to price mortgage-backed securities but simply to estimate their durations. Making the assumption that the duration of a mortgage changes slowly over time, they use recent data on price sensitivity to estimate durations numerically. The technical procedure is the same as described in Part Three. Given two prices and two interest rates, one can compute the percentage change in price for a unit change in the interest rate and use the result as an estimate of duration. The hope is that averaging daily duration estimates over the very recent past may provide a useful estimate of the mortgage's duration. A variation on this procedure is to look for historical periods closely matching the current environment and to use price and rate data from that time to estimate duration.

The implied models have several drawbacks as well. First, they are not pricing models. It should be mentioned, however, that some investors might not find this much of a drawback. If sophisticated mortgage pricing models are beyond their reach anyway, it may be perfectly reasonable to assume that the market price is as it should be and use implied models for hedging and asset-liability management. The second drawback is that mortgage durations may change rapidly over time. As has been discussed and as will be shown more fully, mortgages share many of their interest rate properties with callable bonds. Recall the duration-yield curve of a callable bond (Figure 11.1). When the bond is likely but far from certain to be called, its duration can move very quickly from one resembling the duration of the underlying, noncallable bond to one resembling the duration of a noncallable bond with maturity equal to the call date, or *vice versa*. Similarly, mortgage durations may move quite quickly when small rate moves make prepayments much more or much less likely. Therefore, in the interest rate regions where one most needs accurate durations, recent implied durations may prove a misleading guide.

The third set of pricing models, called *prepayment-function models,* is the most popular among sophisticated practitioners. These models use historical data and any insights the researchers might have to develop predictions about prepayments as a function of several variables. These variables might include the difference between the existing mortgage's rate and currently issued mortgage rates, the age of the mortgage, the steepness of the term structure, the season, and so on. Given the burn-out effect described in the previous section, other popular explanatory variables include *lagged,* or past values of interest rates. Given a prepayment-function model, arbitrage-free techniques can be used to price mortgages. Since this step can be quite complicated, some space will be devoted to this process.

One might think that a prepayment function could be combined with the pricing tree technology developed in Part Two to price mortgage-backed securities. Instead of taking the cash flow on future dates to be the coupon or the fixed mortgage payment, one could use a prepayment function to get the possible cash flows in the two future possible states. Then, pricing would proceed as before. Unfortunately, due to the desire to include lagged interest rates in prepayment functions, the pricing tree technology is not easily adapted to mortgages.

The tree technology assumes that the value of a security at any node only depends on the interest rate level at that node and, by implication, on future possible interest rates. This assumption excludes the possibility that a security's price depends on past interest rates. Say, for example, one is valuing a security at date 5, state 2, in a binomial tree, a node that can be reached by path A, two "up" moves and three "down" moves, or by path B, three "down" moves and two "up" moves. In all previous problems in this book the historical path did not matter because the security's price depended only on current and future interest rate values. But, because of the burn-out effect, the value of a mortgage does depend on the historical path. Mortgage pools are likely to exhibit relatively low prepayments on date 5 if interest rates followed path B, because path B passed through relatively low rates before date 5. On the other hand, if rates follow path A and experience low rates for the first time on date 5, mortgage pools are likely to exhibit relatively large prepayments.

The solution to this problem has been to use *Monte Carlo simulation* techniques in combination with a prepayment function. This procedure, to be discussed more fully shortly, can be summarized as follows.

Step 1: Starting with today's short-term rate, randomly select a path followed by future short-term rates. Example:

Date 0: 4%
Date 1: 4.25%
Date 2: 3.75%
Date 3: 3.5%
Date 4: 3%

Step 2: Moving forward along the path, from today until all principal has been prepaid, use the prepayment function to generate a mortgage's cash flow. Example:

Date 1: $10
Date 2: $12
Date 3: $15
Date 4: $80

Step 3: Find the value of the security assuming that the short-term rate does follow the selected interest rate path. More specifically, starting at the date of the last cash flow, discount all cash flows back to the present using the short-term rates along the selected path. As with price trees, values assume that the payment on each particular date has just been made. Example:

Date 4: $0
Date 3: $80/(1 + .035/2) = $78.62
Date 2: ($78.62 + $15)/(1 + .0375/2)
Date 1: ($91.90 + $12)/(1 + .0425/2)
Date 0: ($101.74 + $10)/(1 + .04/2)

Step 4: Repeat Steps 1 through 3 many times and calculate the average value of the security across these paths. Use that average as the security's true value.

Step 1 of the Monte Carlo simulation requires the generation of an interest rate path. These paths can be thought of as particular paths along an interest rate tree of the kind studied in this book. Valuing a security along many paths and averaging the result, therefore, is in many ways equivalent to valuation using interest rate trees.

As with interest rate trees, the generated paths should exhibit certain properties. Most importantly, if Treasury bonds are priced using the Monte Carlo technique, the result should be the market prices of those bonds. This is equivalent to the arbitrage-free condition that an interest rate tree must correctly price Treasury bonds of all maturities. Put another way, just as the interest rate tree had to reflect the risk-neutral interest rate process, so do the generated paths. If the generated paths reflect the true interest rate process, rather than the risk-neutral process, then the technique just described would be equivalent to discounting expected values. From Part Two, that pricing procedure is known to be incorrect.

The requirement that Treasury bonds be priced correctly suffices for the science of Monte Carlo simulation. But, as in the case of trees, the art consists of selecting "good" interest rate paths. The criteria for "goodness" are the same as described in Part Two.

The advantage of Monte Carlo simulations over the tree technology appears in Step 2. Since the paths are generated from today forward, a prepayment function that depends on past rates can be used to obtain cash flows. In the example, the cash flow of $15 on date 3 might have depended on any or all of the short-term rates on dates 0, 1, and 2. By the way, while the short-term rate on date 4 is never used for discounting, because the last cash flow is on date 4, this rate may very well have been used to compute that the cash flow on date 4 is $80. (This might be the case, for example, if the 3 percent rate on date 4 triggered a prepayment of all outstanding principal.)

It is important to point out that the choice of moving forward in time to generate cash flows is not better than the tree methodology for all problems. Recall that the value of an optimally exercised option at a given node is the maximum of the value of holding and the value of exercising immediately. Furthermore, the value of holding equals the risk-neutral expected value of holding the option one more period. But, in the Monte Carlo technique, this information is not available. One knows the value of the security along one particular path but not the possible values of the security next period. Hence, Monte Carlo techniques cannot be used to value optimally exercised American style options.[75] Given that homeowners don't optimally exercise their prepayment options anyway, this sacrifice is worthwhile in the mortgage context in exchange for the ability to capture the burn-out effect.

Just as the tree methodology can be used to calculate duration and convexity as well as price, so can the Monte Carlo method. In the latter case, each path may

---

[75]An American option can be exercised at any time before maturity.

be perturbed up or down by a small amount. Then, the pricing procedure is repeated to obtain new prices which, in turn, are used to calculate numerical durations and convexities. Alternatively, the original term structure can be shifted, resulting in a new set of paths, cash flows, and prices. Choosing between these approaches involves the same considerations as in the case of trees, discussed in Part Three.

As with any model and any technique, market prices will not always match model prices. There are two possible explanations for this. One, the model doesn't adequately capture the market's pricing mechanism. Two, the market price is too high or too low. Any trader or value investor has to decide between these two interpretations on his own.

Given one has concluded some market prices are too high or too low, there is a desire to quantify the resulting richness or cheapness. The simplest measure is the difference between the model price and the market price. Another very popular measure is a security's *option-adjusted spread* (OAS), motivated by the desire to express richness or cheapness in terms of an interest rate instead of a price.

An OAS is computed as follows. Say that, following the Monte Carlo pricing procedure previously, the model price of the security is $115 while the market price is $110. A certain number of basis points, say 10, is added to all of the short-term rates along each and every path. Discounting the cash flows by those new rates gives a lower model price, perhaps of $112. This still exceeds the market price, so the spread between the original discount rates and the new ones is increased to 15. Say that this spread gives a model price matching the market price of $110. The security is then said to have an OAS of 15 basis points. Adjusting price for all of the security's embedded options, or more generally, interest rate dependent cash flows, the security seems to earn 15 basis points too much. Said differently, if the model turns out to be right, an investor earns 15 basis points more by investing in the underpriced security than by investing in a fairly priced security with similar risk characteristics.

It is important to remember that OAS can be used as a measure of mispricing only after the interest rate paths have been made arbitrage-free. It is incorrect to use OAS as the means by which to adjust for interest rate risk. The proper risk adjustment studied in Part Two is quite complicated, requiring each node in the entire interest rate tree to be moved by the appropriate amount. One spread cannot accomplish this complex job. In fact, say that an investor generates interest rate paths without making sure that Treasury bonds are priced correctly and then calculates an OAS for each security. In that case it is easy to construct examples for which fairly priced securities will have different OASs. More directly, Treasury bonds will have non-zero OASs. Without first controlling for risk in the proper way, OAS is some combined measure of risk and mispricing and, as such, is not particularly useful.

One disadvantage of prepayment function models is that they lack a behavioral model of homeowner behavior. In other words, they model the result of prepayments rather than the motivations behind prepayments. The risk of such an approach is that historical data, on which a prepayment function model is based, may lose its relevance as economic conditions change. An alternative approach is to model the homeowner decision process. The category of models attempting this may be called *option-based* approaches. An example would be a set of assumptions about the costs homeowners face when refinancing, allowing that some homeowners have higher costs than others. Then, one can value the mortgage pool by weighting mortgage values for each cost class by the prevalence of that cost class in the population. While potentially promising, these models have not demonstrated much success in valuing mortgage-backed securities.

PRICE-YIELD CURVES OF MORTGAGE PASS-THROUGHS AND SELECTED DERIVATIVES

Pass-Throughs

A *pass-through* mortgage-backed security is a collection of mortgages whose cash flows are passed from the homeowners, through the banks and servicing agents, to the investors in the security. Figure 18.1 is quite useful for understanding the qualitative price behavior of pass-throughs. The dotted line graphs the price of a mortgage that is not prepayable. Since it is not prepayable, its cash flows are fixed and its price-yield curve has the general shape of all fixed income securities with fixed cash flows: downward-sloping and positively convex.

While not shown in the figure, it is worthwhile to point out, the price-yield curves of mortgages derived from static cash-flow models will also have this same shape. While the static cash-flow models take prepayments into account, they assume that those prepayments are solely a function of mortgage age and, therefore, are fixed with respect to the level of interest rates. In fact, it is not difficult to determine how price-yield curves under these models will appear relative to the no-prepayments curve in the figure. When rates are very high, investors in mortgages like prepayments: The mortgage carries a low rate relative to current economic conditions, is a discount security, and, therefore, prepayment of principal at par increases value. On the other hand, when rates are very low, investors dislike prepayments: The mortgage is paying an above-market rate, is a premium security, and, therefore, prepayment of principal at par decreases value. Hence the price-yield curve based on static prepayment assumptions will have the same shape as the no-prepayments curve but will generate higher prices for higher rates and lower prices for lower rates.

The price-yield curve under the assumption of optimal prepayments is very

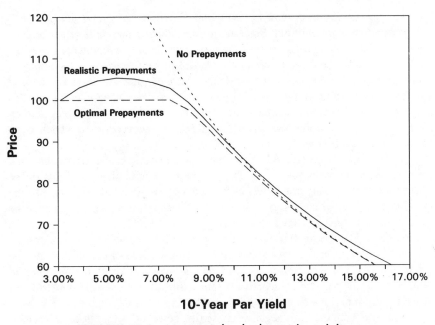

FIGURE 18.1   Mortgage-backed security pricing.

much like that of callable bonds. When rates are very high the curve looks like that of a security with fixed cash flows. When rates are lower and prepayments become more and more likely, the price appreciation of the mortgage is slower, capping out at par. The flattening of the curve at low rates of interest is sharper than that of callable corporates, shown in Figure 17.1, because the latter graph applied to bonds callable some time in the future. Were the callable bond callable immediately, as mortgages are, its graph would also flatten at the call price.

Having discussed the two reference curves, the price-yield curve of a mortgage under more realistic prepayment assumptions can be analyzed.[76] When rates are very low, the value under realistic prepayments is greater than under no prepayments or optimal prepayments. This happens because, for reasons unrelated to interest rates, some homeowners wind up prepaying even when rates are quite high. Since investors like prepayments when rates are high, the value under realistic prepayments exceeds the value under models that predict no prepayments when rates are high.

[76]The graphs in this section were created using a representative, but very simple prepayment model. The reader should use the graphs to better his understanding of their qualitative features rather than focus on particular price levels.

As rates fall, some homeowners will think about prepaying and take appropriate action, but many will not. Since prepayments lower the value of a mortgage when rates are low, the failure of all homeowners to prepay optimally raises the value of a mortgage above its optimally prepaid value. In particular, the failure to prepay can raise the value of the mortgage above par, that is, above the price at which it could, in theory, be called. Eventually, however, when rates have fallen dramatically, all homeowners have heard that rates are low and have been told by friends to prepay. For this reason, the realistic prepayments curve falls back to par at very low rate levels.

There is a very general and useful principle at work in this figure. Optimal prepayments, by definition, imply that the borrower minimizes the value of the mortgage security. Any price-yield curve based on non-optimal behavior, like the two other curves in the figure, will necessarily generate higher prices than the curve under optimal prepayments.

While no duration graph is shown, the lessons about the duration of pass-throughs are easily seen from the price figure. First, as in the case of callable bonds, the right to prepay changes the convexity of the price-yield curve, at intermediate and low rates, from positive to negative. More loosely, unlike securities with fixed cash flows, duration will begin to fall as rates fall.

More shocking than the negative convexity, however, is that there is a region of negative duration or a region in which price falls as rates fall. As mentioned above, this behavior is due to homeowners' eventually realizing that prepayment is their best option. But, unwary investors may be caught by surprise as the price of their securities falls while most other fixed income securities rally. By the way, the reader should not be tempted into reasoning that no one will ever buy the mortgage-backed security in the figure when the 10-year yield is between 5 percent and 6 percent. It is true that price will fall whether rates rise or fall. But, the mortgage is earning above-market interest rates at the same time. Its total return, therefore, which is what really counts, is likely to be competitive with other fixed income securities. Reasoning based on price alone would be as bad as concluding that premium Treasuries should never be purchased because they will eventually decline in price to par.

Strips[77]

Consider $100 face value of a newly issued or current mortgage pool carrying an interest rate of 9 percent. This security can be divided into the following two derivative securities. The first, the *discount strip,* receives claim to $50 of the $100

---

[77]See Roll (1988) for a more detailed analysis.

face value and to $2 of every $9 in interest payments. This effectively creates a security with an interest rate of $2/$50 = 4 percent. Since this rate is well below current mortgage rates, this derivative is aptly named a discount strip. The second derivative, the *premium strip*, receives all that is left over after paying the discount strip. This means that the premium strip receives $7 of every $9 in interest payments and has a claim on $50 principal, for an effective rate of $7/$50 = 14 percent. Since the cash flows of $50 of each strip add up to the cash flows of the underlying mortgage, any term-structure model will predict that the sum of the prices of $50 of each strip will equal the price of the underlying mortgage. Since it is more convenient to work with $100 face values, one may also say that the average of the prices of $100 face value of the two strips equals the price of the underlying mortgage.

Figure 18.2 graphs the price-yield curves of the underlying mortgage and of $100 face value of each of the two strips. When rates are high and prepayments not much of an issue, all behave qualitatively like securities with fixed cash flows. As rates fall and prepayments accelerate, however, the plot thickens. The discount strips continue to rise in value. First, there is the standard effect that falling rates increase present values. Second, since the discount strip is earning less than market rates, investors like the acceleration of principal caused by prepayments. The premium strip, on the other hand, begins to fall in value as prepayments pick up.

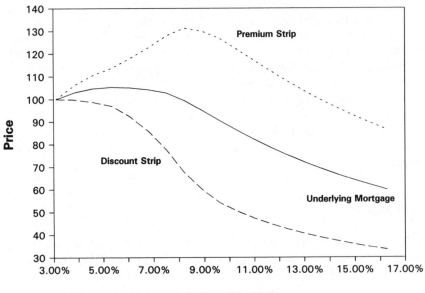

10-Year Par Yield

FIGURE 18.2   Mortgage strips.

Since these securities earn above-market rates, prepayments hurt their value. Principal that used to be earning 14 percent must be reinvested at much lower rates. Another way to explain the fall in price is to use the fact that the average of the strip prices equals the price of the underlying mortgage. If the underlying mortgage price is flattening as rates fall while the discount strip price is rising, it must be the case that the premium strip price is falling. Note that the premium strip has a negative duration over a wide range of interest rates.

Why has a market developed for these strips? Alternatively, what attracts investors to these two derivatives? Many investors dislike what they call *prepayment risk,* the fact that pass-throughs flatten out in price as rates fall. Put another way, pass-throughs do not do as well as many other fixed income securities when rates fall. To expand the market for mortgage-backed securities, it may therefore be useful to have a derivative that does not suffer as much from this feature. Discount strips satisfy this requirement. A salesman can confidently tell an investor that for relatively large drops in rates the discount strip will not suffer from prepayments. Of course, they are not immune from exceptionally large drops in rates.

Whenever one security is carved out of some underlying security to reduce a particular type of risk, the remaining or residual security will necessarily have more of that risk. In the present case, reducing prepayment risk for the discount strip necessarily means that the premium strip will have more prepayment risk. On the other hand, some investors may value the negative duration of the premium strip. When rates are intermediate to low, premium strips naturally hedge a portfolio of more traditional fixed income securities against rate increases.

Investment banks will initially decide to carve up securities and sell the pieces if they can sell the pieces for more than the cost of the underlying security. Competition between banks, however, will quickly bring prices into line, transforming the business into one of earning fees rather than arbitrage profits. From the point of view of investors and capital markets in general, this process is quite desirable. Securities that truly satisfy investor needs will be created. The first investors to satisfy these needs may have to pay a premium for the service, but the securities created, so long as they remain valued, will last beyond the investment banks' original arbitrage opportunity.

IOs and POs

IOs, for *interest-only* derivatives, and POs, for *principal-only* derivatives, are also formed from carving an underlying mortgage into two pieces. In this case, the IO gets all the interest payments made by the borrowers while the PO gets all the principal payments. Figure 18.3 graphs the prices of the underlying mortgage and its derivative IO and PO. The underlying mortgage and the PO are assumed to

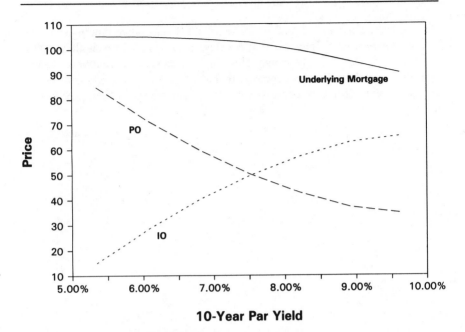

10-Year Par Yield

FIGURE 18.3   IOs and POs.

have a $100 face amount and interest payments to the IO are based on that same $100. So, unlike the figure for premium and discount strips, the sum of IO and PO values in this figure equals the price of the underlying mortgage.

When rates are very high and prepayments not an issue, the PO is like a zero-coupon bond, paying nothing until maturity. As rates fall and prepayments accelerate, the value of the PO rises dramatically. First, there is the usual effect that lower rates increase present values. Second, since the PO is like a zero-coupon bond, it will be particularly sensitive to this first effect. Third, as prepayments increase and are expected to increase, the effective maturity of the PO falls. And, of course, lowering the maturity of a zero-coupon bond increases its value. Together, these three effects make POs extremely volatile securities. Of course, the same argument works in reverse. When rates rise in this region, the discounting and maturity effects substantially lower the value of the PO.

The price-yield curve of the IO follows from subtracting the value of the PO from the value of the underlying mortgage. But it is instructive to explain why the IO falls in value so dramatically when rates fall. When rates are very high and prepayments not a concern, the IO is like a security with a fixed set of cash flows. As rates fall and the mortgage begins to prepay, the cash flows of the IO vanish. Interest lives off principal. Every time principal is paid off there is less available from which to collect interest. But, unlike callable bonds or pass-throughs, which receive principal when interest payments slow or stop, the IO gets nothing. Once again, its cash flows simply vanish. This effect swamps the discounting effect so that when rates fall, IO values decrease dramatically. As mentioned in the discussion of premium strips, investors may like the negative duration feature of IOs for hedging purposes.

References

Amemiya, Takeshi. *Advanced Econometrics*. Cambridge: Harvard University Press, 1985.

Black, Fischer, E. Derman, and W. Toy. "A One-Factor Model of Interest Rates and Its Application to Treasury Bond Options." *Financial Analysts Journal* (January–February 1990): 33–39.

Black, Fischer, and Piotr Karasinski. "Bond and Option Pricing when Short Rates are Lognormal." *Financial Analysts Journal* 47, no. 4 (1991): 52–59.

de Boor, Carl. *A Practical Guide to Splines*. New York: Springer-Verlag, 1978.

Boyce, William, and Andrew Kalotay. "Tax Differentials and Callable Bonds." *The Journal of Finance* 34, no. 4 (1979): 825–838.

Boyle, Phelim. "A Lattice Framework for Option Pricing with Two State Variables." *Journal of Financial and Qualitative Analysis* 23, no. 1 (March 1988): 1–12.

Coleman, Thomas, Lawrence Fisher, and Roger Ibbotson. "A Note on Interest Rate Volatility." *Journal of Fixed Income* 2, vol 4 (March 1993): 97–101.

Conte, S. D., and Carl de Boor. *Elementary Numerical Analysis: An Algorithmic Approach*. New York: McGraw-Hill, 1980.

Cox, John, Jonathan Ingersoll, and Stephen Ross. "The Relation Between Forward Prices and Futures Prices." *Journal of Financial Economics* 9, no. 4 (1981): 321–346.

Duffie, Darrell. *Futures Markets*. New Jersey: Prentice Hall, 1989.

Ho, Thomas. "Key Rate Durations: Measures of Interest Rate Risks." *Journal of Fixed Income* 2, no. 2 (1992): 29–44.

Ho, Thomas, and Sang-Bin Lee. "Term Structure Movements and Pricing Interest Rate Contingent Claims." *The Journal of Finance* 41, no. 5 (1986): 1011–1029.

Hull, John, and Alan White. "Pricing Interest Rate Derivative Securities." *Review of Financial Studies* 3, no. 4 (1990): 573–592.

Jacob, David, and Alden Toevs. "Chapter 26: An Analysis of the New Valuation, Duration and Convexity Models for Mortgage-Backed Securities." *The Handbook of Mortgage-Backed Securities*. Rev. ed. Edited by Frank Fabozzi. Chicago: Probus Publishing Company, 1988.

Jamshidian, Farshid, and Robert Russel. "Evaluation of Complex Sinking Fund Options by Backward Induction Methods." *Advances in Futures and Options Research,* vol. 4 (1990): 83–106.

Kopprasch, Robert, William Boyce, Mark Koenigsberg, Armand Tatevossian, and Michael Yampol. "Effective Duration and the Pricing of Callable Bonds." Salomon Brothers, 1987.

Litterman, Robert, and Jose Scheinkman, "Common Factors Affecting Bond Returns." *Journal of Fixed Income* 1, no. 1 (1988): 54–61.

Litzenberger, Robert. "Presidential Address: Swaps: Plain and Fanciful." *The Journal of Finance* 47, no. 3 (1992): 831–850.

Longstaff, F., and E. Schwartz. "Interest Rate Volatility and the Term Structure: A Two-Factor General Equilibrium Model." *The Journal of Finance* (September 1992): 1259–1282.

Roll, Richard. "Chapter 18: Stripped Mortgage-Backed Securities." *The Handbook of Mortgage-Backed Securities*. Rev. ed. Edited by Frank Fabozzi. Chicago: Probus Publishing Company, 1988.

Stigum, Marcia. *Money Market Calculations: Yields, Break-Evens and Arbitrage.* Homewood, Illinois: Dow Jones-Irwin, 1981.

Tuckman, Bruce, and Jean-Luc Vila. "Arbitrage with Holding Costs: A Utility-Based Approach." *The Journal of Finance* 47, no. 4, 1283–1302.

Index